D0065184

# Answers
# from
# Within

## Spiritual Guidelines
## for Managing Setbacks
## in Work and Life

William J. Byron, S.J.

MACMILLAN • USA

*Also by William J. Byron*

Toward Stewardship (1975)
The Causes of World Hunger (Editor; 1982)
Quadrangle Considerations (1989)
Take Your Diploma and Run! (1992)
Take Courage: Psalms of Support and Encouragement (Editor; 1995)
Finding Work Without Losing Heart (1995)
The 365 Days of Christmas (1996)

# Answers from Within

## Spiritual Guidelines for Managing Setbacks in Work and Life

William J. Byron, S.J.

Macmillan Spectrum
An imprint of MACMILLAN • USA
A Simon & Schuster Macmillan Company
1633 Broadway
New York, NY 10019-6785

*For Tom Donnelly, whose personal and professional integrity I admire; and to the memory of Clif Brown, whose life and death brought Tom and me together in faith and friendship.*

# CONTENTS

*Our very life depends on everything's*
*Recurring till we answer from within.*
*The thousandth time may prove the charm.*

—Robert Frost

# INTRODUCTION

THIS BOOK IS WRITTEN for men and women of faith, who may need a compass to keep themselves on track when things go wrong in the workplace, or in their lives away from work. Faith is the needle on the compass this book will recommend.

Franz Kafka once remarked that a book "should serve as an ax for the frozen sea within us." In your hands you are now holding an ax designed to cut into the sea of your soul, a literary ax meant to crack open the way for in-spiriting ideas that can be internalized and made a vital part of you. These ideas are principles of action, spiritual guidelines that will enable you to cope with setbacks in life and work. These ideas will shape your answers from within, answers that only you can give to the questions that surround you.

Once internalized through prayer and reflection, these ideas can be carried with you everywhere you go. They are particularly potent allies in the workplace (also in the marketplace, where persons from one workplace interact with representatives of another).

These ideas can function as shields against stress, as signposts pointing toward spiritual solutions to personal on-the-job problems, and as reaffirmations of the relevance of religious faith to work and life. Thus transformed, you will become a person who encourages and empowers character-building virtuous actions in others.

# CHANGES

You hear a lot of talk these days about transforming the workplace, making it more humane and respectful of human dignity, but that won't happen until the people who go to work each day are transformed first. That simple, undeniable fact points to the revolutionary potential of a spirituality suited to your workplace as well as your life off the job.

The change I have in mind has nothing to do with organizational restructuring, but just about everything to do with making a personal commitment to the search for purpose, both on and off the job.

# HOW THIS BOOK IS STRUCTURED

This book is presented in four parts, which I will summarize for you here.

Part One offers an introduction to practical spirituality. It's background information, part of the equipment you need to deal with everyday problems. In Part One, you find the basic material—the infrastructure, if you will—that supports what will emerge by way of *Answers from Within*.

Part Two covers experiences that might best be classified as "workplace wounds." This part of the book deals with unpleasant realities, those situations where spirituality is not simply tested, but demonstrates its power to sustain believers who are willing to relate their faith commitments to their workplace responsibilities.

Part Three focuses on personal and family problems that accompany you wherever you go. Managing those problems well is important in maintaining balance in a working person's life, and essential if that person is to be productive in the workplace and peaceful when business hours are over.

Part Four puts spiritual pillars—a supportive foundation—under the person whose faith perspective is wide enough to find God on the job, his or her job, not God's, whose job is to be faithful to those who have faith in God and in themselves, however weak and wobbly that faith may be. This section of the book opens the door of hope for those whose faith has stood the test of time.

## PRACTICAL SPIRITUALITY

Spirituality in work and in life is the thread that runs throughout these pages. The focus is on practical spirituality, one grounded in a sense of vocation. You will know you have found this type of spirituality when you have an awareness that you are "called" to do what you do, Monday through Friday, nine to five (or later), just as much as you are called to family responsibilities and perhaps to membership in a faith community. Grasping a sense of "being called" is not as difficult as you might at first suspect.

### THE PAULINE CRITERIA

You will find the most important ideas supporting this type of spirituality outlined in the early part of this book. You will also find an explanation of how biblically based virtues, which I call the *Pauline Criteria*, can function as spiritual guidelines. These nine virtues can serve as pillars of support when workplace stresses threaten to unbalance a life and derail a career. Here are the Pauline Criteria:

- ◆ Love
- ◆ Joy
- ◆ Peace
- ◆ Patience
- ◆ Kindness
- ◆ Generosity
- ◆ Faithfulness
- ◆ Gentleness
- ◆ Self Control

These virtues might not strike you as the stuff of a strategic plan for getting ahead in the world of work, but keep on reading!

# AFFECTS

David E. Morrison, M.D., founder of Morrison Associates, a suburban Chicago business consulting firm, is a psychiatrist who works with organizational leaders and managers on issues related to workplace stress. He introduced me to the insights of the late Silvan S. Tompkins, whose writings on "affects" influence the approach Dr. Morrison takes to emotional issues that can enhance or impede effective work.

Using Tompkins (author of *Affect, Imagery, Consciousness*, Springer, 1962) as a basis, Morrison identifies nine *affects*, or basic emotional responses, only two of which are positive. One of those, "enjoyment-joy," defines a culture that Morrison sees as supportive of the nine virtues just listed and necessary for a healthy workplace.

The early portion of this book also deals with the "human predicament," an expression that suggests a troubling tension between matter and spirit, joy and sorrow, success and failure—a tension that's felt in every human life. All too often, it seems, people spend the first half of their lives warming up…and the second half wearing out. Just when it all appears to be coming together, we see signs that things are beginning to come apart. That's our predicament, our human condition. We never seem to be able to get life to the perfect point and keep it "just right."

# DAY BY DAY

This book also encourages you to come to terms with the relevance of religious faith to normal, everyday working life. It highlights the relationship between the Sunday-centered preoccupations of believers and their Monday-through-Friday occupations. When faith-based spirituality becomes congregational, when individual faith is nourished by word and sacrament in community—exactly what happens in Sunday assemblies—something surfaces that can be carried over into Monday to enrich life in the workplace.

The search for that "something" leads toward a spirituality that supports busy men and women who want to find a way for their commitments to God and work to become mutually reinforcing.

# A SPECIFIC FAITH PERSPECTIVE

I take a Christian faith perspective in these pages. From that perspective, I invite the reader to carry some of the "boundary" questions of life into that zone of reflection where good Christians, who will inevitably have bad experiences in the workplace and elsewhere, have to search for meaning. My personal faith commitment is Roman Catholic, and my spirituality has been shaped by my nearly 50 years of life as a Jesuit. That background will be evident to you as this book unfolds, as will, I hope, my respect for other faiths.

Prayer is an integral part of my own spiritual life and of this book, too. You will notice dividers at intervals throughout this book, containing prayers I composed for your consideration. Ongoing conversation with God, or just listening to God, is essential to a well-grounded spiritual life. I hope you'll pause from time to time as you move through this book for that kind of conversation, that kind of listening.

How do I know what you might want to say to God? I don't. How do I know if you even want to pause for prayer as you're moving through these pages? I don't. I just thought it would be a good idea to provide a few "pump primers" in case you do choose to pause for prayer while reading this book. The prayers I've composed can be used as bookmarks, or slipped beneath a desktop glass, or just tacked or taped onto a closet door or any workplace wall. Whatever you do with them, my hope is that they will help you center yourself, gain perspective, and restore balance as you try to juggle demands and manage pressures. They can also serve as models to help you compose your own prayers. You are, after all, the world's leading expert on what you might, at any time, want to say to God.

# APPLICATIONS

An important part of my purpose in writing this book is to help you apply spirituality to the realities of workplace life, especially those realities best described by the Bard of Avon centuries ago as the "slings and arrows of outrageous fortune." This book offers short, to-the-point discussions of familiar *workplace wounds*—those often unintended, but sometimes deliberate, blows that can strike at any time. Nursing your wounds isn't the way to maintain balance and move forward. Drawing on spiritual resources to make peaceful progress through the wound toward the goal of healthier relationships is the route this book recommends.

Personal reversals can occur at any time in any place, not only in the workplace, of course. Inevitably, some personal reversals remain for a while and must be managed well if both you and your career are to remain on track. The most common reversals—illness, divorce, the death of a dear one, and the "death" of job loss—are covered in short chapters and tied into the spiritual lifelines available to anyone willing to reach out in faith for help.

Ethical issues underlie most of the problems that surface throughout this book. Having a functioning spirituality makes it a whole lot easier to "do the right thing" when complications or problems arise in the workplace. After reading this book, you will have, I hope, a heightened ethical sensitivity and a deeper commitment to a functional spirituality.

Sadly, and all too often in the workplace today, decision makers are treating human beings like disposable parts in the interest of efficiency and profits. Whatever must be done to reverse this unfortunate trend won't be done, I believe, without the support of a practical, faith-based spirituality.

## ATTITUDES

Attitude is always important. A positive attitude tilts you forward, into the wind, as it were, and that positive tilt is a prerequisite for recovery from any setback. In the later chapters of the book, you'll learn about a rebound-and-recovery route and find out how your spirituality can support and reinforce that positive attitude.

## SPIRITUALITY IS EVERYWHERE— INCLUDING WHERE YOU WORK

The remarkable thing about the current revival of faith-based spirituality is that so much of it is taking place outside the churches. This is not to say that organized religion, as such, is being dismissed as irrelevant by those searching for a meaningful spirituality. Some dismiss it perhaps, but by no means all. There are good people, however, who are finding that religion, as they know it, isn't helping them connect their faith commitments to secular concerns. The aim of this book is to try to close that gap, to encourage anyone willing to make his or her way through these pages to forge a meaningful connection between faith and work.

# ACKNOWLEDGMENTS

MY THANKS TO THERESA MURTHA, former Vice President and Publisher of the Macmillan Consumer Information Group, and to Dick Staron, former Editor-in-Chief of Business and Finance Publications at Macmillan, who saw the need for a book like this and invited me to write it. Dick managed this project and was extraordinarily helpful.

Mike and Pat Snell, of the Snell Literary Agency in Truro, Massachusetts, have a great sense for organization and progression in a project like this; their suggestions and encouragement helped a lot.

My friend John Fontana introduced me to his colleagues David Morrison and David Deacon, of Morrison Associates in Pallatine, Illinois. Their approach to business consulting is unusual, if not unique, and extraordinarily useful. John and both Davids were generous in offering me insights and the benefit of their considerable experience with workplace issues. John Fontana also offered helpful comments on the finished manuscript.

My thanks to HarperCollins Publishers for permission to use in Chapter 11 the quotation from Aleksandr I. Solzhenitsyn, *The Gulag*

*Archipelago* (1974). Scripture quotations are from the *New American Bible*, Copyright 1991, The Confraternity of Christian Doctrine, Inc. All rights reserved.

As a member of the Woodstock Business Conference, I've participated in many rich discussions that have one organizing principle: The desire to probe the relevance of religious faith to business practice. My Jesuit friend Jim Connor, who directs the Woodstock Theological Center at Georgetown and is organizer of the Woodstock Business Conference, which has chapters in various cities across the country, read the manuscript and provided many helpful suggestions.

My assistant at Georgetown, Janet Lychock, was both resourceful and generous in preparing the final manuscript.

Many others offered anecdotes, reflections and general encouragement, and I'm grateful to them. I also look to them for more assistance in the years ahead. This topic is alive today in the minds of these and countless other faith-committed people. As they work, they are all searching for a deeper meaning in what they are "doing." I expect to continue to learn much more from them on the relevance of faith to work. And I hope what they find in this book will offer them some encouragement in return.

# PART ONE

## ON THE RELEVANCE OF FAITH
## TO WORK AND LIFE

*Chapter 1*

# SPIRITUALITY AND THE HUMAN PREDICAMENT

## WHAT IS SPIRITUALITY?

According to theologian Doris Donnelly, spirituality is prayer elevated to a lifestyle. That's one compelling definition of the reality that's prompting countless people in these stressful times to stretch their souls toward God. Our challenges are now "soul size," as playwright Christopher Fry phrased it in *A Sleep of Prisoners*, and "the enterprise is exploration into God."

The question "What is spirituality?" gives rise to another question: What are the roots of the current growing interest in spiritual issues?

More than 50 years ago, *Time* magazine ran a cover story about an event that shook the world, an event that wounded us so profoundly that it has remained to trouble us, mind and soul, ever since. The incident, reported in *Time*'s August 20, 1945 issue, marked both an end and a beginning.

This report was published, as were all *Time* stories in those days, without attribution of authorship. I learned years later that a young (and then relatively unknown) *Time* staffer named James Agee wrote the piece under a very tight deadline. The overarching headline was "Victory." The first subhead was "The Peace," and the second subhead was "The Bomb."

*Time* was covering a big story that week, perhaps the biggest of this century. Agee saw the "controlled splitting of the atom" that produced the bomb used to attack Hiroshima and Nagasaki, and thus bring to an end the greatest conflict in human history, as an event so enormous that "the war itself shrank to minor significance" in comparison. To Agee's eye, "[H]umanity, already profoundly perplexed and disunified, was brought inescapably into a new age in which all thoughts and things were split and far from controlled."

*Time's* readers, still dizzy with the thrill of victory, could hardly have seen, as Agee did, the potential for both good and evil that the atomic bomb represented. That potential bordered "on the infinite with this further, terrible split in the fact that upon a people already so nearly drowned in materialism even in peacetime, the good uses of this power might easily bring disaster as prodigious as the evil.... When the bomb split open the universe...it also revealed the oldest, simplest, commonest, most neglected and most important of facts: that each man is eternally and above all else responsible for his own soul, and in the terrible words of the Psalmist, that no man may deliver his brother, nor make agreement unto God for him."

Then Agee made a shattering observation that rings every bit as true today as it did that memorable August. Here are the words he wrote, words that were available to any reader of the nation's most popular newsmagazine in 1945 and that have gone largely unheeded for more than 50 years:

> *Man's fate has forever been shaped between the hands of reason and spirit, now in collaboration, again in conflict. Now reason and spirit meet on final ground. If either or anything is to survive, they must find a way to create an indissoluble partnership.*

These powerful words were perceptive and prophetic. Appearing just before the so-called "baby boomers" were born, they explain the cause of the "split" that has been troubling us for half a century. We have not yet forged the "indissoluble partnership" between reason and spirit; we are even more adrift now than we were then on a sea of materialism. We may, however, be beginning to notice what Agee saw when the bomb split open the universe—namely, that each of us is responsible for his or her own soul.

Men and women in the world of work who are restless and wondering about the relevance of their Saturday or Sunday faith to their Monday responsibilities are, I believe, being nudged now by the Spirit, the Holy Spirit, to begin an exploration into God.

4

# WHAT SPIRITUALITY ISN'T

"Spirituality" is not to be confused with the everyday sense of the word: "spirit" as in "school spirit," "pioneer spirit," the "spirit of capitalism," or the "spirited" response someone might have to an event or action. To be spirited in such contexts is to react to something completely human, something finite. That which is truly spiritual isn't material or tangible, so it can't be fully grasped by our limited human minds. It cannot be measured, counted, weighed, or touched; it is seen only in its effects.

*Spirit* in a faith-based spirituality rooted in the Christian tradition is identified with the Holy Spirit, the Third Person of the triune God, present and active in the human soul. As scripture puts it: "This is how we know that we remain in [God] and he in us, that he has given us his Spirit" (1 John, 4:13).

In his Letter to the Galatians, Paul addresses people who are converts from paganism. He instructs them in the exercise of their newfound freedom in the Holy Spirit and urges them to "live by the Spirit" in their normal secular surroundings. This method of incorporating spirituality into their everyday lives is precisely what serious Christians at work in the world today are concerned about doing.

In other words: How can you know that you're "guided by the Spirit?"

# THE PAULINE CRITERIA

Paul offers in Galatians 5:22–23 what I call the "Pauline Criteria" for judging the consistency of your own (or anyone else's) behavior with the presence of the Spirit in a human life. These nine criteria, which are listed in Galatians in the following order, constitute what Paul calls the "fruit of the Spirit":

1. Love
2. Joy
3. Peace
4. Patience
5. Kindness

6. Generosity
7. Faithfulness
8. Gentleness
9. Self-control

Examine what you do at home or in the workplace against these criteria, and judge another's oppositional or supportive behavior in the light of these norms. These are non-market values that can humanize every marketplace and workplace.

Notice that Paul hasn't outlined unattainable goals. All nine of these Pauline criteria are within your reach; normal people leading ordinary lives can succeed in gaining them.

In contrast to these ingredients of a faith-based spirituality rooted in Christian revelation, Paul mentions the "works of the flesh," that is, human activity only, activity not influenced by God's Spirit dwelling within us. The works of the flesh are what we're left with when we reject the Spirit and set out blindly on our own. These rebel elements are "obvious," Paul notes, and he identifies them as follows: "immorality, impurity, licentiousness, idolatry, sorcery, hatreds, rivalry, jealousy, outbursts of fury, acts of selfishness, dissensions, factions, occasions of envy, drinking bouts, orgies, and the like" (Galatians 5:19–21). At the end of this catalogue, Paul puts it bluntly: "I warn you, as I warned you before, that those who do such things will not inherit the kingdom of God."

# THE PRESENCE OF THE SPIRIT

After examining Paul's second list, you might be forgiven for thinking, "Well, except for the orgies, that's actually a pretty fair description of the workplace as I know it." True enough, so that's all the more reason to focus on the first list of positive Pauline values.

If spirituality is to mean anything at all for you in the workplace, the Pauline Criteria signaling the presence of the Spirit must become the very infrastructure you carry with you into the world of work. They should be guiding principles, pillars that support your working life. Once internalized, they can serve as answers from within.

The Pauline Criteria can transform you, and with them you can transform the workplace. If you hope to change the world around you, change yourself!

Sober reflection on the absence in your surroundings (and perhaps even in yourself) of these positive criteria can be unsettling. So can the occasional presence of what Paul listed as negatives. These experiences *should* be unsettling. Welcome the discomfort—it can serve an eviction notice on the complacency that stifles the Spirit and the spirituality waiting to energize you from within your soul.

The following sections cover each of the nine Pauline values in more detail.

# LOVE

The word *love* means many things to many people. Popular culture debases love in song and story, forever confusing it with physical passion. Great literature and great lives throughout history, however, illustrate the profound beauty of truly selfless love.

At its core, love is service and sacrifice. It is the willingness to lay down your life literally or figuratively for another. When you think about love, you should be thinking about your willingness to offer up your own true self for the benefit of another.

# JOY

Joy is another profound reality that shouldn't be misunderstood or confused with pleasure and hilarity.

Those who replace "the pursuit of happiness" mentioned by Thomas Jefferson with "the pursuit of pleasure" will find lasting joy always eluding them. Joy is an inner assurance that your will is aligned with God's will— that you are favored, graced, and gifted beyond anything you could merit on your own. Joy is balance, an abiding contentment.

# PEACE

Often mistaken for whatever follows a truce, peace is actually tranquility.

St. Thomas Aquinas described it as the "tranquility of right order." Those who "bury the hatchet" but keep their grudges are not at peace, but those who retain their emotional balance and agree to disagree can live in harmony.

# PATIENCE

*Patience* literally means "suffering." The agent acts; the "patient" receives the action.

How a person receives the action—especially an unwelcome action—is the test of patience. Tests of patience come from countless sources: a dentist's drill, a honking horn, a fist pounding on the table, a spoken contradiction, an unmerited rebuke. The question is "How do you respond?"

# KINDNESS

Many have remarked that apparent kindnesses can, in fact, be acts of cruelty. This means that weakness or timidity can slip into virtue's clothing and provide cover for an escape from responsibility or right action. Many a selfish or hypocritical act has been justified by a bad motive wrapped in counterfeit kindness.

Kindness does not depend on the perceptions of others. True kindness is respect for human dignity in every circumstance of life; it is both courtesy and courageous attentiveness displayed toward other people.

# GENEROSITY

The opposite of all that is small, closed, petty, ungiving, and unforgiving, generosity points to largeness of soul. Generosity doesn't come naturally to human nature, but it can be learned by observation and acquired by practice. When it's practiced, genuine generosity demonstrates the truth of the saying that "virtue is its own reward."

# FAITHFULNESS

Dependability and reliability are the prerequisites of friendship. Keeping commitments—commonly thought of as "promises" and theologically understood as "covenants"—is the "stuff" of faith.

For the believer, faith is the habit of entrusting oneself to God. In the workplace, faithfulness is friendship, trust, and the security that comes from keeping commitments. These two varieties of "promises kept"—vertical, so to speak, to God, and horizontal toward fellow humans—might seem distinct from one another, but they actually reflect a single ongoing reality in the life of the believer. In either case, you put your authentic self on the line.

# GENTLENESS

Lee Iacocca was once referred to by a speaker at a black-tie dinner in New York as a "gentle" man (aren't all who attend such functions "ladies and gentlemen"?). Donald Trump, following the speaker to present an award to Iacocca, ridiculed the suggestion that there was anything at all "gentle" about the then-chairman of Chrysler.

Does being a "gentle" man (or woman) imply refinement? Withdrawal? A retiring personality? What does it mean to be gentle? Gentleness is so often linked with timidity that we are confused by the very meaning of the word and of the place of gentleness in the workplace.

In actuality, gentleness is strength. The gentle person is neither insecure nor arrogant; he or she is self-possessed, in quiet control of self and the surrounding situation.

# SELF-CONTROL

Self-control, a test of personal integrity, involves the practice of saying no to yourself.

A young mother once held up her infant son in the presence of the legendary Confederate general Robert E. Lee and asked for his blessing on the child. Lee offered an apt, but unusual, blessing: "Teach him he must deny himself," he said.

9

A person "out of control" in matters large or small is a diminished person. To have "lost it" in any circumstance of life is to have abdicated what makes you human; it is to have invited the curse of self-centeredness and rejected what Robert E. Lee saw as a blessing—a life lived generously in the service of others.

## WELCOMING THE SPIRIT EVERY DAY

Anyone seriously concerned with the challenge of changing workplace negatives into faith-based positives, or with welcoming the Spirit to dwell within his or her own soul, might well begin with Paul's nine-point checklist, making it an instrument of daily self-examination. These nine pillars can support an ongoing commitment to developing a personal spirituality.

A practical spirituality for life and work can become a part of you if you simply follow these suggestions:

◆ Write these spiritual guidelines down in tabular form as a nine-point checklist.

◆ Reflect on them prayerfully for a few moments in the morning as you ask God's blessing on your day.

◆ In the evening, during another few moments of reflective prayer, review your checklist and mark your slippage or progress on each point as you give thanks to God for all the gifts that are yours at the close of another day.

Such a routine is quite simple: a morning and evening expression of gratitude accompanied by a checklist review. As simple as it is, however, this approach to spirituality—or any approach vaguely resembling it— is all too rare in modern life. What a difference it would make for any home or workplace if everyone there attended to Paul's checklist at the beginning and end of every day!

## A PERSONAL CHECKLIST

Before your working day begins and at the end of the day before going to bed, compose yourself for a few stock-taking moments of prayer. You might want to use the following example as a starting point for developing your own routine, but avoid the rote repetition of empty words and phrases. Be sure to allow for your own formulation of questions and selection of points for emphasis.

◆ Recall that you are in God's presence and thank God for the gift of life and any other gifts that come to mind.

◆ Ask for light to see yourself as God sees you, to see your day in the light of eternity.

◆ Review your role in the day just unfolding, or just ending, against these norms:

---

### Love

*Morning: Am I prepared to share, serve, and sacrifice for others today?*

*Evening: Did I open up toward others? Where did I hurt anyone or hold back?*

### Joy

*Morning: Is my will aligned with God's? Do I cherish the graces, the gifts of God to me? Do I recognize the difference between pleasure and happiness? Am I in balance?*

*Evening: Where did I turn in on myself today? When and why did sadness touch me today? Did I lose balance?*

### Peace

*Morning: What image of tranquility can I carry with me into this new day?*

*Evening: Why was I upset? What grudges am I carrying? Did I disturb the peace of others? Did I make anyone angry?*

### Patience

*Morning: Am I prepared to suffer today, if God wills it or is willing to permit it?*

*Evening: When and why did I "lose it" today? Did I overreact? Did I lose my temper because I was about to lose face? Do I really believe that everything depends on me?*

11

### Kindness

*Morning: Am I prepared to be considerate today? Will courtesy and civility accompany me through the day, and will attentiveness mark my relationship to others?*

*Evening: Did I contribute any rudeness, abrupt demands, or insults to the rubble of this day?*

### Generosity

*Morning: What will I be today, a giver or a taker?*

*Evening: Was I petty, ungiving, or unforgiving in any way today? Did meanness enter the world today through me? Did I make anyone smile? Did I listen generously?*

### Faithfulness

*Morning: If God is God, he cannot be anything but faithful to me today and always. I resolve to remain faithful to God today and, with God's help, to keep all my commitments in faith and friendship, in dependability and reliability.*

*Evening: Was anyone let down by me today? Did I lose any faith in God or in myself? Did I violate any trusts?*

### Gentleness

*Morning: I am capable of being rude, rough, and domineering. I want to be gentle. I hope the source of all gentleness will work through me today.*

*Evening: Was I harsh toward anyone today? Did I hurt anyone in any way?*

### Self-Control

*Morning: I may have to say no to myself today; am I ready?*

*Evening: Did I leave any space for others today? Was I selfish or indulgent in ways that diminished the world's supply of human dignity?*

Again, give thanks and, as needed, express not just regret but resolve to make amends.

Consider developing a daily sheet for monitoring your activity in each of the nine areas. You can use blank spaces on that sheet to monitor your own progress on each of the Pauline values.

One item or another on the list of nine might call for special attention at a given stage in your life. You can highlight any category you like, and you can also add other criteria that suit your purposes. Remember: The point of any exercise involving the Pauline Criteria is to heighten your awareness of God's presence in your life and your responses to or rejections of God's promptings to you in the course of any day.

As you will discover later in this book, you are a vocation. As a person with a calling, you must learn to listen for the specifics of that calling in the earthbound conversations of the secular settings where you are called to live the life God has given you. You have been called by God. God never stops calling; that means you must never stop responding. Although the call isn't in the familiar tones and patterns of speech you're familiar with, you simply have to learn to "hear" these calls or "read" them in the circumstances that surround you. God's initiatives toward you are an essential part of your life; after all, wherever you are, you are there by God's providence.

If these Pauline Criteria for the presence of the Spirit in a human life are internalized—if they become part of who you are, regardless of where you are and what you do for a living—you will always carry them with you. Wherever you happen to be in work or life will become a better place for your presence there.

## SPIRITUAL RESOURCES

Imagine that your spirituality provides you with a personal bank account to be drawn upon in troubled times. This is really not so wild a proposition. Have you noticed how often theological terms, such as *providence* and *trust*, are used to name financial institutions?

The spiritual guidelines that the Pauline Criteria give you can function as deposit slips for the spiritual capital that is yours by God's providence. You can always trust the God who knows you and calls you by name (no PIN needed) to maintain a positive balance in your account. You don't make the deposits; all you can do is have the good sense to make withdrawals as needed.

# CONNECTIONS

So here you are with a book in your hands and a desire, or at least a curiosity, to connect your religious faith to work and life.

The point of this chapter, and those that follow, is to help you act on that desire or that curiosity. The pages that follow aim to show you how to deal productively not only with the wounds and reversals that are part of life, but also specifically with your challenges in the workplace. My goal is to help you do so in such a way as to make God present in this world, to make life better for others, to use your time in a manner that aligns your life with God's will for you.

Integrating religious faith and workplace responsibilities will bring balance to your life. And if you are called to a position of managerial or executive responsibility, you can create a workplace culture where those you lead can themselves lead a balanced life.

I believe that you can overcome your personal share of the lethal "split" between faith and reason, matter and spirit, that Agee identified as a developing characteristic of society. Once you do, your healing will move society one notch closer to the balance in these areas that it so conspicuously lacks. You will have done your part to create the "indissoluble partnership" required to hold these split realities together as the human community struggles to maintain its sanity and live in hope on "final ground."

You will also, I believe, have unlocked the secret of a happy life in an imperfect world, a world that can deal with you harshly and unfairly at times. The source of this unhappiness in a less than perfect world is your ongoing effort to align your free will with God's will for you. This exercise of human freedom brings balance—peace—to a human life.

# GRADUAL PROGRESS

Your progress will depend on your willingness to let these spiritual truths sink into your soul, just as moisture seeps into the earth. It won't happen right away or all at once. Let these lines from Robert Frost's poem "Snow" set the pace for assimilating the wisdom principles that will keep you and your career on track in stressful times:

*Our very life depends on everything's*
*Recurring till we answer from within.*
*The thousandth time may prove the charm.*

Those answers "from within," from the depths of a personal faith-based spirituality, are wisdom principles. They don't surface immediately when things go wrong. They have to push their way up through emotion, and ambition, and anger, and pride through the negatives that will appear on your checklist during the recommended nightly review I sketched out for you. Developing a strong and functioning spirituality will take a while; the thousandth time may indeed prove the charm.

# "IT'S A JUNGLE OUT THERE!"

You might be thinking that the principles of spirituality outlined in this chapter will, if assimilated, arm you with little more than a simple slingshot when it comes to dealing with the unpredictable assaults you face in your daily working life. Well, think about that for a moment: David did quite well against Goliath with that kind of equipment! Don't be too quick to discount or disregard the practical value of spirituality, a weapon both "offensive" and "defensive."

Here is an important point for the hard-charging competitor who wants to succeed both in business and in the spiritual life: Whenever you go on the offensive and activate your properly aggressive, competitive energies in the workplace, make sure your style of assertiveness reflects the presence of the Pauline Criteria. Keep your competitive cool!

Spirituality is your invisible means of support, your ever-reliable resource in keeping yourself and your career on track when the going gets rough.

Perhaps your relationships with others in the workplace are going quite well at the moment. Perhaps you have no enemies; it's simply not a "jungle out there" for you. All is serene and successful, so you might be wondering about the relevance for you of wisdom principles designed to sustain you when things go wrong.

That, of course, is the point: Things will go wrong eventually. It wasn't raining when Noah began to build his ark. The harmony and purpose in your workplace now should certainly be celebrated, but they probably shouldn't be relied on to endure forever.

In love and war, in spiritual and material combat, in religious and business ventures, fortune favors the well prepared. Even a minimal time investment in your personal spirituality will go a long way toward keeping you centered when events threaten, as they inevitably will, to pull you apart.

Your commitment to personal spirituality will also help you overcome complacency and reawaken courage from within. If you see yourself now as both serene and successful, consider this note of caution: You might not be feeling the tension or experiencing any war in the workplace because you haven't started to reject what's wrong in that "jungle out there." "No war" for you could mean no spiritual growth.

# AFFECT

I mentioned in the book's introduction that management consultant and psychiatrist David E. Morrison sees a "fit" for the Pauline Criteria in the workplace. He sees people from a wide variety of work environments. They come to him because they want to manage stress better; often their bosses want them to fit in better with functioning workplace teams. Morrison begins by focusing on a client's *affect*—an emotional state, the fundamental feeling an individual expresses through eyes, voice, and body language.

Since managing people means managing feelings, the people at Morrison Associates in Palatine, Illinois find themselves assisting clients who manage others by helping those clients identify and deal with feelings, the very feelings that are typically denied or ignored in the workplace.

Examples you will encounter later in this book will show that affect is an area that can be managed—not manipulated, but managed.

There can be appropriate or inappropriate reactions to feelings in the workplace. Often, if you are willing to listen to them, your feelings can help you identify what's really going on.

The image of a horse and a jockey is used by Morrison Associates to explain how feelings can impair thought. The area where affect operates is like the horse, and the area where thought works is like the jockey. Sometimes the horse gets out of control and throws the jockey; similarly, the affect can become too powerful, not only for the person experiencing it at home or work, but also for those who are just observing or trying to understand the "horse" in others.

In an interview, Dr. Morrison explained to me that affect is the foundation on which feelings, thought, and, eventually, behavior rest. A stimulus doesn't gain your attention until it triggers a response—the affect. If someone has a persistent unmanageable affect, he or she should see a health professional, says Dr. Morrison. If an organization has a persistent unmanageable affect, its leaders would probably be well advised to contact an organization like Morrison Associates.

Following the lead of the late psychologist Silvan S. Tomkins, Morrison identifies nine affects. One is neutral because it affects all people immediately and in much the same way: Surprise-Startle. Two are positive: Interest-Excitement and Enjoyment-Joy. Six are negative: Fear-Terror, Anger-Rage, Distress-Anguish, Shame-Humiliation, Disgust, and Contempt. I see each of the hyphenated pairs as something of a "one-two punch" or a "two-stage rocket." An amplifying force is at work in these affect pairs. Interest builds to excitement, enjoyment leads to joy, fear develops into terror, and so on. The stimulus triggers an affect that expands.

Perhaps the most important point David Morrison made when I mentioned the Pauline Criteria was that every one of them fits comfortably into the Enjoyment-Joy category; they lead to (amplify toward, extend into) a balanced self-possession, a kind of serene contentment at the center of an active life. (Indeed, the Pauline value of joy is half of the descriptive label placed on this affect.)

The two positive affects, Interest-Excitement and Enjoyment-Joy, can be used to define a culture, says Morrison. Cultures, of course, are defined by dominant values. Interest-Excitement, he explains, describes a pervasive phenomenon in contemporary American culture, as well as in the American workplace. We live in settings of excessive hype and accelerated pace. We are overamplified. The cultural thrust is toward excitement, but this excitement can't be sustained.

Just consider the music, tone patterns, inflections, facial expressions, and staccato communication style characteristic of, say, five consecutive minutes of television news delivery. This example gives you a window on our stress-inducing world. We sit in front of that window on a daily basis and unconsciously adopt it as the backdrop for the daily drama (or, more accurately, daily melodrama) of the harried lives we create for ourselves.

Here is how Dr. Morrison explained the two positive affects: "If there is an optimal rise in the level of stimulation, you get Interest-Excitement. It starts off as interest and becomes excitement if the stimulation continues. This is a pleasant affect, so when someone finds the right level, he or she will move to it and seek to maintain it. This ranges from the interest of reading a book to the building excitement of sex." He added that this affect can be a great motivator; it's one of the important reasons we return to work each day. (A daily workplace routine that features no interest or excitement, of course, relies solely on monetary or other inducements, not all of them pleasurable, to keep people coming back to work.)

Morrison explains Enjoyment-Joy this way: "Imagine someone listening to a joke. That person is stimulated by the story. Often it is an odd or awkward situation being described; there is an element of discomfort. Tension builds and then suddenly, with the punch line, it stops. That's when there's laughter, i.e., enjoyment. When the uncomfortable stimulation, the suspension, stops, joy settles in. You see the same thing in people getting off a roller coaster. Enjoyment-Joy is there after the stress or distress is relieved and the need for comfort, for balance, has been met."

The notion of contentment—a positive, abiding kind of balance—suggests itself as I think about this Enjoyment-Joy affect. I see it as serenity; you can be intensely active but your activity can be rooted in serenity. You have an anchor. You know where you stand. You know yourself.

This is the affect that's needed when people are hurting. However, Enjoyment-Joy is not, according to Morrison, fashionable in the contemporary workplace, where the dominant culture is Interest-Excitement. "This Interest-Excitement pattern just doesn't do it for the human person," says Morrison. "Think of the guy who drives up in a BMW and comes in here wearing designer clothes. He wants me to tell him how to manage his stress and put balance in his life. The Interest-Excitement culture tires you out." In other words, the affect in many working people leaves them exhausted, rather than energized, so it's up to the individual to cultivate consciously the Enjoyment-Joy affect. To ignore or minimize the importance of this task is, in my view, tantamount to ignoring or minimizing your own role in preparing your soul for a better relationship with God.

# WHERE WE COME FROM, WHERE WE ARE GOING

If you move about in the workplace without giving any thought at all to your origins (from God) and your destiny (to be with God for all eternity), you are foolish indeed.

I hesitate to use the word *fool*, but anyone who ignores or denies a day-to-day dependency on God demonstrates impressive qualifications for full possession of that title. Psalm 14 offers this gentle reminder: "Fools say in their hearts, 'There is no God.'"

Human dependency on a living, caring God is not passivity, just as serenity is not passivity. Nor does it point to the absence of freedom, for freedom and the ability to reason set us so-called rational animals apart from all other living beings. Moreover, acknowledging this dependency is not declaring yourself to be religious; it's simply conceding that you are not the sum and substance, let alone king or queen, of the universe. You might choose to realize this dependency without the help of church, synagogue, mosque, or shrine of any kind. You are free to make that choice. Such an acknowledgment would, however, still be an exercise of spirituality, the spirituality that is, as I mentioned, emerging everywhere you look, even outside the churches.

Religion and spirituality are separate realities. Some good people view formal religion as an unappealing stained-glass abstraction, far removed from the demands of daily living. As worthy of attention as such criticisms might be, it's difficult to comprehend how any good person can be truly good without some consciously forged spiritual links to the source of all goodness. These links could be forged apart from any involvement with formal religion. In fact, commentators on religion—some to their dismay, some to their delight—are noticing that spirituality (the focus on ultimate origins, ultimate destinations, and the ultimate source of power and virtue) is not dead in contemporary America. It is simply happening as much or even more outside churches, mosques, shrines, and synagogues as within them.

# TOWARD BALANCE

Think of the nine elements in the Pauline Criteria as stretching across the Enjoyment-Joy spectrum that Dr. Morrison uses. The goal, the term, the end, is a deep and lasting joy that should reside deep within your soul.

The other positive affect, Interest-Excitement, could move you toward ever higher levels of excitement into a perpetual state of agitation, which would also reside in your soul. There lies much of the discontent that troubles us today. It's already there in our mass-media culture; you don't have to make any effort to find it.

Beyond agitation, behind the ever-rising "thresholds" of excitement and adrenaline, there is no such thing as a state of fulfillment. There is, however, enjoyment in what I recommend as elements for the infrastructure of your spirituality. There is a positive, satisfying quality associated with each of Paul's nine virtues: love, joy, peace, patience, kindness, generosity, faithfulness, gentleness, and self-control.

Coming from within yourself, or seen in the effects of others' actions, each of the Pauline elements has an expansive capacity. The expansion or enlargement moves you toward balance; it leads the soul toward security. You know very well how events can whirl around you; that will surely continue. You also know how you can get caught up in activity; that will

20

not change. What you might not know, however, is the capacity of this spirituality to keep you rooted in joy because it roots you in God, while setting you free for the pursuit of all good things.

# LIMITATIONS

An image that catches the tension between human freedom and dependency under God, while providing a window of sorts on what I like to call the human predicament, is that of a puppet on a string.

Of course, a person under God is more than a puppet, and God, although certainly not a puppeteer, is more than a mere observer of human activity. Events aren't simply random, out of divine control; human beings are not completely autonomous and fully in charge of their own destinies.

Thoughtful believers acknowledge God to be all-powerful, and they celebrate the fact that God endows each person with the freedom to act and choose as he or she pleases, whether wisely or foolishly. The reflective person of faith is left, however, with the theological problem of figuring out the relationship between divine foreknowledge and human freedom.

Freedom of choice is part and parcel of the human predicament. You are a contingent being who is free to choose. Your choices can result in gain or loss, life or death. No matter how wisely and well you choose, however, limits surround you every day at every turn. The ultimate limit— the ending of life as you know—is always a possibility, usually regarded as remote, but undeniably inevitable.

History gives you perspective on the human predicament, on the contingent state of being (the condition of dependency) that's yours simply because you're human. Two hundred years ago this world was filled with people, not one of whom is alive today. Two hundred years from now, no one now on earth will still be alive. Two hundred years is a very, very short time in the long view of history. Cut that span of years by 100 and you face the same conclusion: Your journey through life is short.

Yet, caught as you are in the human predicament, you kick against limits, struggle to achieve, and act as though you hold permanent title or a perpetual lease on life, health, and possessions. Even in serious illness, it's a

21

rare person who is ready to concede that he or she might be among the "PUDs," physicians' shorthand for a *patient's unconquerable disease.*

Some would say: You only go around once. I would elaborate on that by saying the human predicament points to the inseparability of growth and decline in the unrepeatable onceness of a human life.

# LIVING AND DYING

It has been said that people may or may not believe in God, but they all believe in death and do all they can do to defer it.

There's just no escaping it, however. You start to die when you begin to live. You move toward the end the moment you set out on the journey. Everything in you reaches up, even as the gravitational pull of human limitations holds you down. At different stages of your life, that weight is so light that you hardly notice it; you can easily forget it's there—but it always is.

At many mileposts on your journey, the absolute endpoint is remote and far from view, and you fail to notice it. Your attention is fixed on immediate goals that take on dimensions of importance and permanence, labels that are laughable when you understand the insignificance of those short-term goals in relation to your ultimate goal and purpose in life.

That understanding is the by-product of a functioning spirituality, which, as I noted at the outset, is a by-product of prayer. Busy people have to be encouraged to "waste" more time with God in prayer. Trapped in the human predicament, believers typically turn to God with prayers of petition, in search of a "fix" when things go wrong. They rarely associate their musings, ponderings, and puzzlings over their relationship to a higher power with the act or practice of prayer. Those mental meanderings happen, however, in moments that most people cherish: time spent walking along the shore, staring into a fireplace, looking at the stars, gazing at the mountains, listening to a symphony, watching a baby crawl. Those reflective moments can, of course, happen in a cathedral or a subway station, in sacred space intended to be conducive to prayer or in ordinary lunch-hour surroundings. Those reflective moments will, if you let them, happen naturally.

Whether human architecture or natural beauty provide the setting, believers need to find the space and time for permitting God to become more fully present in their conscious minds, more fully resident in their hearts. Once you do that, and take the next step of letting the effects of this consciousness manifest themselves in your attitudes and external behavior, you have a functioning spirituality.

Prayers of petition, not at all to be denigrated or disregarded, can be a proving ground for the higher level of meditative communication with God. Caught in any one of a million predicaments that come with the human condition, believers typically and spontaneously beg for assistance. "God help me" is more than an idle phrase useful for giving punch to a narrative. "Please, God, let…" "Dear Lord, help…" "Oh, God, don't…" are all ways that prayers of petition can begin. When you make a prayer of petition, your prayer is like the rope thrown from a boat to the dock when you're ready to come ashore. You catch the rope on a cleat not to pull the dock to you, but to pull yourself toward the dock.

The point of your prayer of petition should be to line up your will with God's so that you can be "pulled" by grace toward God to accept whatever it is that God regards as best for you. Not "my will," but "thy will be done" is the qualifier that should accompany any request for divine help. If you understand this, you will have opened up your soul for a fuller stretch toward the God who cannot be anything but faithful to you, and who will be there for you in any wound, reversal, or recovery you experience as you work your way through the human predicament.

For the intellectual, the human predicament is the troublesome split between science and religion, or more broadly, between faith and reason. For the artist, it's the split between mind and heart. For the ordinary person trying to figure things out, it's the tension between the conscious experience of being personally affected by growth and decline, and the often unconscious anxiety associated with a personal, sometimes lonely journey that stretches from birth to death in an environment of risk, on an unfamiliar road called life.

With the nine Pauline Criteria as guideposts for the journey, you can move ahead with confidence and courage to meet the challenges that lie ahead.

23

*Everything does not depend on me. In making this admission, I'm not saying anything profound, Lord…or am I?*

*I think of prayer as something I should do, if only I take the time to do it. That's because I come to prayer as if, in fact, everything depends on me, but who ever said it all depends on me?*

*I depend on you, Lord, for life, breath, and thought—for everything. Too often I live, and breathe, and think the opposite— that I depend on me. Fortunate as I am to have a Declaration of Independence to support my citizenship on earth, it would be foolish of me to try to declare independence as the foundation of my citizenship in the City of God. Dependent then, and knowing it, I cry out, my God, to you. Save me from the foolishness of living as if everything depends on me.*

*When I sit, or stand, or kneel, or walk, or stretch out flat on my face to pray, let me wait for you to do it all. Lift me up, mind and heart, to you, Lord. Fill me with your presence. Let your love and your power touch me. And may your wisdom convince my oh-so-busy, all-too-centered self that there is nothing better I can do than "waste my time" with you in prayer.*

*Take my emptiness; fill it with your presence. Here is my dependence, Lord. It is all you expect. It is all I have to give.*

# Chapter 2

# MIXING FAITH AND WORK

It might be hard for you to believe that what happened to John Koepke, a friend of mine in Chicago, ever happened, and even more difficult to believe it could happen to you. But it did happen to John, and it could happen to you. If it does, you might find yourself wondering about the relationship of faith to work; you may, in fact, find yourself searching for a spirituality to help you cope.

John was president and chief operating officer of a small graphics company in a Chicago suburb. He reported directly to a working chairman. A few years ago, just before he was ready to leave for work one morning, John's wife, Pat, passed along some bad news she had received the day before: She had breast cancer.

John was stunned, saddened, and understandably upset. He wanted to stay with Pat that day, but it was simply impossible. An important meeting was scheduled with people coming in from out of town; he absolutely had to attend.

When he arrived at work, the chairman saw that something was wrong and said, "John, you look upset. What's the problem?"

"I just got some bad news," John replied. "Pat told me this morning that she has breast cancer."

"Well, John," the chairman announced, "maybe you ought to get all your bad news on the same day. I'm afraid I've got to let you go."

John was reeling for the second time in only a few hours. Although he had gotten a handsome raise just weeks before, he decided not to fight the dismissal. He later told me that he realized he had been trapped for some time in a dysfunctional situation. Best to break away promptly, he thought, and get home to take care of his wife. As if he needed further proof that he was working for a crazy outfit, John soon learned that his contractually assured, 12-month severance period had been unilaterally cut to six months, and the 100 percent compensation that was to continue for a year after an involuntary separation had been cut in half.

After reviewing all the options, John decided not to litigate, choosing instead to get on with his life and help Pat get on with hers.

Both, by the way, are now doing fine. John is running his own company and Pat is in remission. "We were the best of friends when we got married," John told me (in Pat's presence) one night not too long ago, "and having been through all this together, we're better friends today."

# VOCATION

Ed Willock, editor of the long-defunct magazine *Integrity*, composed the following verse around the end of World War II, just as James Agee was noticing that split between reason and spirit, and just as the great American business machine was returning to the task of meeting peace-time economic needs:

> *Mr. Business went to church,*
> *He never missed a Sunday;*
> *But Mr. Business went to hell*
> *For what he did on Monday.*

That dart might have been amusing five decades ago. However, despite horror stories that John Koepke and many others can still tell, it's wide of the mark now, as more and more Americans find unacceptable the notion that work should be compartmentalized from one's spirituality.

Why are you there, wherever you show up for work on Monday, in the first place?

This is a question of vocation. What is your calling? Everyone has one—what is yours? If you have a vocation to business, how can you treat your associates in the workplace with anything less than dignity and respect, knowing that God called both you and them to be there?

As a youngster growing up in Philadelphia, I frequently heard the word *vocation*, but it was typically used in one of two ways. The first was in reference to a "vocational school," like Dobbins, a secondary school where students uninterested in or unqualified for enrollment elsewhere on an academic track took carpentry, printing, or other vocational courses. The second sense of the word referred to some form of religious ministry.

I learned that in a religious context, Protestant ministers were "called" to serve a particular congregation, and that young Catholics were urged to consider a "vocation" to priesthood or religious life. Both situations represented something special that was given by God; the call was not to be taken lightly. If accepted, a vocation was, in the pious imagination, carried around much like a piece of air-travel luggage that could be "lost" at almost any point on the journey. Anyone who refused or lost this higher calling was thought to be running no small degree of personal, spiritual risk.

This use of the word has fallen out of fashion nowadays. Young people are encouraged to think not in terms of "having" or "losing" a vocation, but of being a vocation. The theologically correct approach is reflected in a very direct statement of identity: You are a vocation.

You are, in other words, responding to a call from the God who formed you in your mother's womb, called you then, and never stops calling. It's not as though God placed a call to you, left a message, and then hung up. To the contrary, you are being called, person-to-person, at every moment of your life. Do not, however, expect to hear a voice in this communication. You will hear this call in the circumstances of your life, in the people who nurture or disappoint you, in the opportunities or frustrations that present themselves, in your temperament and talents, in your physical and intellectual capacities, and in your aspirations and desires.

All of these are gifts to you from God. Faith instructs you to use them according to God's will for your salvation, for his glory, and for the service of your fellow human beings. That is what you are "called" by God to be and to do. Because God calls you to do it, the work—whatever form it takes—has inherent dignity.

Martin Luther King once said, "If a man is called to be a street sweeper, he should sweep streets even as Michelangelo painted, or Beethoven composed music, or Shakespeare wrote poetry. He should sweep streets so well that all the hosts of heaven and earth will pause to say, 'Here lives a great street sweeper who did his job well.'"

# ANSWERING GOD'S CALL

There is a genuine vocation to business and to the daily working life. Men and women are called by God to serve one another in the context of buying and selling, producing and consuming, supplying and demanding the material goods and services that sustain and enrich human life. Financial benefit resulting from a transaction is hardly evidence that God is absent from the lives of those conducting the transaction.

There are, of course, many other callings you might consider. The trick is to determine which call is for you, and this determination requires prayer.

You must freely choose the place and the occupation where your prayer suggests that God is calling you to be. You'll never know for certain, but faith has a way of convincing you that you are where God wants you to be. If you feel otherwise, that in itself could be a message to move on. Keep in mind, however, that you are not a random fluctuation in some complex system of occupational distribution. You are a person who is known and cherished by a creator-God who has something special in mind for you. Even if prayer were the furthest thing from your mind when you prepared yourself for a particular way of life—taking this job or that, selecting one profession over another, living here or there—God wasn't disinterested or absent from the process. God's providence was there, at least permitting, and perhaps promoting, the outcome of your unreflective choices. Regardless of the presence or absence of prayerful reflection on your part as you moved through life to where you are now, you can decide to begin listening more attentively to the God who calls; you can try to read more carefully the will of God in your current circumstances.

You are a vocation.

# PURPOSEFUL VOCATION

I've always liked the following reflection-prayer of John Henry Cardinal Newman. It's one of the ponderables that belongs in any workplace spirituality, an assertion of purpose and vocation even when you're tempted to believe that your compass is gone and your life is devoid of meaning.

*I am created to do something or to be something for which no one else is created; I have a place in God's counsels, in God's world, which no one else has; whether I be rich or poor, despised or esteemed by man, God knows me and calls me by my name.*

*God has created me to do Him some definite service; He has committed some work to me which He has not committed to another. I have my mission. I may never know it in this life, but I shall be told it in the next. Somehow I am necessary for His purposes....*

*I am a link in a chain, a bond of connection between persons. He has not created me for nothing. I shall do good; I shall do His work. I shall be an angel of peace, a preacher of truth in my own place, while not intending it, if I do but keep His commandments.*

*Therefore, I will trust Him, whatever, wherever, I am, I can never be thrown away. If I am in sickness, my sickness may serve Him; in perplexity, my perplexity may serve Him; if I am in sorrow, my sorrow may serve Him. He does nothing in vain.... He knows what He is about. He may take away my friends, He may throw me among strangers, He may make me feel desolate, make my spirits sink, hide my future from me, still He knows what He is about. (Meditations and Devotions, "Hope in God Creator," March 7, 1848)*

It might be true that week after week, for most of their working lives, millions of Christians who worship on Sunday move back into the Monday world of the workplace without giving much thought to the relevance of their religious faith to business practice. It's also true, however, that theological reflection, practical pastoral advice, and a renewed interest in spirituality are encouraging committed Christians to integrate their religious commitments with their business responsibilities for a unified, grace-filled life. The resulting spiritual benefits are all the more important when the walls of the workplace begin to close in and stifle the spirit of the person employed there, or worse, when accumulated stress causes those walls to start tumbling down, crushing the human spirit.

A friend of mine once remarked, "If you feel called to what you are doing, and if you really like what you do, you'll never work a day in your life!" The integration of faith and work can make that joyful conclusion possible. When linked to faith, a working life becomes a life that's really worth living!

# WHAT IS THE PURPOSE OF BUSINESS?

The material in this book of reflections on workplace spirituality will help you come up with your own answer to the question of what it means for you to be a Christian in a secular workplace setting, Monday through Friday, nine to five. Are the Pauline Criteria in evidence there? Are they present as a result of your presence—not your preaching, mind you, but your presence? Are they instinctive to you?

These are all fundamental questions that lead to another fundamental question: What is the purpose of business?

"To maximize profits," is no answer; "to optimize profits" isn't particularly helpful, either. Neither answer explains the deeper purpose of business activity, nor is it fully satisfying to couch the purpose of business in terms of maximizing the firm's long-term viability.

Business, I would argue, deals essentially with exchanges. If you're in business as an owner, a manager, or a worker, somewhere down the line, you are doing something for others on condition of receiving something of fair value in return.

People in business relate to other people whose needs, preferences, and desires are met, to some degree of satisfaction, by the product or service the business supplies at a price. To meet that need, preference, or desire is the purpose of business. To do so at a price (and thus differentiate the activity from voluntarism or altruism) means receiving in exchange enough payment to cover, at the very least, the costs (including risk) of providing the service or product. This compensation gives the provider the income necessary to meet his or her own legitimate needs, preferences, and desires.

Otherwise, the business system, the network of relationships where need and satisfaction meet as question and answer, could not attract and hold you, the provider; you would have to find some other way to make a living.

Why you choose business to occupy your reimbursable time, instead of earning income in another of the many ways open to you, is a good question. Could it be that you chose business because you were chosen for this way of life, called to it? This question points to the possibility of business as your calling, your vocation; it suggests that business has a special place in the divine plan for you.

The business organization is there to meet, on the buyer's side, a human need for products or services. For the seller, business generates necessary income. The business environment, with all its market intermediaries, makes it possible for buyers' and sellers' needs to be met in a reliable, predictable, organized fashion. Such a system, of course, allows people in our society, and societies like ours, to get on with the daily activities of life.

Business organizes the material basis for human existence and well-being, so it's seen as a foundation for constructing a community's material relationships. Besides the material, however, business also brings a range of social, cultural, and personal goods to the construction of a good society.

If you're in business, you should take proper credit for fostering a human good that wouldn't be accomplished without you and the others who form the business community.

Your purpose for being in business is rooted in a great deal more than simply making money. Sure, just as food is necessary for life, profit is necessary for the life and health of a business. No argument about that. But who would recommend that you maximize your intake, stuff yourself full of food, at every opportunity?

If you are a leader in business (or any other kind of organizational environment), your purpose is to help create a culture in which your associates can lead a balanced life. You have an opportunity to make life (quite literally) richer for others, to do something that makes this world receptive for a kingdom that is coming, a promised kingdom of justice and peace.

# NEEDS, PREFERENCES, DESIRES

Need, preference, and desire are separate categories or stages of demand to be considered by suppliers in providing goods and services.

If, for example, you're organized to make available essential food, shelter, clothing, education, medicine, security, and health care, you are in the business of meeting basic needs. If your business is directed toward meeting preferences, as opposed to needs, your product or service will go beyond the essentials and move from a focus on *vivere* to *bene vivere*, from survival to comfort. Consumer preference invites the supplier to move toward the fancy, but not the frivolous, product offering. If desire only is active on the demand side, you're probably operating in a luxury market-place. Of course, what's viewed as necessity at the high end of the market might be luxury to the eyes of consumers at the lower end.

In your estimate of all this, if you grant priority to need over both preference and desire, you might say that meeting material human need is the immediate and fundamental purpose of business. All the same, meeting preferences, not basic needs, accounts for most of the volume of business activity and is, of course, in most settings, a worthy purpose.

Most human desires are healthy, wholesome, and normal, but not all of them. When business aims to satisfy unreasonable and even harmful desire, or worse, promotes and stimulates personally and socially harmful desire, the purpose of business is perverted. If you're carrying a faith-based spirituality into the workplace, you will surely find yourself becoming more sensitive not only to what that workplace is doing to those employed there, but also to what impact that organization's product or service is having, for good or for ill, on its clients and customers. If the place or the product is hurting people, you have a choice: Change things or get out. Otherwise, you shrink into a person of diminished integrity if you remain in that job. Each believer must make his or her own choices on this score, but certainly any commitment to a career based on increasing the sales of harmful or addictive consumer products, say, or pornography (to offer an obvious example), needs reexamining in light of the nine Pauline values.

Unreasonable desire can be at work on the supply side of the exchange, too. When greed, far removed from need or legitimate preference, drives the income motivation of the provider (the seller), the business mechanism is abused for unreasonable personal gain. Society is not only ill-served, but also seriously injured by abuses on either side of the exchange. If you notice this happening in or around your organization, that should motivate you to change it, if you can. If change isn't a realistic option, your discomfort with a greed-based corporate culture should be enough to send you packing.

## EMPLOYMENT...AND GOD'S ACTION

Another purpose of business is to provide employment, an organized environment in which people can come together, on a regular and stable basis, to supply service to others and earn income for personal and family support.

It would be difficult to exaggerate the value to society of giving working people and those who depend on them economic security. We look to business to do just that, although few today expect any single business organization to provide uninterrupted employment for all its workers throughout their working lives.

From a theological perspective, business can be seen as relating in a privileged partnership to the Creator. From the very beginning, all creation is God's action. All created things depend on God and God's continuing activity. This critical point was emphasized not just for Catholics, but for the whole world by the Second Vatican Council:

> *"For without the Creator the creature would disappear. For their part, however, all believers of whatever religion have always heard His revealing voice in the discourse of creatures. But when God is forgotten the creature itself grows unintelligible,"* (Pastoral Constitution on the Church in the Modern World, No. 36)

Everyone has the opportunity to participate, through work, in the Creator's ongoing activity. Those who work in business can hear God's revealing voice "in the discourse of creatures," no matter how earthbound and material that discourse might be.

# RELATIONSHIPS IN BUSINESS

All business activity has a dual relationship: to God, the Creator of what's transacted or exchanged, and to those who engage in the variety of transactions that constitute business activity. The first relationship is really worship (an obvious opportunity for Sunday to spill over into Monday); the second is actually a vocation, the call to work with others in advancing God's creative activity.

This dual relationship opens up yet another theological perspective. Men and women in business are not, strictly speaking, creators, but they are stewards. Stewardship is a human responsibility, and the business environment is an ideal setting in which to meet that responsibility.

The idea of stewardship is rooted in the first verse of the 24th Psalm: "The earth is the Lord's, and the fullness thereof." In this context, the "earth" means that all material creation belongs to God. So does the "fullness thereof": the fruit, the yield, the extract, the product, the construct, the artifact, or whatever emerges as the formed, forged, or finished result of human interaction with the resources of the earth. All of it belongs to the Lord, and people are the managers, the stewards.

Legal conventions assign and protect ownership rights, but in the theological perspective, ownership rights are, in fact, stewardship responsibilities. What we own is the Lord's. What we do through human work is done by the Lord at work within us. This perspective supplies a solid theological foundation for releasing your human potential in full-time business activity.

Business supplies the context for human interaction in pursuit of all the worthy purposes mentioned previously; it also comes as close as anything I can imagine to the definition of stewardship.

There is theological significance in making available, through fair exchanges, the goods and services people need, prefer, and, in some cases, simply desire. There is also theological meaning in your managerial and entrepreneurial function of making employment available for others—helping them to be more active and productive human beings.

# UNION WITH GOD, UNION WITH OTHERS

Your ultimate purpose, theologically speaking, is union with God and others in the human community. Your journey begins with God and, make no mistake, is intended to end with God after experiencing sin, grace, and the gift of redemption through a covenant community called *church.* Your journey is, of course, in, of, and through a material world that theology sees as "good." The purpose of your business activity, from a theological perspective, is to serve people on the way to salvation by organizing the material and social basis of their transit through life. This is something to think about on your way to work and any time you hear yourself praying, "Thy kingdom come!" The Kingdom is indeed coming, and what you are doing Monday through Friday, nine to five, is intended in God's great plan for the world to be part of that reality.

On Sundays, those Christians who emphasize the sacramental life are conscious of themselves as communicants, bread-breakers. They remember their Lord in the breaking of the bread. Rarely do they reflect on the linguistic link between the companies that employ them on weekdays and the Eucharist they celebrate on Sundays. The Latin phrase *cum pane* ("with bread") describes both their Sunday "companionship" and the "companies" to which they return, refreshed and rested, on Monday mornings. Also, Christians can infuse these companies with a spirit of cooperation and, yes, genuine companionship.

In families, there is association by kinship; in faith communities, there is association by conviction. In corporations (even those that call themselves "families"), kinship is not what holds people together. But conviction could work that way, particularly the kind of conviction that stems from a deeper religious faith.

Businesses, then, are organized to serve the material needs of the community, and working there can easily be viewed as "just a job." But it can also be seen, with the eye of faith, as a vocation to work not only in companies, but also in companionship. It can be viewed as service not simply to clients or customers, but to people destined, like you, for eternal life.

This perspective moves the believer beyond considering only the bottom line to appreciating the relevance of religious faith to business practice. It stretches Sunday into Monday, and beyond. It suggests that retirement benefits for the "faithful steward" (see Luke 12:42) are quite literally out of this world.

That is something worth thinking about right now and incorporating into the "whole nine yards" of the Pauline Criteria mentioned throughout this book. Love, joy, peace, patience, kindness, generosity, faithfulness, gentleness, and self-control belong in the business environment to humanize it, sanctify it, restore it to emotional balance, and render it truly efficient and effective for the long haul. That's the silent but compelling statement you make when you carry them with you as you go to work on Monday morning.

Recall my suggestion to view these nine spiritual guidelines as spanning Morrison's Enjoyment-Joy category, that is, as expanding from the initial affect of enjoyment to a deeper sense of abiding joy. Enjoyment engages you with your work; continued application of your talents to the task can lead to genuine joy, a deep joy within your soul. That, in my view, is the meaning of those words we wish we could say all the time, "I really love my work."

Love it or leave it, I would add. If there is no room in your workplace for the first of the nine criteria, how can you believe that God really wants you to be there? It might not be realistic to expect your work always to be pleasurable, but it should be joyful, with that deep-down joy of knowing it's a place where you can find God and where God wants you to be. It's possible, of course, to be "stuck," by God's permissive will, in work you simply can't love and feel that you can't get out. Read on, and you will see how the spiritual guidelines outlined in these pages can become sustaining lifelines in dealing with such situations.

"…or wherever your final destination may be." The flight attendant is welcoming us all to Pittsburgh (as travelers are welcomed on airborne arrivals every day into airports across the country). "May you have a pleasant stay here in Pittsburgh, or wherever your final destination may be."

I know for sure my final destination is not Pittsburgh. It is not Chicago, or Denver, or San Francisco, either. Faith tells me the "final things" are death, judgment, heaven, and hell, and you, Lord, will be there in only three of those four possibilities. Lord, I want to be with you—finally and forever.

"To be with you." Love songs play that theme for us as we sing and dance our way through life. Curious, isn't it, that only hymns, not love songs, pick up on that theme's eternal dimension: To be with you, Lord, safe and secure, at peace and happy forever. That's what I want deep down. That desire underlies my restlessness; it is part of me. I want salvation for those I love, also, for those you've entrusted to my care. I want it, Lord, for everyone, friend and foe alike. How could I hope to see you face to face and not want that for them?

I have your promise that eternal life, everlasting union with you, is out there waiting for me. I have that promise on your word. I take that promise on my flimsy faith.

And so I pray, Lord, now and always, keep me faithful. Bring me home safely to you, my final destination, who is now, and will be forever, faithful to me.

# Chapter 3

# PREPARING FOR ADVERSITY IN LIFE AND WORK

NOT LONG AGO, AN OUT-OF-WORK Wall Street executive called me for advice. His job search was going nowhere. His divorce had just been finalized. His battle for weekly visitation rights to his only son was bogged down in red tape and made all the more painful because his son didn't really care about seeing him.

This man told me he wanted to develop a deeper sense of spirituality in his life. He had become convinced, he said, that "organized religion is for people who are afraid of going to hell, but spirituality is for those who have already been there." He is a very good and decent person. Why, he wanted to know, were all the negatives piling up on him?

## BAD TIDINGS

Rabbi Harold S. Kushner's wise, warm, and wonderful book *When Bad Things Happen to Good People* (Schocken Books, 1981) addresses just such difficult questions. It is written from the heart of a deeply religious man who has encountered great adversity in life. Kushner's son Aaron was diagnosed in infancy with *progeria*, which means rapid aging. The rabbi learned that his son would never grow much beyond three feet tall or have any hair on his head or body. The boy would have the appearance of a little old man, and he would die in his early teen years.

Rabbi Kushner spoke of his son in the introduction to his book. "This is his book," Kushner wrote, "because any attempt to make sense of the world's pain and evil will be judged a success or failure based on whether it offers an acceptable explanation of why he and we had to undergo what we did." Two of Kushner's chapter titles reflect questions that are part of the human predicament: "Why Do the Righteous Suffer?" and "What Good, Then, Is Religion?"

These questions are on the minds of most thinking people in the face of human tragedy and remain unexpressed by many. It's important for your spiritual and mental health not only to bring these and similar questions to the forefront of consciousness, but also to talk them over with trusted friends. Keep in mind, however, that these questions can be answered only in the vocabulary of spirituality, as Rabbi Kushner demonstrates toward the end of his book:

> Let me suggest that the bad things that happen to us in our lives do not have a meaning when they happen to us. They do not happen for any good reason which would cause us to accept them willingly. But we can give them a meaning. We can redeem these tragedies from senselessness by imposing meaning on them. The question we should be asking is not, "Why did this happen to me? What did I do to deserve this?" That is really an unanswerable, pointless question. A better question would be "Now that this has happened to me, what am I going to do about it?" (p. 136)

As I read those words, I wondered what meaning a Christian spirituality might impose on them. Is there a Christian perspective, I asked myself, that might enlarge the interpretive framework needed to figure these issues out and decisively respond to the question, "What am I going to do about it?"

## MEANING

From my Christian point of view, I wondered whether some "bad things" might not have a meaning when they happen. (The crucifixion of Jesus comes to mind.) Such events could indeed, I found myself thinking, be accepted willingly for a very good theological reason. There is, of course, an unacceptable reason that I would dismiss, as Rabbi Kushner does; namely, that something someone did makes him or her "deserve" this truly horrific outcome. That kind of thinking turns God into some kind of mean-spirited umpire anxious to call you "Out!" at the plate, instead of waiting, like the father of the prodigal son in Luke's gospel parable, to welcome you home.

Both Jewish and Christian spirituality are careful not to put the blame on God when reversals occur. "Acts of God" are really acts of nature. It's true, of course, that God is the creator of all things natural, but nature's laws—the law of gravity, for example—play themselves out without divine interference. Kushner is particularly good on this point, refusing as he does to blame God for the agony of a particular cancer patient, but insisting at the same time that the action of God is clearly visible in the "gifts" bestowed on such patients: "The strength to take each day as it comes, to be grateful for a day full of sunshine or one in which they are relatively free of pain."

According to Kushner, the vexing questions that enter the minds of those who find the world closing in on them—the victims of disease or downsizing, the survivors who mourn the death of a spouse or child—will surface in every life and recur in every generation. "The questions never change," he observes; "the search for a satisfying answer continues." That is where I found myself pausing as I read this insightful book (a book I readily recommend to anyone burdened with tragedy and distress) and coming to a different conclusion, one that I had the opportunity to mention to Rabbi Kushner at a White House prayer breakfast early in 1997.

# SEPARATE CONCLUSIONS

For me, and for those who believe as I do, the search has ended in Christ. This is not to say that I, or we, or anyone else has all the answers. I mean only to say that the reflective Christian has met Christ, as a serious questioner meets a satisfying answer. Christian spirituality savors the satisfaction of the answer in a challenging, but never complacent way. The challenge is what Christians call the *Paschal Mystery*, an intriguing notion explored later in this chapter.

Any person of faith, Jew or Christian, can agree with Kushner's observation that the success in your search for answers depends a lot on what you mean by "answer." If you expect fully satisfying explanations,

Kushner says, there is "probably no satisfying answer," so the pain "will still be there."

But so will you still be there, and life will be there challenging you to get on with it, to face up to the future, to help others, to love and smile and grow, and to believe that God is there with you, right there at your side. "That's the spirit," you might find yourself saying to someone else who is trying to rebound bravely and recover from a shattering reversal. The "spirit" you admire is, in fact, a functioning spirituality; it is evidence of the presence of the Holy Spirit in the human soul.

# Soft Solutions to Hard Problems

The spirituality that underlies this book equips you with some admittedly soft solutions to life's hard problems. As I mentioned earlier, this book gives you an invisible means of support. You might try it out, as Peter tried walking on the water (Matthew 14:28–31), only to lose heart and start to sink. Or you might stick with it and adopt the spiritual solutions offered in these pages as forces that imperceptibly supply balance, coherence, and consistency to all you do.

Peter's problem related to shaky faith. He and a boat full of disciples of Jesus were quite a distance from shore on a windy night in very choppy waters. Matthew's gospel (14:28–31) recounts that Jesus "came toward them walking on the sea." When the disciples saw him walking on the water, they were terrified, but Jesus said to them, "Take courage, it is I; do not be afraid." He then invited Peter to come toward him to walk on the waves. As the gospel account tells it, "Peter got out of the boat and began to walk on the water toward Jesus." For the moment, Peter's faith sustained him, but when he saw how strong the wind and the waves were, he faltered, began to sink, and cried for help. The gospel account, in words that have found their way into the hearts of countless Christians, says: "Immediately Jesus stretched out his hand and caught him, and said to him, 'O you of little faith, why did you doubt?'"

Belief in Jesus as Son of God and the Messiah sets Christians apart from Jews; it's a fundamental difference between the faiths. The difference lies not simply in an assent, on the part of Christians, to the proposition that Jesus is divine. It's more complex than that. The difference works itself out in a spirituality that integrates, however incompletely, the dimensions of the Paschal Mystery.

This expression encompasses the reality of Easter: the sufferings, death, resurrection, and ascension of Jesus. The Paschal Mystery allows the eye of Christian faith to "see" that there is life through death, a notion rooted in the Hebrew scriptures that relate the story of the original *pasch*, or "passover." The Paschal Mystery offers an interpretive framework through which the Christian comes to believe that the route to glory passes through shame and humiliation. In this faith-based value system, loss is the price of gain; defeat is the preface to victory. For those who believe this, personal hardships, including those encountered on the job, do have meaning, and transcendent meaning at that.

This specifically Christian perspective raises a host of intriguing issues. For example, in his book *Why Work* (Simon and Schuster, 1988), Michael Maccoby plays on Lord Acton's famous saying, "Power tends to corrupt, and absolute power tends to corrupt absolutely." Maccoby offers as a corollary "the equally certain law that powerlessness perverts" (p. 67). Christians, however, have a basis in faith for not overlooking the power of powerlessness.

Dealing with workplace difficulties can be a spiritual exercise, one that adds meaning to life and work. Just as the Father raised Jesus from the dead, the Christian's Easter faith maintains, so those whose baptismal commitment "plunged" them sacramentally and symbolically into the death of Jesus will also rise with Jesus for eternal glory. The process begins with baptism, which lets the baptized symbolically "die" with Jesus and then "rise" to walk in "newness of life" (Romans 6:4), the life of grace. In that death is a faith-based reality that puts the sorrows and setbacks of life into proper perspective, where they can be seen as preludes to glory.

Belief in the resurrection of Jesus is central to the Christian faith. To try to figure out exactly how that event happened is to reduce a mystery to a problem to be solved. The only "solution" is faith, which Christians use to make sense out of pain, suffering, illness, disappointment, defeat, and death. They know, by faith, that resurrection recoveries are available to them, by God's grace, in the aftermath of any reversal on their journey through life. They know that when they eventually die, they will rise from death to eternal life, again by God's grace.

# AMAZING, INDEED

Knowing all this by faith, Christians find themselves at Easter time singing "Amazing Grace" and giving thanks to God in Christ for making their redemption possible. If all this is true, they find themselves thinking, then this life with all its difficulties is something worth living to its fullest. Sure, it has its ups and downs, but all of it—pain and gain, sorrow and joy, defeat and victory—is good precisely because God chose to make it so in Christ.

So when bad things happen to good Christians, they can call on their own interpretive framework to search for a deeper meaning, a meaning available only to the eye of faith. This is not a grin-and-bear-it exercise or a matter of "carrying your cross." The meaning comes from a quiet conviction that the glorified Jesus, the victorious Jesus, lives now in glory. He is an eternal winner who is at the side of every believer at every stage of the believer's life. Christ's victory can never be reversed, and there lies the basis for the Christian believer's hope.

There is no room for smug complacency here. It's not that you have picked a winner, but that a winner has picked you. All you can do is be grateful and remain faithful, which requires you to act according to the law of love.

Let me close this circle that opened with an excerpt from Rabbi Kushner's book by recalling the words of the prophet Micah, words that are applicable today to all of us:

> You have been told, O man, what is good,
> and what the Lord requires of you:
> Only to do right and to love goodness,
> and to walk humbly with your God.
> (Micah 6:8)

That sounds to me like the basis of a spirituality capable of transforming both people and workplaces in a world where bad things can happen to anyone, but where everyone can survive and even prosper by simply choosing to "walk humbly" with God.

So here I am, Lord, trying to remember your goodness to me, trying to be grateful, trying to remember that it is the human condition to be "much obliged."

Lord, help me realize and recognize that I depend on your power for my very existence here on earth and for the life I hope to live with you forever.

When I pause to think about it, I have to conclude that not to be grateful is foolish; it's the practical equivalent of pretending not to exist.

Let me avoid pretending that I am not contingent, dependent, gifted, and graced. Let me avoid acting as though I were not something created. Let me avoid deluding myself into acting as though I brought myself into being; don't let me think I can propel myself through life on my own power.

I'm created and carried by you, Lord…so I'm grateful.

# PART TWO

## DEALING WITH WORKPLACE WOUNDS

# Chapter 4

# CRITICISM

Is there anyone alive who has never been criticized unfairly, misunderstood, passed over, forgotten, betrayed? Probably not, and an incalculable number of these "wounds" are inflicted in the workplace every day.

Criticism can be harsh and all too often compounded by false accusations and subtle forms of sabotage. Feelings of fear, anger, and shame often accompany workplace criticism; singly or in combination, these emotions will always be there. How, then, should you prepare to deal with any of these workplace wounds?

Spirituality can help you handle problems arising from criticism on the job; it gives you strength and helps you keep these setbacks in perspective. Spirituality provides answers from within—that is, from within your own soul.

## COMING TO PSYCHOLOGICAL BLOWS

Conflict is a given in the workplace, you're told. That may be so, but the nature of the conflict, and the way you respond to it, often speaks volumes about your relationships with those around you. A young woman who had worked as an administrative assistant once told me that an exchange with a rude, overbearing female bank manager nearly led to inflicting physical wounds.

The assistant was working with adding machine tapes and happened to have scissors in her hand when she was berated unfairly for a mistake in computing the total of a column of numbers. As it happened, this young woman hadn't been responsible for the error in question. All the same, a high-decibel volley of verbal abuse issued forth from the manager's desk.

This prompted the assistant to stand, tapes and scissors in hand, to attempt a clarification. The manager recoiled in horror, thinking she was about to be stabbed!

"I could never have done that," the assistant told me, "although I wanted to!" Instead, she dropped everything, including the scissors, and quit on the spot. Perhaps the reaction was extreme, perhaps it wasn't. Make no mistake, though; such tense situations in the workplace represent forms of spiritual and psychological violence, even if no physical blows occur.

After some reflection and soul searching, the young woman decided to use the concept of "human dignity" as her range finder in the search for new employment. Now she works as an office manager in a family-owned construction company, a place where, in her words, "they treat you like a human being." Career counselors can tell you that the failure to develop conflict-management skills is a significant hazard to career growth. This might be true, but ignoring the "treat me like a human being" standard in the workplace could be an even more serious career hazard.

# BEYOND THE STIFF UPPER LIP

"It's all part of the job. Either you can take it or you can't." This commonly expressed sentiment is not, perhaps, the most effective in formulating a long-term strategy for dealing with invasive, painful workplace criticism.

It's worth remembering that homicides occasionally happen in the workplace. They are rare enough to be considered newsworthy, so they become, paradoxically, major influences on the way some people view the workplace. ("If it bleeds, it leads" is the principle of selection guiding the decisions of many television news editors, a philosophy consistent with the values of the Interest-Excitement culture that drives that industry.) More often than not, though, workplace violence is related to off-the-job problems.

The wounds discussed in this and the following short chapters happen on the job; they are caused by emotions and events in the workplace. They are not physical, and neither are the bandages that spirituality can offer to help you tend to them. They are nevertheless quite real, and ignoring them or trying to pretend they don't exist can be a huge mistake.

50

In considering emotional wounds in general, I think of Shakespeare's words in *Othello*, act 2, scene 3, in which he has Iago say to Roderigo, "How poor are they that have not patience!/ What wound did ever heal but by degrees?" Iago's sinister role in the play shouldn't blind us to the wisdom of these words. Here, as elsewhere in the play, the Bard makes the creative choice of using perhaps his greatest villain to pass along eminently sound counsel.

Any wound, physical or psychological, needs time to heal. (Later in that same speech, Iago refers to it pointedly as "dilatory Time.") If an injury is to heal, it must indeed heal "by degrees." It takes patience, one of the Pauline Criteria, to permit this to happen.

Patience, you will recall, implies a certain amount of suffering. No one instinctively welcomes suffering (even in the relatively mild form of patience), but suffering is easier to bear if it's accepted as necessary to heal a particular wound. Patience, you must never forget, implies full acceptance of a problem, not an attempt to rationalize away its existence.

## RESPONDING TO CRITICISM

In one of George Gordon Lord Byron's poems, there is a memorable description of an eagle being wounded by a "fatal dart," a dart guided in its lethal trajectory by one of that eagle's own feathers. Bear in mind, in dealing with the problems of workplace criticism, that you can bring, or help to bring, the wound on yourself. Clearly, this is a point to be pondered as you consider the "darts" others may send your way during the working day.

Listen to Lord Byron:

*'Twas thine own genius gave the final blow,*
*And help'd to plant the wound that laid thee low:*
*So the struck eagle, stretched upon the plain,*
*No more through rolling clouds to soar again,*
*View'd his own feather on the fatal dart,*
*And wing'd the shaft that quiver'd in his heart;*

*continues*

51

*continued*

*Keen were his pangs, but keener far to feel*
*He nursed the pinion which impell'd the steel;*
*While the same plumage that had warm'd his nest*
*Drank the last life-drop of his bleeding breast.*
*("English Bards and Scotch Reviewers," lines 819–828)*

The recognition of your own "genius" as something capable of enhancing a wound is a very healthy, if humbling, gift.

As the recognition that you are responsible for how you react to the darts of others dawns on you, it can indeed give rise to some keen pangs. Usually, the wounds you associate with criticism aren't exactly fatal; you can surely "soar again," if not through "rolling clouds," at least along the high road of reconnection and recovery. But it will take time.

Perhaps some of your habitual ways of evaluating workplace situations enhance or strengthen cycles of criticism you experience from others in the workplace. If you've become accustomed to saying, "Time is money," why not try a variation on that theme? Try this experiment. Say, if only to yourself, "Time is patience, and it takes both time and patience for any wound to heal."

## THE POWER OF PRAISE

"Spray the place with praise," a wise elder executive once advised a young manager. The older man was not suggesting flattery, just honest recognition, positive reinforcement, respectful affirmation, and constructive appraisal.

Criticism usually takes the opposite route. Public criticism makes the negativity visible and audible, to the embarrassment of the person being criticized. Unfair criticism (rarely regarded as such by the busy or preoccupied person issuing it) compounds the humiliation by adding the dimension of injustice.

Even someone who is "addicted" to criticism can be transformed by a few moments of heartfelt, reality-based public praise from a colleague. (If you never receive it, you can hardly know how to give it!) This strategy is fully in keeping with the Pauline notion of love, and worth considering closely as you reflect on your day-to-day dealing with hypercritical colleagues.

# FORMAL EVALUATION, INFORMAL EVALUATION

It is routine in the workplace to assess performance against pre-established norms and mutually understood expectations, which can be an ideal forum for constructive criticism. Most supervisors tend to put assessment off, however, simply because they're uneasy doing it. Excessive supervision is often found in organizations suffering from an absence of corporate vision. So a tendency to postpone formal assessment of the people a manager is responsible for supervising isn't necessarily a bad thing. It could happen with managers caught up in forward, visionary thinking; they communicate vision and enthusiasm and prefer to cheer employees on as a team, rather than measuring individual performance step-by-step with a formal performance review. This kind of manager exhibits trust, which, in turn, almost always stimulates productivity.

Such a manager, however, like the parent of an adolescent, has to face the problem of figuring out where trust ends and neglect begins. This task is never easy and might best be regarded as an ongoing series of adjustments, rather than a single policy that can be "implemented" and then forgotten.

Some species of "formal" constructive criticism are always a part of workplace life. If this criticism has the following characteristics, then it's unlikely that any but the thinnest of skins will be wounded in the process:

◆ It's balanced
◆ It takes place in a supportive, informal workplace environment
◆ It takes the form of a formal, scheduled, straightforward exchange
◆ It's handled professionally and with a measure of encouragement by the person passing along the information

Both the giver and receiver of formal constructive criticism must make an effort to remain calm and clear during these exchanges. A minimal amount of strategic preparation for the meeting usually does the trick.

Don't assume the worst before any meeting meant to help you focus on performance issues; if you do, you might bring about the worst. Just as you can't see the bottom of a pool or lake when the waters are agitated, you will never see assessment issues without distortion if either party to the evaluation conversation is emotionally upset. By the same token, if nothing about measurement norms is set out clearly beforehand on paper, for both to see, then agitation or emotional turmoil is much more likely to result.

# A Marathon Session

David Morrison told me an interesting case history that originated in a performance evaluation and led to the discovery of a very deep wound.

An organization that prided itself on its policy in never laying off top managers referred a man to Morrison for evaluation. The manager wanted, whenever possible, to work away from corporate headquarters. He appeared to be anxious and deeply troubled about something. Just as troubling to his supervisors, he tended to begin work late on Monday and end his workweek early on Friday.

His supervisors suspected alcoholism. His immediate supervisor spent eight hours with him discussing a performance appraisal, one with which the subordinate didn't agree. He took the "step up" approach by appealing to the CEO, who, remarkably, spent a total of 18 hours with him in some focused sessions meant to evaluate his performance.

Although the CEO directed him to have an outside consultation with Dr. Morrison, the distressed manager delayed making the appointment for several months. When the meeting finally took place, however, it didn't result in the findings the senior executives at the company had anticipated.

The evaluation found that the manager was not an alcoholic, although he certainly was very anxious. "I feel like I'm walking on a razor's edge all the time," he confided to Morrison. The causes and expressions of this feeling were, it turned out, more complex than his superiors expected.

He was deeply troubled, for example, by the traffic he encountered going to and coming from the workplace, just one of a series of symptoms indicating the profound dislocation this manager associated with his workplace. He had been raised on one coast in a rural setting with close family attachments and was now working on the opposite coast in a pressure-packed urban environment. He showed signs of an unmet need for close family attachments.

Toward the end of their session together, Dr. Morrison was chatting informally with this anxious manager and chose to take that relatively innocuous time to raise a potentially serious issue. "I notice," Dr. Morrison said, "that when you were 14, one of your brothers died. Can you tell me about that?" The manager's whole demeanor changed. A story then unfolded that had never been shared with anyone else, not even with the troubled man's wife. Morrison had established a nonconfrontational relationship that permitted the manager to share his experience.

When he was 14, he had wanted a rifle for Christmas but hadn't gotten one. A close friend of the family who was about his age, however, did receive a .22 caliber weapon. He and his brother played with this gun; they always did exactly what safety requirements dictated because both wanted to prove to their parents that they could handle the responsibility.

The two families visited a lake house on vacation. The two brothers took the borrowed gun and rowed across the small lake for target practice. Usually, they would not put more than one shell at a time in the rifle, and they never walked with the gun loaded. For one exercise they were doing on that particular day, however, they needed to shoot two shots, so they put two rounds in the rifle. Just as they fired the first, they were called from across the lake to come for lunch. They stopped, put the gun in the boat, and began to row back to the lake house.

As they came to the shore, the boat hit a rock. The gun went off and the bullet went right through his brother's heart.

There he was, the boy who had always done everything exactly right; his parents, who loved both their sons, were trying to help this one while they were mourning the loss of their other son. It proved to be a job that was just too big for them.

It was at this point in the narrative that the man started crying and said to Dr. Morrison, "I've never told anybody else this story—never."

In the aftermath of the tragedy, the poor youngster had never talked about it in detail with his grief-stricken parents. Now, so many years later, this hapless fellow said to Morrison, "It just wasn't fair; it just wasn't fair. I've gone over it again and again. I've tried to make it logical; I've tried to make it fair. But it just wasn't fair."

Morrison saw to it that the man was referred to someone who could help him work through the confusion, grief, and anger, and in three months, he was functioning well on the job. A few months after that, however, the firm faced for the first time in its history the pressures of downsizing. The CEO said to Morrison, "We've got too many people at his level. We've got to get rid of somebody in that part of the organization, and he's right there at the bottom. He's doing better, but he's on the bottom. I've got to let him go."

Morrison commented, in relating this story to me, that the decision appeared to be unfair to everybody, even the CEO, because the economy, rather than any single individual, was forcing the decision. Yet the fundamental, unspoken message this manager received was a clear one: "You're not needed; you don't count." Talk about workplace criticism! Although no one in the organization was trying to send such a message, it was nevertheless what was being received.

The man was notified of the decision to let him go. He reacted badly, refused the firm's offer of outplacement services, protested the decision, and threatened to sue. He was referred back to Morrison for help. Not surprisingly, his bitter summary of this reversal was, "It's not fair; it doesn't make any sense."

Morrison's response to this manager was in complete agreement with the Pauline notion of patience. He told the man:

*"No, it's not fair. And your job is to forget about it being fair. Fairness is something you do for other people, but when it comes to yourself, you don't need to worry about it being fair; you have to worry about you getting out of life what is the best for you. If you sit here and worry about making this fair, right here and now, then you'll get out of life what isn't good for you."*

The patience to accept the reversal, to process it and move on, was going to be an integral part of this worker's obedience to the laws of growth. "He didn't like that," Morrison told me, "but he listened to it and did it well, got another job and moved on with his life."

56

That unusual story shows how workplace interactions can sometimes lead to the discovery of old wounds that were never attended to. In these interactions, as in so many, what you bring to the situation often dictates what you get out of it.

## SERENITY: THE BEST RESPONSE TO WORDS MEANT TO HURT

Workplace wounds induced by conscious, hurtful criticism can be incubated in jealousy and spite, transmitted by direct verbal attack, or passed along indirectly through anonymous (almost always cowardly) notes or cutting remarks overheard or reported at second or third hand. If you encounter such criticism, how will you react?

Fighting vitriol with vitriol is not a good idea. Serenity (not to be confused with stony silence) is an excellent defense, firmly rooted in the Pauline value of self-control.

Don't pursue conflict for its own sake. If others are present, a simple question directed to them—"Do you agree with that?"—can help put everything in the proper context.

If you're faced with unfair, even abusive, criticism from a colleague who approaches you one-on-one, your strategy is simple: listen. Be sure you hear what's being said. Repeat it aloud.

If what is being said is untrue and a threat to your career, reduce what you heard to writing, add your explanatory or defensive commentary, and ask to have a conversation with your immediate supervisor. Also, cultivate the habit of "listening generously," a quality that career expert Lynne Waymon recommends, in good times and in bad, for all who interact in the workplace.

In the matter of unfair criticism, as in so many other unpleasant workplace situations (particularly when you are caught in an ethical dilemma), your best response, one that will be made easier by your reliance on and cultivation of self-control, is to avoid responding in kind to your accuser. Beyond that, if you face a truly serious situation, you should consider taking the one-level-up route: Talk to your immediate boss. If your immediate boss is the problem, go up another level or more until you connect with a responsible person who can hear you out. If you're the CEO and the problem is your chairman, take it to your board!

If what is being said is untrue but not a threat to your employment, or not worth alerting higher-ups about, reject the criticism firmly. Do this without emotion and without discussion. If someone rolls a ball in your direction, you don't have a game of catch unless you pick up the ball. Once again, self-control is an essential part of your response. Usually, it's easy to reject the criticism but difficult not to reject the person. Try always to keep the door between you open. Face up to the difficulty as best you can, and leave yourself open to an apology...always.

If what is being said is true, even though the message was rudely served up by a person who has no right to criticize you, talk it over with a trusted friend in or out of the workplace. Hard as it is to take at times, the truth can always help you.

If the message was anonymous or communicated to you by a third party who received it in confidence, give it the same validity test outlined in this chapter and act accordingly. Either take it to heart, or toss it in the wastebasket...and then move on.

If you have high visibility as a manager, there are ways of getting the word out that you never read anonymous mail. Provide an ombudsman if your organization is large and complex; anonymity should always be offered to conscientious whistle-blowers. But if it is known throughout your organization that anonymous communications will be filtered and normally not get through to you, crank complaints will diminish as will interference with your sleep. And take this tip: A good sleep-preserving principle for the busy manager is never to read any mail after 5:00 p.m.

There's nothing wrong with you if you are sensitive, even thin-skinned. Thin-skinned people can benefit from the reminder that spirituality emanates from within, from within the soul. If the skin, as the saying goes, "is the surface of the mind, and the mind is the surface of the soul," thin-skinned people have an advantage—faster access to the soul, which is the ultimate repository for answers from within.

# INNERCISE

Just as physical exercise tones up both the muscles and the skin, spiritual exercise (some call it *innercise*) can strengthen the soul against any possible workplace wound, including the wound of criticism.

Fitness-conscious people are conscientious about working out, often every day. Anyone concerned about spiritual fitness should be just as conscientious about working in. This commitment means a regimen of some form of daily prayer. Your commitment should also include reflective reading and ongoing reminders to yourself about the importance of listening to God's voice in the circumstances of your life and seeing God's hand in the wonders of creation.

If the physically fit, because of repeated physical exercise, enjoy a longer life expectancy, it seems logical to suggest a spiritual parallel. The inner spiritual life might have been on Robert Frost's mind when he wrote:

*Our very life depends on everything's*
*Recurring till we answer from within.*
*The thousandth time may prove the charm.*

If, in the face of criticism, you find that you have nothing to draw upon from within, the situation you face is clear: You have some innercising to do. The thousandth time could indeed prove the charm.

In anticipating future criticism, give some thought to these words from the famous peace prayer of Saint Francis of Assisi: "Grant that I may not so much seek to be understood as to understand." And from that same prayer: "Where there is hatred, let me sow love." Let these petitions sink into your soul so that they can become principles to guide your response to workplace criticism.

*Chapter 5*

# FEAR

Fear is usually a self-inflicted wound.

It is intimately related to worry, and worry almost always arises over something that doesn't exist (or, at the very least, no longer exists, or doesn't yet and might never exist). Many wise people have observed that fear is the opposite of love, the first Pauline principle. Not all our workplace exchanges, of course, are driven by love. It's hard to imagine a workplace relationship, however, that wouldn't benefit from a commitment to renew the value of nonexploitive, accepting love, the kind of love that reflects God's love for us.

## FEAR REFLECTED ON ITSELF

A perceptive man who runs a high-technology firm was described to me as someone who knows people as well as he knows technology. He understands the people who create, use, and are affected by that technology. On one occasion, he wondered whether an employee, who was experiencing serious performance problems and whom he was eager to help, was suffering from some kind of attention-deficit disorder.

Psychological tests revealed no problem. The employee tested well cognitively and gave no evidence of being out of touch with reality. He lacked confidence, however, and was distressed because he always seemed to be convinced that something was wrong with him.

This employee was worrying about his worrying. Only after medical and psychiatric evaluations validated his health could the employee be persuaded to use the knowledge that he was healthy to free himself from worry. Before this reassurance, he was both healthy (although unconvinced that he was) and distressed (because he thought he had something to worry about). Once convinced that he had no health problems, he could accept a physician's instructions and the unremitting encouragement of his boss to stop worrying and take control. It took him a while to learn that worry typically looks to a past that is dead or a future that might not happen as the worrier envisions it. Worry has an insidious capacity to pull the worrier out of the present, the only place where he or she does, in fact, exist.

Recall that President Franklin Delano Roosevelt, in his inaugural address on March 4, 1933, said that "the only thing we have to fear is fear itself." Roosevelt immediately added that fear is a "nameless, unreasoning, unjustified terror which paralyzes needed efforts to convert retreat into advance."

Having nothing to fear but fear itself could have been what Ralph Waldo Emerson was suggesting in the poem "Borrowing," which is included in his *Quatrains*:

> *Some of your hurts you have cured,*
> *And the sharpest you still have survived,*
> *But what torments of grief you endured*
> *From evils which never arrived!*

You can save yourself a good deal of the grief Emerson mentions by simply maintaining a sensible, prudent, and balanced orientation in the present. Embracing the present moment with love (the first Pauline value), patience (the fourth), and faithfulness (the seventh) can help you to banish fear and worry from your workplace life.

## FEAR TAKES MANY FORMS

Workplace fear can take the form of fear of discovery, fear of failure, fear of criticism, fear of loss of job, or fear of what others might think.

If your fear of discovery relates to criminal behavior, get a lawyer. If it's fear of something actually or possibly unethical coming to light, talk first to an adviser you trust, and next to a responsible person in the organization.

Understand, however, that most of us spend too much time worrying about the discovery of minor lapses and honest errors in judgment—problems that take more effort and energy to conceal than they are worth.

If the actions that concern you fall into this category, remind yourself that nobody's perfect and then address this question to yourself: "What's the worst that could happen if I shared this problem openly with all the affected parties?"

If it's failure you fear, recognize that not everything depends on you. You have associates (the preferred term now for *employees* in many organizations) ready to work with you if you let them know you're open to collaboration. A workplace touched by the spirituality discussed in Chapter One, "Spirituality and the Human Predicament," will be an increasingly collaborative, rather than a destructively competitive, place. Your own experience and commitment to spiritual values can free you up to begin the "ally relationship" your current project might demand. Remember: The spirituality I've invited you to consider will sustain you in the midst of uncertainty; it will shore up your faith in yourself as well as in God.

Unbelievers never try, but even believers of long standing have difficulty in accepting as personally applicable to themselves the word of God in scriptural expressions like these:

*I have the strength for everything through him who empowers me.*
*(Philippians 4:11-13)*

*Entrust your works to the Lord and your plans will succeed.*
*(Proverbs 16:3)*

Any believer can bring these words to bear in daily life by grounding them on the absolute, faith-based conviction that God is with and within him or her all the time.

God is interested in and engaged with you in whatever is happening to or through you at any particular moment. The spirituality you bring with you into the workplace can heighten your awareness of an active God at work in the world, who wants to work through you. You have nothing to fear. Recall that fear itself is all you have to fear, and then say, with the psalmist:

*Prosper the work of our hands! Prosper the work of our hands!*
*(Psalm 90:17)*

If you take this approach, criticism and censure, and even the possibility of career disruptions, will seem less threatening than they would to a person with lots of fears and little faith. Know that God is with you at all times, and that your conscious concern to reflect God's love in the world will help you clear the hurdles and overcome the obstacles that are always a part of working life.

# A LESSON

Take a lesson from the life of my friend Lillian Brill. This lesson came to me directly from her, by word and example, shortly before she died. It embodies a spiritual principle that served her well both in life and death, but especially in life, in the many workplaces that were enriched by her competent and caring presence as an army nurse.

Lillian had an abiding conviction that God could never let her down, could never be anything but faithful to his promise to love her and be with her, no matter what.

She was ill, more so than I realized, when she gave me a cheerful telephone call one morning to say she wanted me to officiate at her funeral. "Nothing sad or solemn," she said, "I want it to be a happy celebration." She asked that I drive over from Washington to see her at her home in Annapolis a day or two after her next monthly blood transfusion ("my cocktail party") that was part of her battle against Hodgkin's disease.

Lillian wanted me to help her plan the funeral liturgy. She asked that I bring another friend, Elaine Walter, dean of the School of Music at The Catholic University of America where Lillian had studied nursing.

"I love the violin," Lillian reminded Elaine as our planning session began in her brightly decorated waterside cottage. It was a very pleasant, sunny morning in the middle of the week. Elaine assured her that the violin would have a prominent place in the program of music; Lillian specified selections she would like included in the program.

Turning to me, this retired Army colonel, who looked vibrant and not at all close to death, asked if the Mass could be celebrated in the nearby Naval Academy Chapel where, in retirement, she often worshipped. I assured her that this could be easily arranged. Then she said, "As I told you on the phone, no gloom, no doom. Keep it light and make it a genuine celebration. You see, for years I've been paging through the Bible and pausing to underline those sections where God makes promises to his people. You'd have trouble counting all those promises of fidelity and salvation."

Then she came to her central point: "And if God is God, he can't be anything but faithful to his promises. So what do I have to fear?"

She died three weeks later. Her funeral went exactly as planned. I had the honor of letting Lillian deliver the homily at her own funeral. All I did was spell out for those who gathered in remembrance and celebration of her life the invaluable lesson Lillian taught me when she uttered those two memorable sentences about God's promises to his people.

## OVERCOMING FEAR

Each time you overcome fear of any kind—picking up the telephone to make a call you're afraid of placing, seeing your physician when you fear the news won't be good, asking for the sale when you're worried about a turndown, exposing yourself to the possibility of criticism or rejection, facing up to whatever it is that tends to immobilize you—it makes you a freer, fuller person.

On a completely worldly, totally secular level, you're a better, more productive person, more fully engaged with practical reality. On the spiritual level, facing up to fear is a way of affirming your belief that God is there at your side, standing by you in the troubling circumstance, with you all the way.

The collected spiritual wisdom of the ages puts this simple question to you every moment of your waking life: If God is with you, who can be against you?

Take a moment now to think about that question. I believe that once you do, you will be inspired to live the rest of your life with the obvious and only possible answer to that question echoing in your heart. Let your response activate the love, patience, and faithfulness that will, along with the other Pauline principles, become for you a matter of habit rooted deep in your soul.

# ATTITUDE

Dealing with fear through the values of love, faithfulness, and quiet courage, as Lillian did, is all a question of attitude, and you are in charge of your attitudes.

The word *attitude* suggests a tilt, a slant, a leaning toward. You can choose to be positive or negative, upbeat or downcast, hopeful or pessimistic, fearful or peaceful. No one but you can determine how you will "trim your sails" to navigate the troubled waters that can swirl around you at any time.

The following anonymous reflection was under the desktop glass close to the telephone Kevin Dolan used during his transition period from a good job just lost to another not yet found. It helped to overcome the fear he felt that he would never find another good job.

**Attitude**

*The longer I live, the more I realize the effect of attitude on life. Attitude is more important than facts. It is more important than the past, than education, than money, than circumstances, than failures, than successes, than what other people think of, say, or do. It is more important than appearance, giftedness, or skill. It will make or break a company, a school, or a home. The remarkable thing is we have a choice every day regarding the attitude we will embrace. We cannot change our past…. We cannot change the fact that people will act in a certain way. We cannot change the inevitable. The only thing we can do is to play on the string we have. And that is our attitude. I am convinced that life is 10 percent what happens to me and 90 percent how I react to it. And so it is with you…. We are in charge of our attitudes.*

There is no question about it: You *are* in charge of your attitudes. You're doing yourself no favor by permitting an attitude of fearfulness to paralyze you.

Repeat the questioning process outlined in this chapter as many times as necessary, and don't be surprised to learn that "necessary" means at regular or irregular intervals for the rest of your life. If God is really with you (your faith assures you this is so), who can be against you? The answer to that question has to come from within. Search your soul for the answer. If you find yourself coming up empty, keep searching. You might discover the need to do some prayerful listening to scripture: to the Psalms, to the Sermon on the Mount, or to other sources of reassurance in the inspired word of God. Use them to fill up that seemingly empty center of your soul; it won't stay empty for long.

I have often thought about how perceptive playwright Robert Bolt's observation is: "It is with us as it is with our cities: an accelerating flight to the periphery, leaving a center that is empty when the hours of business are over." Fear often indicates an empty center, a vacuum in the soul. Surely, God intends no one to live this way. God does intend, however, that you listen to his word, internalize it, and let it drive fears from your soul, shape your attitudes, and guide your choices.

I can think of no better way to close this discussion of fear than to repeat this advice from Proverbs and urge you, too, to repeat it often.

*Entrust your works to the Lord, and your plans will succeed.*
*(Proverbs 16:3)*

*Boost my spirits, Lord. I would be a walking optimist, if what I really believe would only penetrate my outlook and propel my movement through life. But I'm not, and it doesn't.*

*When I think of faith, Lord, I don't think of a collection of statements that say what I believe. I think of the circus and an empty trapeze, swinging empty, back and forth. I imagine myself on another trapeze, hanging on, and swinging back and forth, in rhythm with the empty trapeze bar that seems to be inviting me to let go and make the leap. That's faith for me, Lord: letting go. I count on you to provide the safety net.*

*I'm not expecting to hear the roar of the crowd, Lord; I just want to get the gift of hope that comes with faith. I'm hanging on, but you keep swinging empty trapeze bars in front of me, asking me to keep on letting go and trusting. I'll try. I want to. But boost my spirits, Lord, so I can know you more as promise, protector, and presence in all my letting go's and catching on's.*

*Chapter* 6

# BETRAYAL

The workplace wound of betrayal can be interpreted and treated within the framework of Christian spirituality more readily than most. When the average person, religious or not, hears the word *betrayal*, he or she tends to associate it more or less automatically with the name Judas.

Anyone even vaguely familiar with the story of Jesus' life knows that Judas betrayed him and that some equivalent of the gospel's "thirty pieces of silver"—in other words, some form of greed, gain, or self-promotion—can usually explain a betrayer's motivation. Weakness of character, such as that shown by Judas Iscariot, can also contribute to the betrayer's unprincipled act.

Whatever the explanation, betrayal happens in the workplace, and its victims suffer. Put yourself in the shoes of anyone who has experienced betrayal—you might not have to go far beyond your own clothes closet to find a good fit!

If you need an example, however, I can offer one. A manager I know is a seasoned professional who was encouraged to be candid and completely frank with the selection committee reviewing internal candidates for promotion to an executive-level position reporting directly to the CEO. As requested, she was disarmingly direct in assessing her strengths and weaknesses, as well as the strengths and weaknesses in the substance and style of the CEO's approach to management. She did this to lay out a framework in which their relative strengths and weaknesses could be matched up and some judgments made concerning the likelihood of a good fit, a positive working-relationship, if she were selected for the position.

Someone on the selection committee broke the presumably unshakable commitment of confidentiality that had been touted during her interview as an integral part of the selection process. That unknown someone disclosed to the CEO all the "negatives" in the candidate's assessment of his management record. Instead of a promotion, the candidate got a summons to appear before the CEO, explain her disloyalty, and defend her right to continued employment in her present job.

Needless to say, she felt betrayed. She remains on the job, considering herself now to be "unpromotable" in that organization and doomed to a distant but "correct" relationship with the boss as long as she remains there. She may well leave the firm someday. When and if she does, she probably won't get a glowing reference from the CEO. Perhaps more important, now she will be less trusting and more careful. Sad.

For another example of workplace betrayal, consider the case of the designer of a major corporation's information management system. He was given confidential orders, in light of a board-level downsizing decision, to reconfigure the system and write out (that is, eliminate) many jobs. He carried out this sensitive assignment well and without breaching the trust that had been accorded him. He was well aware that his own job title would be eliminated in the restructuring, but it never occurred to him that he would wind up on the street. He simply assumed, because the application of his talent to this assignment would save the corporation $6 million, that there would be a place for him on the scaled-down organization's management team. Not so. They let him go. He went away mad, feeling betrayed.

# TRUST LOST

Trust is almost always a casualty in any betrayal situation.

Betrayal of trust means broken promises, trashed agreements, and reversal of assurances. It means abdication of the basic responsibilities of friendship: dependability and reliability. At bottom, betrayal is a refusal to love, but that dimension of the reality is hardly ever recognized when it happens.

Curiously, the victim of betrayal often feels shame, a shame that's much like that sometimes felt by those who experience rape. Some people, for example, react to job loss that is totally without fault on their part with a feeling of profound shame.

Shame is a very tricky affect; it lowers the eyes, drops the head, and promotes withdrawal. Shame tends to immobilize a person, so it can be profoundly debilitating.

Shame is not the only possible reaction to betrayal, of course. Workplace betrayers might send their victims into sudden torrents of fury. The anger triggered by betrayal often precipitates an immediate but unwise response to the situation.

When betrayed, you must not yield to either shame or rage. You have to find a way to let the Pauline value of self-control guide you back toward a necessary balance.

If you permit the emotional volcano that follows betrayal to turn in on itself, you run the risk of depression. If you release that energy in the form of anger, and strike back at the betrayer or simply vent your rage, you lose control (and thus diminish your humanity). You also further pollute the very workplace environment that your vocation is calling you to make more civil, cordial, and human.

What, then, are you to do when you are betrayed?

# THE EXAMPLE OF JESUS

Jesus knew who his betrayer was, but he permitted Judas to greet and kiss him. Listen to what Jesus said to the man who sold him out: "Friend, do what you have come for." (Matthew 26:50) There is sadness and resignation in that line, but no hint of anger or revenge. Sure, it saddened him to know that a member of his trusted inner circle was about to do him in, but there you have a clue: A managed sadness, far stronger than anger, is the appropriate response to betrayal.

Jesus moved on with what he had to do, but he remained wide open and completely ready to forgive. Asking for or receiving forgiveness was not his problem; that was up to Judas. Being prepared to forgive, and being ready to deal constructively with the effects of betrayal, is the challenge that can be met only by the one who was or is about to be betrayed.

Just a few lines after this account of the exchange between Jesus and Judas in Matthew's gospel is Jesus' famous saying: "Put your sword back into its sheath, for all who take the sword will perish by the sword."

(Matthew 26:52) If you have experienced betrayal first hand, this gospel message is worth considering closely. If you try to live by the "sword" of retaliation in the workplace, you will surely die a workplace death by someone else's sword.

Recall the Pauline Criteria: love, joy, peace, patience, kindness, generosity, faithfulness, gentleness, and self-control. These values (especially self-control, in this case) are your arms and armor. Using them will not only preserve your workplace life, but also encourage others there to equip themselves in similar fashion.

# WHAT TO DO

As in the case of unfair criticism, the one-level-up approach should be taken as you move on with life, choosing the higher road as your route to recovery from the damaging effects of betrayal. Consider the following true story, however, where the problem existed one level up with a hostile board of directors, and there was no higher level where the score could be settled. There was no principled, neutral superior to whom to appeal, so the betrayed person just decided to move on.

He was a chairman and CEO who had hit all performance targets, met the goals set for him by the board, and delivered impressive results to the bottom line. When he asked the board for reciprocity and complained about the hostility they were showing him, the ranking member snapped, "What did you expect me and the rest of us to be, a friend? If you want a friend, get a dog." The CEO's many contributions were reduced to a single, sadistic, and not-all-that-original joke. Ever since millions of moviegoers first heard it in the film *Wall Street*, the "get a dog" rejoinder is commonly used to justify inhumane and abusive treatment in the workplace.

Some workplace environments are poisoned and not worth saving. You simply have to move on. Once you move on, you can further free yourself by exercising the self-control that allows you to stop talking about it. Let it ride. Get on with your life.

A really well-functioning spirituality frees you up enough to forgive. Remember that the virtue of self-control is the one you rely on most heavily in betrayal situations, and use it to overcome the temptation to attack the motives and character of your betrayers. You should even be able to boast (to yourself, at least) about your willingness to forgive. Your refusal to speak ill of those who turned against you will bear quiet, eloquent witness to your forgiveness and provide a measure of your largeness of heart and the depth of your humanity. Every betrayal carries with it an opportunity for growth.

## "AND ON THE NIGHT HE WAS BETRAYED, HE TOOK BREAD..."

If you need a story to help you wrap your mind around the issue of betrayal and how to grow through it, recall the gospel story of the betrayal of Jesus. What can you learn from this unparalleled example?

Christians, in their eucharistic celebrations, remember Jesus "in the breaking of the bread." They give thanks for the good that came to them out of his betrayal. They focus on the verbs in the scriptural accounts, a focus that can be helpful to anyone trying to deal with betrayal. The gospel accounts say he "took," "blessed," "broke," and "gave" bread to his closest friends—his associates, his companions—after first "giving thanks" to the Creator of everything: bread, friendship, and life itself.

You, too, in your own time, have to give thanks, even in the wake of betrayal. Take hold of the "bread" of daily existence, even when it includes the experience of betrayal, and bless it. A blessing means saying something good about that which is blessed. (Literally, a blessing is a *bene-dictio*, a well-saying.) Whatever you face, it somehow comes from God, who at least permits it and can, therefore, draw good from it. Then break the loaf of reality that's yours, break it open so you can give it (and yourself) to your brothers and sisters in the human community. You will encounter your segment of that community in workplace, or family, or wherever you happen to be. That's precisely where you have to share—to give fully and generously of yourself.

## BEYOND THE PAIN

Betrayal, badly managed, can become an enemy within—and that's the only way it will ever truly hurt you. "We are betrayed," wrote the poet George Meredith, "by what is false within."

You can be hurt only if you let that falsehood—the injustice, the hatred—reside within. Remember, betrayal is, at its core, a refusal to love. If you find yourself, when betrayed, refusing to love, you are not only ignoring the first of the Pauline principles, you are also falling into a trap set for you by the Enemy.

Your spirituality is there to remind you that you can do far, far better than that!

*Straight are the paths of the Lord; in them the just walk, but sinners stumble in them. (Hosea, 14:10)*

Chapter 7

# FALSE ACCUSATIONS

A false accusation is always unjust. It differs from criticism because there's no element or even possibility of truth in a false accusation. Such accusations are a form of betrayal, but they aren't necessarily related to the prior condition of trust or friendship that makes betrayal so hard to take.

A false accusation is simply a lie…and it wounds.

## IMMEDIATE RESPONSES

It was not a false accusation, just an unspoken question, when a high school teacher, a friend of mine, turned quickly and caught the eye of a student who could possibly have tossed a wet wad of paper that had just hit the blackboard.

"It wasn't me, sir," the student blurted out.

"It wasn't I," said the teacher in his unflagging commitment to correct grammar.

"I know it wasn't you, sir, but it wasn't me neither," said the anxious youngster, for whom, at the moment, establishing innocence was clearly more important than speaking correct English.

There will be moments in your life when, with or without fault on the part of another, you will be falsely accused—not just questioned or suspected, but charged falsely. You might be totally convinced, absolutely sure, that "It wasn't I," but someone will assert the contrary. Although your instinct will be to brand your accuser as a liar, that person might not be lying. To say something that turns out to be incorrect isn't necessarily lying. A lie is a statement (or an expression, like a nod of the head) that conveys to someone who has a right to know the opposite of what, in your mind, you know to be true. When you say you spoke to someone last Tuesday, and the conversation actually took place on Wednesday, you aren't lying; you're just confused. If you stole a sum of money and deny it when authorities question you, you are both a thief and a liar.

There is a genteel kind of false accusation that floats like a feather in almost every workplace. More gossipy than accusatory, attributions of motivation, for instance, are blithely made without any knowledge at all of what's actually happening in the mind and heart of the person who is presumed, for some unflattering reason, to be doing this or that. Public figures live with this gossip and have no recourse to legal protection from slander or even libel, but private persons intent on minding their own business are often wounded by others who prefer not to mind theirs, and act, for all the world, as though they were omniscient.

They think they can read the minds and motives of others and disclose whatever they think they have "read" in others. This curious reading habit isn't prompted by a love of learning. It can be explained only in terms of pettiness, insecurity, envy, curiosity, boredom, jealousy, hatred, or some combination of these elements, and more.

More destructive forms of false accusation, in the style made famous by "honest" Iago, happen all the time. These accusations not only wound— they kill. Othello believed his trusted friend, so Desdemona died. There might not be workplace fatalities associated with false accusations, but the "death" of your ability to trust and deal openly with others is certainly at issue in such situations. Your good name, too, of course, is under attack.

Your proper and immediate concern, after learning that you have been falsely accused, is with reputation, if you are lucky; it could be your career that's now in danger. You have to act to defend yourself whenever reputation, career, or more is at stake.

# JUST THE FACTS

There's nothing like a fact to dispose of a falsehood.

If you're accused of having said or done something you didn't, post proofs that will defend you. It isn't always possible to prove what you did not say or do; it's easier to find documentation for and witness to what you *did* do or say.

These are steps you must take when you're under direct assault. Your aim is to defend yourself, not to retaliate or prove to the whole world that you know why your accuser acts as he or she does. Avoid mud-wrestling in the motivation pit.

Just as others cannot with certainty read your mind, you can't know for sure why they are doing this to you. Better to let your character stand up in your defense. At the end of the day, your own integrity will prove to be your best shield.

The way you conduct yourself in the workplace is, in fact, your character in motion. People will have noticed this, simply because it's impossible for you to go unnoticed wherever you work. You might be unappreciated, but not unnoticed. Others have been observing you every day, just as you have been observing them. They make judgments about you, just as you make judgments about them, and those judgments can be wrong, either way. Moreover, these judgments are so much a part of human nature and so often neutral in their evaluative dimensions that you don't give them a second thought. They do, however, contribute toward you gradually forming an impression of another person, distinctive if not detailed. The way you carry yourself and the emotional reaction you bring to the accusations you face say a great deal about you to others who draw their own conclusions from your accuser's charges.

Just as you should gather proofs in your own defense, a false accuser should be challenged to post proof in support of the false charges. In the absence of proof, however, the jury of your workplace peers will always find in your favor because of the person they know you to be.

When the Pauline values become part of you, you are, unlike Iago, an honest person of integrity. You don't merely seem trustworthy, as Iago did; you are. (About Iago, the tragically misled Othello said: "This honest creature doubtless/ Sees and knows more, much more than he unfolds.") Your reputation and your career can withstand the assault of any false accusation not because of what you say, but because of who you are.

Someone who is not guided by love, joy, peace, patience, kindness, generosity, faithfulness, gentleness, and self-control is a person for whom issues of character and integrity are of secondary (or even lower) importance. Someone who isn't honest probably overreacts to accusations; such a person "protests too much" and quite likely loses some ground in both reputation and career, regardless of the accusation's truth or falsehood.

Keep in mind Horace Greeley's wise observation: "Fame is a vapor, popularity an accident, riches take wings. Only one thing endures, and that is character."

Most people are good people, but most people also believe what they want to believe. They want to believe you, if they see you as a person of integrity. They can grow skeptical, however, if you give them reason to believe you're a hypocrite, presenting only the image of a positive character while dishonestly defending yourself against what might be a true accusation. The truth or falsehood of the charge pales in significance when compared to the truth or falsehood of who you are.

## SPIRITUAL FOUNDATIONS

Unfortunately, some bad people—not just selfish and mean-spirited people, but evil people—are out there. They are capable, for motives you might never discover, of knowingly speaking falsely about you. Practically, how are you going to handle that? You can only speculate about that now, but you can also plan to build a spiritual infrastructure that includes peace, patience, and self-control, upon which any practical plan of action or inaction can rest.

I sat in a federal court room not long ago for one full day to observe part of what proved to be a six-week trial. The defendant, a personal friend, is a public official who was falsely accused by persons of questionable credibility, and later acquitted of bribery and extortion charges.

The prosecution put his ex-wife on the stand and subjected her to extensive questioning about family and financial matters. Her former husband, the defendant, was visibly angry at the government lawyers for putting her through this ordeal. If looks could kill, there would have been murder charges leveled against him as he stared at the prosecuting attorney when all of us rose for a recess as the witness was excused.

78

My friend had been angry over the false accusations that led up to this trial, but now he was outraged over the grilling to which his former wife had been subjected. During the break, he and I spoke briefly. I said, "Come up with an image of tranquility. Fix it in your mind and have it there when the trial resumes and you sit down again at the defense table. Don't let them see how upset you are; control the impulse to fight back. Think of a calm lake, a snow-capped mountain, a bed of yellow roses, a sunset, a field of wheat. Think of anything that will calm you down and enable you to sit there in some semblance of peace and dignity."

I didn't want him to risk upsetting anyone else, particularly the judge and jury. Two weeks later, after the acquittal, several jurors told reporters that they thought this witness had been treated badly and that her divorce from the defendant had nothing to do with the issues to be decided in the trial. Moreover, one juror added that when the defendant eventually took the stand in his own defense, he, as she perceived him, was "incapable of lying; mistakes in judgment, maybe, but no lies."

If, in response to false accusations and treatment that you know is unfair, you lose control, you could be giving away your best chance for eventual vindication. That's not to say never protest, but never choose, under emotional pressure, to lose your balance. Choose instead to fix your attention on an image of tranquility, and give some thought to an act of forgiveness.

*The vengeful will suffer the Lord's vengeance, for he remembers their sins in detail. Forgive your neighbor's injustice; then when you pray, your own sins will be forgiven. (Sirach 28:1–2)*

Lord, I know I cannot know you now. That you are, yes; but who you are, not now, at least not fully now. Yet I persist in thinking and praying that perhaps I can. I know you are there, somewhere. Here and there, inside and out…everywhere. I know you are there, but I also know, as C.S. Lewis put it, that "He whom I bow to only knows to whom I bow."

No one else knows fully; only you do. Only your triune self knows to whom I pray. Yet pray I must, and do, with the certainty of faith, knowing not completely you, but that you are there. You are there for me and for anyone who calls out to you.

Faith assures me that you are there no less for me because you are there for all. I know I cannot know you fully now, but I also know that you are always there for me, with me, in me to be known. That's all I need to know for now. Your Christ has come to show you forth, to tell me what you are like. He helps me know to whom I bow.

And so, I bow.

# Chapter 8

# SABOTAGE

Sabotage is malicious destruction. It is commonly associated with war, and war certainly has defensive as well as offensive strategies. Is the workplace a war zone? It doesn't have to be, but often is.

Careless workmanship, or malice intended to harm an employer or owner, are not the forms of sabotage under consideration here. What's at issue is directly intended destruction of another person's work.

For example, a student in a laboratory, driven by ambition, could sabotage another student's experiment. Why? To get ahead of the other student, to outrank a competitor, and thus achieve an academic advantage—an advantage that can, presumably, be translated immediately into enhancing prestige and postgraduation economic gain.

There is another form of academic sabotage, one that's rare but all too real. In this variation, the saboteur steals or hides a reference book needed by others, or pages containing information needed by all are secretly removed from reference books. The purpose is to deprive students preparing for the same examination of access to key information they would need to score well on the test. The most recent variation on this theme is injecting a virus into a rival's computer.

These tactics are, of course, easily transferable to the workplace. Your own work could be the target of a saboteur, usually a co-worker intent on getting ahead of you or, at least, making you look bad. You might experience what happened to an editor I know: A person abruptly fired by the organization, but permitted to remain on the job for a week or so, found ways during that week to sabotage others' work, including all the paperwork the editor had prepared for a contract to be signed with an author. In this case, there was nothing personal against the editor, and certainly no career benefit to be derived. These were simply acts of vengeance against the publishing house, soon to become the saboteur's former employer.

# VIGILANCE

The workplace saboteur is an enemy whose identity might be unknown to you. This is war, and you have to be vigilant. You have not only the right, but also the responsibility, to defend yourself against any potential enemy, seen or unseen. But how?

It's interesting to recall that the modern wartime weapon known as a land mine gets its name from a centuries-old tactic of digging (mining) under the wall of a fortress, buttressing the base of the undermined wall with timbers, and, at a strategic moment, pulling away the timbers, causing the wall to collapse. The walls quite literally come tumbling down. However, the underground digging can be observed, so those holding the fortress should be able to prevent it, if they remain vigilant.

Deceit thrives in secrecy and darkness. Openness and light—qualities nurtured by the Pauline values of patience, generosity, and self-control—are the defensive weapons of vigilance. Modern land mines, real or metaphorical, won't be there to blow up in your face, if vigilance detects any attempt to plant them in the workplace under cover of secrecy and darkness. To defend yourself, you must use the workplace weapons of lock and key, password and PIN number, and the normal precautions that, even if there were no danger of sabotage from within, must still be taken against the possibility of theft by anyone inside or outside the organization.

# INFILTRATION

Would-be saboteurs first have to infiltrate the organization. There can, of course, be instances in which someone joined the enterprise with good intentions but became disaffected and used sabotage as a "get even" strategy. In either case, the probability of harm can be reduced if appropriate screening takes place before employment begins. Credentials, employment histories, and references should always be checked. It's important, too, to have some measure of emotional stability as part of the application process. Problem people can, of course, always slip through the screen. Interestingly, however, employment experts report that the more open and positive workplace relationships are, the more likely that people prone to sabotage (or any other form of destructive behavior) will be noticed. An open, congenial workplace pays off in enhanced productivity and other benefits, not the least of which is detecting saboteurs.

## DEALING WITH ADVERSITY

Whatever happens, however unfairly, to you in this regard, a functioning spirituality attuned to the theme of Chapter Three, "Preparing for Adversity in Life and Work," can shore you up and not just save the day, but save your sanity and career to boot.

To turn this consideration around for a moment, imagine a situation where you might be asked by someone higher up in your organization to sabotage the work of a competitor. The proposition might not be made quite that bluntly; it could, however, be wrapped in the vocabulary of "gaining a competitive edge" or "increasing market share." You could be encouraged to misrepresent comparative test results, lie about or tamper with another's product, or otherwise throw sand into your competitor's gears.

Can you conceive of ever doing that? To reinforce the conviction I hope you feel that you never would, take stock now of your willingness to conduct all your business in the sunshine and of your resourcefulness to balance open-air competition with appropriate protection of your own competitive "play book."

Business saboteurs are usually clever, secretive (by definition), and rarely up to the demands of fair competition. They resort to sabotage precisely because they don't have the personal and organizational characteristics required for success supported by ethics and social responsibility, the characteristics that thrive best when grounded in the principles and values of a workplace spirituality.

Saboteurs, in short, take immoral shortcuts; they are strangers to integrity who are completely unfamiliar with the benefit and even the meaning of persistence. How could you defend yourself against someone like that? The answer is simple and straightforward: Take precisely the opposite approach.

Being open and alert, operating in the light, avoiding the darkness, and adopting persistence as your basic business strategy—all these strategies protect you from your enemies, within or without, and enhance your ability to recover from and prevail over any saboteur's assault on you or your work. You won't recover from the assault or prevail to go on working in peace without a special quality that only a functioning spirituality can supply: forgiveness. Some thoughts on that strategic weapon are in Chapter 30, "Forgiveness"; in that chapter, notice that those who forgive are not only spiritually stronger, but also practically wiser and better able to defend themselves against the injury that caused the opportunity to forgive.

# THE ETHICS OF "INTELLIGENCE"

Meanwhile, the importance in the workplace of "competitive intelligence" is emerging. Observers are noting a gradual drift from what we've been calling an "information economy" to an "intelligence economy." Competitors are using both new technology, such as the Internet, and some very old snoop-and-search methods, like checking phone logs and jotting down license-plate numbers, to get information about one another. In this way, information not readily available, or available information that has been intensely analyzed, becomes "intelligence."

You might be tempted (or even instructed) to cross what you know to be ethical lines to get intelligence on your competitors so you can outsmart them. If you have internalized the Pauline Criteria, they can help you resist this temptation. Theft is always wrong; you may never steal the other team's play book. Scouting may be perfectly acceptable, but spying—using deception to get what you want—carries you well over the line. The means used (lying, misrepresentation, deceit, and fraud) can indeed pollute the discovery process. The ends pursued, not just the means, can also be unethical, even evil.

So what can you to in the interest of both success and survival? Take a do-unto-others approach. Evaluate strategies you might use as though they were strategies being used against you. If a given strategy used by your rival worked to your disadvantage, would you consider yourself a victim of injustice or a runner-up in a fair but tough race? Think about this in both personal and corporate—that is, organization-wide—terms. You or your organization, or both, can be unfairly and unethically undermined, victims of sabotage. By the same token, of course, you or your organization can undercut the competition unfairly and unethically.

*Business Week*, in its October 28, 1996 issue, stated clearly and compellingly the distinction between intelligence and spying: "Corporate intelligence becomes illegal espionage when it involves the theft of proprietary materials or trade secrets." This guideline, then, represents a valuable yardstick to consider as you review your intelligence strategies.

The article went on to list a few legal, illegal, and "gray area" examples. "Digging through a rival's trash on public property (although local laws may vary)" would be legal. "Stealing price sheets from a corporate office" would not, and "expressing interest in a job to find out a rival's plans" would, in the view of *Business Week*, be a gray area.

# PROTECTING YOURSELF AND YOUR ORGANIZATION

In football, the sideline sages say that the best offense is a good defense. Similarly, workplace strategies that emphasize defensive tactics work best for both individuals and organizations. It's more difficult, however, to protect your play-book in a sophisticated "intelligence economy," where protection against computer break-ins challenges the ingenuity of both public- and private-sector managers. In an exploding electronic-commerce marketplace, tensions and concerns are bound to multiply on all sides.

Public-sector planners, particularly those concerned with national defense (like the National Security Agency) and law enforcement (like the Federal Bureau of Investigation) are now at odds with Silicon Valley's private entrepreneurs, who are creating jobs and making fortunes by selling encryption software to millions of users concerned about data security. The FBI fears misuse by terrorists. Encryption applied to cellular phones, as well as to criminal computers, makes electronic eavesdropping, a standard law-enforcement tactic, difficult, if not impossible, to do. The NSA's code-cracking efforts aimed at protecting the nation against foreign enemies can be hindered by *cryptoware*, the scrambling software produced here but used for data protection overseas.

While waiting for the software specialists to improve the security of your digital signature, think about protecting yourself whenever you have phone in hand or files open to inspection by another's eye.

During World War II, workers in possession of information even remotely capable of assisting the enemy were constantly reminded that "loose lips sink ships." The admonition is just as pertinent today, although the "ship" in question is now your career or your organization's comparative and competitive advantage. You should always use your phone (especially your cellular phone) with care. Although there may be virtue in being able to say, "My life is an open book," keep your files closed, your desk clean, your e-mail and voice-mail storage bins empty, and all your medical, financial, and personal records, along with your proprietary interests, protected in secure storage areas. These steps, when combined with a commitment to personal integrity on the job, will leave you in the clear and in the light—an environment that saboteurs prefer to avoid.

This is not to say they can never get to you; despite your best efforts, they can and sometimes will. So think of sabotage as theft and do what any prudent person would do by way of protection against a thief. It's wise to acknowledge your vulnerability, and you should let this acknowledgment bring you to your knees in prayer. Your spirituality will recognize this as a position of strength. It's an ancient posture. It worked for the psalmist; it will also work for you.

> *Keep me, Lord, from the clutches of the wicked;*
> *Preserve me from the violent,*
> > *who plot to trip me up.*
>
> *The arrogant have set a trap for me;*
> > *villains have spread a net,*
> > *laid snares for me by the wayside…*
> *Do not let their plots succeed.*
> *(Psalm 140, 5–9)*

# Chapter 9

# INGRATITUDE

When those who supervise your work or receive the services you render never express appreciation, you notice it. You resent the ingratitude, which can hurt. Your reaction can range from annoyance to anger, from silence to sarcasm.

No one likes to be taken for granted.

What's more, no one, deep down, wants to be regarded as "only being in it for the money." The money is not unimportant, of course, but the purpose of work is a great deal broader than simple financial remuneration.

This broader purpose relates to meeting a need, want, or desire of another, and it's nice to be thanked for doing that well. It also involves using your time and talent productively, and it's satisfying if the employer who purchases your time and directs the use of your talent expresses gratitude for your efforts.

## THE CIVILIZED "CITY" OF THE WORKPLACE

We are, all of us, social beings. We all know that the nice thing, the polite thing, to do in any human interaction is to express gratitude when appropriate.

The word *polite* derives from the Greek word for city, *polis*. In a city—that is, in a civilized community—people are "polite." They are necessarily "political," and they are governed by "policies" that make life in the city more human, more livable. So it should be in the workplace.

Ingratitude signals a breakdown of politeness, leading to a depersonalization of the normal politics of the workplace and resulting in a situation where policies no longer represent guidelines for ordered behavior, but fences to contain individual excesses. Any attempt to build a social order based on constraint is, ultimately, doomed to failure.

It can be argued that gratitude is a foundation for obligation. In the old American vernacular, "much obliged" was a way of saying "thank you." Not to thank another is, in effect, to regard oneself as unfettered by any obligation toward that other, free of even the basic social obligations of civility and courtesy.

# CULTIVATING GRATITUDE IN YOUR OWN LIFE

If you're sensitive enough to notice the absence of gratitude in your workplace surroundings, and if you are personally (and perhaps deeply) wounded by ingratitude, the best remedy for your condition might also prove to be the beginning of a cure for the larger problem. Simply take it upon yourself to be very careful not to miss any opportunity to thank someone else: coworker or customer, superior or subordinate, or anyone you meet in the workplace. Your courteous consideration, your civility, will become contagious. The gratitude you give, but might not yet have received yourself, will eventually come back to you.

When this return of thanks begins to happen, your workplace will begin to turn around. When gratitude becomes a habit, the workplace will be a more humane environment, a better place to be, as well as a better place to work.

How many parents have said to their children over the years, "What's the magic word?" That question comes at the opening of countless parent-child negotiations on any given day. The magic word is, of course, "please." Not far removed from that pleasant sound of politeness, there is always an opportunity for an expression of gratitude. This reminder, of course, is not just for children. Civility and appropriate gratitude are important parts of any adult's identity as a social being. A thankless workplace diminishes those who work there.

Quiet inventory should be taken from time to time in every workplace: How often are the words *please* and *thank you* heard? Anyone who finds the tally disappointing can easily add to the inventory by starting the workplace trend (revolution?) of using these expressions regularly and encouraging a return in kind from others. If you are a thanks-saying, thanksgiving person, you won't have to wait long to hear a word of thanks, even from those whose refusal to say "thank you" really bothers you now.

Many years ago, I took a Sunday morning train from New York City to White Plains for a visit with old friends. I knew they would be waiting at curbside, so when I arrived, I moved quickly down the platform, through the waiting room, and outside to the pick-up area. On the way through, I noticed a hobo, a "knight of the road," to whom I nodded and said hello. He followed me out of the station.

When I noticed him approaching me as I stood by the curb, I reached into my pocket for some change. He waved me off, declining the contribution, and said, "I just wanted to come out here and thank you. You're the first person who has said anything at all to me in two days." That mumbled expression of gratitude for the elemental gift of human contact has stayed with me for years. How sad that both the contact and the thanks can be so rare in a person's transit through life.

Can anyone, anywhere, really believe there is nothing at all for which to say thanks?

Recently, I've noticed an interesting vocabulary development in the way we respond to expressions of thanks. It happened three times in an hour as I moved about on the Georgetown University campus; three times I heard, "No problem," as the pleasant response to my expression of gratitude.

Someone held open a door; I said, "Thanks," as I walked through and heard, "No problem," in reply. Someone else turned in an assignment at my desk and I said, "Thank you." "No problem" was the immediate rejoinder. Still another person delivered some good news by phone. "Thanks for calling," I said, as we ended the conversation. "No problem" were the words I heard before the click of the receiver at the other end of the line.

Curious, isn't it, how "You're welcome" has been lost somewhere in translation and is being replaced by a simple declaration of the absence of any problem? There is "no problem," presumably, connected in any way with the transaction at hand. Nor is there any apparent problem anywhere on the immediate horizon. Could it be that this new usage is coming into style because the young are now more in need of reassurance of freedom from problems than they were formerly in need of being made to feel welcome? Who can say?

I don't mean to suggest that too much should be read into this semantic shift. I'm just indulging in a playful juggling of words, which have a way of changing all the time. Words come in and out of fashion without our noticing, but no one can fail to notice the absence of a word of thanks.

Familiar expressions of gratitude, unlike familiarity, have no potential whatever for breeding contempt. Unfamiliar expressions of gratitude will eventually catch on and find a place in the vernacular; I certainly have "no problem" with that. All of us will be "much obliged" if the new expressions serve the cause of civility and courtesy by ensuring a place for thanks in all circles of human interaction, not just in the workplace.

"Better open reproof than voiceless love," says the Book of Proverbs (27:5). Voiceless love is an issue that often needs attention in the family circle; voiceless thanks is a problem to be addressed in the world of work. Fortunately, anyone with a voice has all the equipment necessary to take that problem on.

"Bend my heart to do your will, and not to love of gain." (Psalms 119:36) The psalmist must have been thinking of me, Lord, when those words were written. Whoever wrote that verse could never have known me, of course, but those words belong on my lips. "Bend my heart to do your will, and not to love of gain."

Steer me away, Lord, from the love of gain. Not from all gain altogether, just from the love of gain. I'm counting on you to point me toward gain in many forms, especially real, measurable, financial gain. But I don't want any part of any gain that you don't will and want for me. Gain, yes; greed, no. May I come by it honestly, share it freely, and be grateful for it always.

No pain, no gain, the saying goes. Help me, Lord, to handle both pain and gain according to your will.

# Chapter 10

# BEING PASSED OVER

There is no single English word that catches the full sense of the workplace wound described in the phrase *being passed over*.

*Forgotten* doesn't quite do it because often the pass-over is quite deliberate and fully conscious. Your higher ups want to keep you where you are, or even drop you down a notch, or encourage you to go away. This knowledge can hurt.

*Jilted* is another nominee that fails to communicate the meaning of this workplace reality (although it seems to work well in explaining why some youthful romances fail). There is often more direct human contact in being jilted romantically than there is in being passed over in the workplace. A consultant friend told me of a manager he knows who remarked that he "can handle headcount reduction" but just "can't deal with firing people." In other words, depersonalization first, and then attend to the dirty work.

Many bosses prefer to walk right past the emotional ruins they know they're creating as they assign new responsibilities, promoting some subordinates while marooning or setting others adrift. We are all capable of walking over the lives and sensibilities of others and being quite oblivious to the damage we leave behind. The probability of that happening in civilized settings is reduced by virtue of the civility cultivated there. Cold, formal civility, however, with its separation of emotional attachments from workplace relationships, can encourage career pass-overs. Unlike the historic Passover preserved in Jewish memory and ritual, workplace pass-overs feature no sense of rescue. They are often lonely, painful affairs marked chiefly by a sense of profound abandonment.

Forget about the "This hurts me more than it's going to hurt you" preamble; if directed at you, you won't even hear it. You might not hear anything but the news that someone else got the promotion. You have been passed over, so how should you react?

# BEYOND THE REPLAY

I didn't deserve this. Why did this happen to me?

Repeated questions prompt your internal review of any workplace pass-over, as you run play-by-play dissections of what happened and why. The poet Samuel Hazo has a line I like: "Can days of making sense/ of days that make no sense/ make sense?" Of course not. The anger roiling up within you encourages you to play and replay reels of "what might have been" scenarios; "if only" you had done this or that, or "if only" someone else had done or not done something else. I can assure you of this: The replay phase, if you indulge it, just sinks you deeper into the quicksand of self-pity.

What, then, should you do? First, give thanks for all the gifts you do have, especially the talents that might be unnoticed or unappreciated by the higher ups who passed you over. Subject your personal career assets—your knowledge, experience, education, skills, contacts, achievements, ideas—to careful review. This self-examination should focus first on how well you have used your assets. If you haven't been using them well, you might find in this assessment an answer to the question of why you were passed over. (Do not, however, use this possibly valid explanation for your workplace pass-over as an excuse to kick yourself around the block, to denigrate yourself endlessly.)

Next, review the steps you took to let others see who you are, what you have done, and what you are capable of doing. Jesus had some good advice about the relative position of lamps and bushel baskets. Perhaps you have inadvertently kept your light hidden under a bushel basket? Not only is that practice not doing you any good, but it's also inflicting harm on your career. When that review is done, take some time to examine the human relationships that are part of your working day. Leave aside, for the moment, questions of your own competence so that you can examine issues of interpersonal chemistry. How do you get along with others? Do others perceive you as likable and pleasant to be around? Does your side of a typical conversation tend to focus on you or the other party? Is your learning

94

curve a closed loop, or are you really open to the ideas of others? Is your workplace personality closed or open, supportive or suspicious, competitive or cooperative?

Once you've completed this review, it helps if you sit down with a few trusted friends to review your personal talent-and-skill inventory. Let them look at the scores you gave yourself in your private self-assessment and the reasons you laid out, with all the objectivity you could muster, for this missed opportunity for an advance in your career. You will be both surprised and, yes, grateful to your friends at the end of such an exercise.

## THE BAD BOSS

I know a person who was treated shabbily by a bad boss. My friend is now convinced that such a problem can actually become a significant career advantage: "Bad bosses can make your career. It gets so bad that you quit, and before you know it, you find yourself in a better job!"

If you (with some help from your trusted friends) conclude that your experience of being passed over is caused by problems that relate to your boss, not to you, that knowledge could well open up a new door to a better future for you.

## ON ADVANCING

There are also people whose ambition for advancement is driven by the expectations of others. When such a person is passed over, the reaction can be complicated by criticism, even scorn, from those whose expectations have raised the bar higher than the affected individual ever really wanted to jump.

Dr. David Morrison describes the case of an executive he calls Tom. Tom's wife, Anne, came from a family of uniformly high achievers in the male ranks. She put constant and heavy pressure on Tom to succeed. He was motivated more by her expectations than by any other drive. In effect, Tom was working for his wife, not his employer.

On the job, he succeeded in building a reputation for pushiness and excessive risk taking. His insatiable appetite for recognition (recognition he could bring home for his wife to see) alienated everyone else in the workplace.

Tom was thoroughly disliked. His focus on upward advancement at any and all costs led him to ignore opportunities for cultivating his own competence and pursuing his genuine interests.

Since work, in and of itself, had no meaning for Tom, it provided no basis for personal gratification, except as a fulcrum for status and an anchor for marital stability. Consequently, Tom didn't work well with others. Any "success" that came to him worked against the company's best interests.

It's no wonder that people like Tom will eventually be passed over because, in Morrison's words, "They will provoke cynicism and distrust when they push others to be concerned about quality or commitment to the organization. Their own true values will be communicated by their behavior and mixed messages. As they focus on short-term gains on their way up the corporate ladder, others will have to clean up the longer-term consequences of their actions." I call the syndrome from which Tom suffers *career tyranny*.

Career tyranny relates to expectations. It can be imposed on you by the expectations of others or by the unrealistic promises you make to yourself. Those who are disinclined toward self-examination are particularly vulnerable. Honest self-assessment is absolutely necessary to deal productively with a workplace pass-over. At the point of pass-over, a crisis for any sensitive human being, the self-assessment trigger must be pulled. If you've been wronged, your spirituality will see you through. If you are wrong and they are right, your spirituality, especially its Pauline dimensions of patience, faithfulness, and self-control, will put a platform under you to support you in the setback and in your push-off toward the next realistic opportunity for advancement. In the process, you will find yourself giving humility a good name!

# WHAT WE DO, WHAT WE ARE

Being passed over is not as bad as being laid off, of course, but it can cause some of the same kind of psychological damage. Regrettably, Americans are psychologically conditioned to believe that what they do is what they are. When they're doing nothing (as a consequence, for instance, of being fired or laid off), they falsely and unfortunately conclude that they *are* nothing. Similarly, when they're passed over in the workplace, they tend to conclude that they have nowhere to go but down or out. Simply staying in place where you are marking time, letting the clock run out, is a sign of failure.

Simply being isn't enough to support one's self-esteem. You must do more and more, and the doing has to keep rising to new levels of achievement, compensation, and prestige if it's to sustain your sense of self-worth.

This approach to life and work is not just dangerous; it's crazy. You are, after all, a human being, not a human doing! You have to come to terms with that simple truth when reversals shake your self-confidence.

You should be able to draw reassurance on this point from that bank account your spirituality provides. If you can't, something of extraordinary value hasn't yet been deposited there. It is, after all, a question of value— your bedrock, non-negotiable values—that's at stake when you struggle with the doing-versus-being problem. If there is no answer from within when you seek reassurance on who you are and what you're worth, your inner account is missing a fundamental value: the unshakable conviction that you are unique, regardless of what you do, and that you belong to a personal, knowing, loving, caring, and all-powerful God who can never be anything but faithful to you. He holds your destiny in his hands.

# FAITH OR FATALISM

Several years ago, I learned a lot from a 51-year-old unemployed marketing executive, who said he had decided it was time to leave his job with a major pharmaceutical company. (Others wonder whether the choice was really his.) Here is just one paragraph from a five-page letter he sent me two years into an unsuccessful job search:

> *Unemployment has had a positive effect on my life in that it has made me a much more sensitive and caring person. I have been humbled and that is good. Last year, for a time, I was driving an airport limousine to make twenty dollars a trip (every little bit helps). On one occasion, I*

*continues*

*continued*

> *picked up one of my former peers who still works at my last company.*
> *That was humbling! I keep telling myself that someday I will find finan-*
> *cial security and I will look back with gratitude for having had the chance*
> *to become a better person. I remain hopeful, but my trust is only in my*
> *own effort. I expect no help and want (and deserve) no sympathy. My*
> *situation is the result of the choices I personally made. I have no one to*
> *be angry at, including myself. I am proud of my strength but I do fear*
> *despair. If someday I did lose hope, the result would be final.*

I am happy to report that he never lost hope and that he toughed it out for two more years before finding full-time, satisfying employment. In the same letter, he disclosed that he found no "comfort or nourishment from religious faith, although I confess that I have occasionally asked for God's help, but always with the expressed thought that 'if you are listening,' or 'just in case you hear me.' If I am wrong, and God does intervene selectively, my lack of conviction dooms me. I do believe in God, but I do not know him or understand him. He is not personal, so there is no reason to be angry with him."

Those sad words left me pondering what his outlook would be like if he had only learned the Pauline value of faithfulness and let it work within him.

Without faith, scripture is an unlighted torch; spiritual guidelines can't help because it takes the spark of faith to activate them. The gift of faith is available to anyone who decides to take it. Remember this whenever you are passed over (or confronted by something worse). Let faith go to work for you. It will surely make a difference.

Meanwhile, search within for the faith to say "amen" to these ancient words from the Book of Wisdom (15:1–3):

> *But you, our God, are good and true,*
> > *slow to anger, and governing all with mercy.*
> *For even if we sin, we are yours, and know your might;*
> > *but we will not sin, knowing that we belong to you.*
> *For to know you well is complete justice,*
> > *and to know your might is the root of immortality.*

# Chapter 11

# BEING MISUNDERSTOOD

As with the situation of being passed over, there is no single word that catches the essence of being misunderstood. It's a universal experience, a common workplace wound that can be extraordinarily painful. Misunderstanding is an unavoidable part of the condition of being human.

Because you depend on others not only to disclose what's on their minds, but to communicate it clearly, you can always misread, mishear, and misinterpret what others communicate to you. By the same token, you're always vulnerable to being misheard, misread, and misinterpreted by them. The intractable problem with interpersonal communication is the assumption that the communication has even taken place!

During World War II, as a young draftee fresh out of high school, I found myself at Camp Wheeler in Georgia. Wheeler was an Infantry Replacement Training Center. One of the lessons I learned there in 1945 was that the original content of spoken messages can easily lose precision and accuracy in oral transmission. We were probably set up to fail when ten of us were spread across a simulated skirmish area and the training officer whispered a fairly uncomplicated message into our squad leader's ear with instructions to pass it down the line. What made it through the bushes and ditches down to the tenth trainee bore little resemblance to the original message.

The experiment was amusing to a pack of teenagers who had been carefree civilians a month or so before. The snickering stopped, though, when a distinctly unamused sergeant made the point that misunderstood messages can kill people in combat. That simple drill was aimed to correct a human tendency to listen carelessly and communicate casually. However, it's a habit that's hard to break.

# FILTERS AND ASSUMPTIONS

In the workplace, the probability of misunderstanding rises as judgments are made not on what was directly communicated, but on what was filtered through another's judgment, or inferred from shaky presuppositions, or simply imagined without any grounding in observable fact. There is no malice aforethought here, so misunderstandings aren't false accusations. They can, however, be fathered by rash judgments.

The famous prayer of Saint Francis of Assisi would have you say, "Lord, make me an instrument of your peace." Among the blessings you request in this prayer, so that your work for peace is effective, is this: "that I may not so much seek to be understood, as to understand." This bit of wisdom—combined with the Pauline values of peace, gentleness, and generous listening—supply the first step of your strategy to handle being misunderstood: Become intent on correctly understanding others—not yourself, but others. Focus on the feelings and ideas of others.

An overall strategy for achieving peace of heart and a happiness that doesn't ride in and out of your life on the waves of emotion is quite simple. Be more concerned with easing the burdens of others than with having your own burdens eased. Selflessness, rather than selfishness, is the way to go. This guideline is particularly applicable to those situations in which you're personally wounded by misunderstanding. Understandably, you want to nurse your wounds. You feel sorry for yourself. How could anyone as well-intentioned and nice as you be misunderstood? How could you be thought of as anything but the good person you really are? How could your generosity be mistaken for self-interest, your explanation be taken to be self-serving, your hard work be seen as personal ambition?

Take a self-assessing moment or two to test your honesty in asserting (even though you are speaking only to yourself) your virtue. Your goodness, veracity, high intentions, generosity, fairness, dedication: Is this really you, or is it the image you're trying to project?

# "IF ONLY IT WERE ALL SO SIMPLE!"

"I credited myself with unselfish dedication," writes Aleksandr Solzhenitsyn in a section of *The Gulag Archipelago* where he, as a prisoner in the hands of

Soviet authorities whom he chooses to call "executioners," is musing on his former self-righteousness.

> *If only it were all so simple! If only there were evil people somewhere insidiously committing evil deeds, and it were necessary only to separate them from the rest of us and destroy them. But the line dividing good and evil cuts through the heart of every human being. And who is willing to destroy a piece of his own heart?*

> *During the life of any heart this line keeps changing place; sometimes it is squeezed one way by exuberant evil and sometimes it shifts to allow enough space for good to flourish. One and the same human being is, at various ages, under various circumstances, a totally different human being. At times he is close to being a devil, at times to sainthood. But his name doesn't change, and to that name we ascribe the whole lot, good and evil.*

> *Socrates taught us: Know thyself! Confronted by the pit into which we are about to toss those who have done us harm, we halt, stricken dumb: It is after all only because of the way things worked out that they were the executioners and we weren't.*

Anyone unable to find tracings of his or her own character in Solzhenitsyn's sketch is suffering from a serious deficit of self-knowledge. Such a person is, I believe, particularly vulnerable to the wounds of misunderstanding. Unable to comprehend how someone else might find grounds for awarding him or her anything but high marks, such a person presumes that he or she has been misunderstood. The problem lies completely on the other side.

Look for that line dividing good and evil in your own heart, and acknowledge the full range of your own potential for good or evil. Admit, at the very least, that you're capable, sometime in the future, of making a present misunderstanding, based in some other person's mistaken judgment, come true. With that recognition of your fallibility renewed, get on with your life. You will find, I believe, that a protective mind-set like this also works to prevent you from spinning off misunderstandings that could be harmful to others.

# OLD WOUNDS, NEW MISUNDERSTANDINGS

Here is an example of how an unnoticed and unattended childhood wound can heighten the probability of workplace misunderstandings. Morrison Associates had a contract to do team-building work with a group of highly autonomous traders. Their leader, to his credit, recognized that the "old cutthroat stuff" just wasn't going to work; they had to work better as a team. Accordingly, this senior executive set higher performance and earnings standards for the group. If any one member impeded the team's ability to meet team goals, that person would be gone. If the team met the higher standards, all members would earn more.

At the beginning of this "executive consultation," David Morrison asked each team member (in private), "What are your personal goals?" One individual, already targeted by the boss for likely layoff because he wasn't working well with the team, replied, "I want to help you (Morrison Associates) with the group dynamics of our team." He was all cerebral, Morrison recalled, when discussing this case; he had no emotions. Morrison, throughout a long interview that got into the man's early family history, was trying to figure out some way to get this team member "attached" to other people, especially to his workplace team. He mentioned to Morrison his "frustration" with the team members at work, and Morrison asked, "Did you ever talk to them about this?"

"No," he said, "my degrees are in finance; I'm not articulate. I can't talk. I can't express myself."

"Oh, you're wrong," Morrison assured him. "You are more articulate than most of the people who come in here. You *are* articulate." Then drawing on what he had learned earlier from this man, Dr. Morrison continued: "The fact is that you had a mother who thought more about her own needs than yours. Whenever you spoke to her, she rephrased whatever you had to say for you. You concluded you couldn't say anything right."

Morrison told me that as an adult, this man played recreational basketball with police and firemen, "nice fellows, but not noted for their ability to articulate." The consultation further revealed that the man was quite convinced that half the human race—women—did not understand him. Speaking of the woman who later became his wife, he said to Dr. Morrison: "The first time I saw her, she wasn't all that attractive. But by the second or third time we were together, she was the most beautiful woman in the world. She listened to me. She's the one and only person I can talk to."

By becoming uncharacteristically assertive (and strongly supportive), Dr. Morrison convinced this non-communicator that he could speak well and that he should speak up with constructive suggestions and informed opinions to establish himself as part of a functioning team. His withdrawal and reticence had been misunderstood as an aloof, nonsupportive, hypercritical, and judgmental working style. Fortunately, he overcame the wound and established himself as a positive contributor to a successful team.

## GREETING MISUNDERSTANDING WITH STRONG CHARACTER

Literature is replete with examples of the tragic dimensions of misunderstandings. For any member of the human race, to be is to be misunderstood (eventually). Those painful moments and their extended consequences test your endurance; they are the stuff from which wisdom flows and character is built.

Trying to avoid all possible misunderstandings with people in your workplace is plainly unrealistic; it could even be dangerous to your career. Sam Rayburn, the late Speaker of the U.S. House of Representatives, simply refused to let misunderstandings and differences of opinion get to him. It was his view that, "when two people always agree about everything, it just goes to prove that one of them is doing all the thinking."

Another insight worth incorporating into the set of Pauline principles that constitute a supportive spirituality is this one from *Further Paradoxes*, a book by the late French Jesuit theologian Henri de Lubac:

> *"To differ, even deeply, one from another, is not to be enemies; it is simply to be. To recognize and accept one's own difference is not pride. To recognize and accept the difference of others is not weakness. If union has to be, if union offers any meaning at all, it must be union between different people. And it is above all in the recognition and acceptance of difference that difference is overcome and union achieved."*

*Right in the eye. That's where I look, Lord, right in the eye of anyone I hope to connect with in conversation. To explain, to ask, to persuade, to apologize, I look them right in the eye.*

*Is that presumptuous, Lord? Is it pride to raise the eye, if not the eyebrow, and connect in this way? Or is it simply a good uncomplicated way of establishing contact?*

*With you, though, it has to be different. Where is your eye? Who am I to even search, let alone hope for contact? "Eyes right, eyes left," the military marchers say. "Eyes down" is my command to myself before your altar, before your throne, before you, Lord, at whatever altitude I imagine you to be.*

*But I have to admit, Lord, that I am waiting for you to open my eyes, touch my outstretched hands, and fill my soul with your all-powerful presence and your never-failing love.*

# Chapter 12

# PREJUDICE

Samuel DeWitt Proctor, a distinguished academic administrator who served, during his long career, as president of Virginia Union University and North Carolina A&T, and also held professorships at Duke and Rutgers, was born into a middle-class African-American family in 1921. "My daddy would go to work everyday," he once recalled, "around white people who treated him like he was a boy. But when he came home at 4 o'clock, he would practice his violin, go to his Masonic meetings and church meetings, and he was a new person. He taught us this kind of transcendence: the ability to rise above whatever people thought or said about us."

*The Substance of Things Hoped For* is the title, borrowed from the Letter to the Hebrews, of Proctor's fine 1996 book written to inspire young black people, whom he urges "to give up the paralysis of analysis and feelings of hopelessness." Proctor's grandmother, once a slave, earned a degree from Hampton University in 1882. Of her, he recalls: "My grandmother was born into slavery, but I never once heard her say anything evil about anyone. That's how they got by then. It wasn't escapism, as some would say today. That was faith." This kind of faith, embodied in the seventh Pauline value, is a firm foundation for a functioning spirituality and is all the protection you need when prejudice strikes in the workplace.

## PREJUDICE: A CONTEMPORARY REALITY

Prejudice is evident in every corner of the American workplace. It is targeted singly or in combination on race, religion, ethnicity, accent, national origin, sex and sexual orientation, age, disability, and educational and economic status (regardless of whether that status is perceived as too high or too low).

Prejudice is irrational. Prejudgment, the essence of prejudice, is an exercise of deliberate, calculated shutdown, usually triggered solely by external appearances. Based exclusively on characteristics like those just listed, and others not catalogued here, abilities and motives are attributed to people without any regard for objective truth. Prejudice reflects an arrogant conviction that the targeted person would be "better" if he or she were exactly like the one making the prejudgment!

What if you are the target of another's prejudice? Well, begin by acknowledging that you can never make someone like you. You look foolish when you try. Distinct personal likes and dislikes are normal and universal. Chances are you will be more likable in the eyes of most of the people with whom you interact if you successfully assimilate the nine Pauline Criteria within the core of your personality. Once you have, these values will not only support you but also show through to others. And yet, there will always be some who simply won't like you.

You can reasonably hope that these people won't hate you or do you any harm; you can be happy and productive even though you don't win their vote. You can easily overcome the adolescent impulse to think life isn't worth living simply because you don't get universal affection and approval. Moving on in the face of this kind of reality is what it means to be a mature and emotionally well-balanced person. But the question remains: How do you deal with prejudice?

Many of the workplace wounds discussed in previous chapters originate in prejudice. Because of prejudice, you might experience criticism, betrayal, sabotage, false accusations, and a host of other problems. In dealing with those problems along the lines suggested in this book, you are, of course, dealing with prejudice. But the point to be made here, in this brief consideration of prejudice itself, is that only a functioning spirituality will help you, as an individual, transcend—literally and effectively rise above the age-old problem of prejudice.

There are legal remedies to the problem of prejudice that can and should be pursued. Tools and tactics of confrontation, and strategies of organization and negotiation, are better used by groups, however, than by individual victims of prejudice. Some victims are provoked to violence singly or in mobs; there's no room for that, of course, in a nine-point program that includes gentleness and self-control.

Nonviolence is, in the metaphor I used earlier in this book, a slingshot strategy that can overcome prejudice. It can reinforce your personal stand against prejudice. The believer simply has to believe that love, joy, peace, patience, kindness, generosity, faithfulness, gentleness, and self-control are pillars of strength against the crushing potential of prejudice. When prejudice threatens to get you down, these values lift you up. That is the meaning of transcendence: You can rise above it all.

Consider once again the words Samuel Proctor wrote about his grandmother: "I never once heard her say anything evil about anyone. That's how they got by then. It wasn't escapism, as some would say today. That was faith."

But often that won't be enough.

## CAN YOU FEEL IT? CAN YOU TRANSCEND IT?

Imagine yourself to be the target of flat-out, hands-down prejudice, the kind of prejudice African-Americans experience in the housing markets, the kind that women in business literally bump up against when they hit the so-called glass ceiling. Would you be able to summon up the spiritual resources to meet the challenge without sacrificing your own principles and diminishing your own integrity?

If you have never had any real experience of prejudice, try this classic experiment: Do a simple role-play in a circle of friends where, for example, blue-eyed people are arbitrarily designated as inferior. Their rights can be violated with impunity. They are denied equal access to facilities. They are just walked over by those whose eyes are brown, or green, or anything but blue. Play that game for more than a few minutes, even among friends, and your blue eyes will soon be seeing red!

I would argue to the end that, for the preservation of your own humanity, you, like Samuel Proctor's grandmother, must never say anything evil about the people behind the prejudice. I would also argue, however, that you should speak out in truth against the injustice and speak

107

up without apology for your rights. (First, however, be sure to filter that speech through the Pauline Criteria for assurance that it's the Spirit speaking from within you!) Remember that, in the workplace, how you speak up is important; style can be supportive or destructive of the substance you feel compelled to communicate.

## INSIDE ANOTHER'S SKIN

Harper Lee's *To Kill a Mockingbird* is a great novel about prejudice, the struggle for justice, and the unfolding awareness of these realities in a child's mind. As if to prepare the reader for what's to come later in the story, and as he is preparing his child for life, the lawyer-father Atticus has a chat with his six-year-old daughter Scout, who has just announced, at the end of her first day in school, that she will not return to school. Her unenlightened first-grade teacher, the reader discovers, told her that morning that she would have to unlearn the reading skills already learned in the lap of her father (where, the now adult daughter-narrator recalls, "reading was something that just came to me.... I could not remember when the lines above Atticus's moving finger separated into words, but I had stared at them all the evenings in my memory"). Her father patiently explains a lesson that all of us have trouble putting into practice:

> *"First of all," he said, "if you can learn a simple trick, Scout, you'll get along a lot better with all kinds of folks. You never really understand a person until you consider things from his point of view..."*
>
> *"Sir?"*
>
> *"...until you climb into his skin and walk around in it."*

So that's the first thing any of us has to do, even in the midst of hurt and the heat of anger. Try to climb inside the skin of the person who is harming you to see the world from his or her perspective (even though, in the case of prejudice, you will find it to be a distorted view). As I indicated, prejudice is, by definition, a prejudgment. That mind is already made up. What is blocking the vision? What might you be doing to prevent those other eyes from opening or, if open, seeing clearly?

If you walk around inside the skin of another for awhile, it will affect your style of reaction; you might begin to see that person's problem and then be better able to figure out the best next step. This is not to suggest that you were somehow wrong and that you can now make a return trip "to your senses." Not at all! It simply means that by allowing yourself to think for a moment as the other person thinks you might get a better handle on the problem to be solved. It also increases the probability that you will be more inclined to treat the person behind that problem as you would treat yourself.

I mentioned this exchange between Atticus and his daughter Scout to former Pennsylvania Governor Robert P. Casey while he was still in office and recovering from the life-saving surgery that transplanted a liver and heart from a black man's body into his own. He had read *To Kill a Mockingbird* many years before, and noted with appreciation that some well-wisher had given him another copy while he was recuperating from the transplant surgery.

"You didn't climb inside your donor's skin," I said. "His organs were transplanted into yours. Does that have any effect at all now on your view of race relations?"

"It sure does," he replied.

Mrs. Casey told me how, a few months after the surgery, when everyone across the state knew that the governor was doing well, an African-American woman who was a total stranger greeted her warmly in a Philadelphia department store, expressed her joy at the governor's progress, then added: "And we're so glad we were able to help!"

The governor, always on the side of victims of racial injustice, intensified his efforts during his remaining years in office to reduce both the unemployment and drug traffic that set the stage for his donor's death by gunshot in an economically depressed western Pennsylvania town. Casey continues today to work on establishing an endowment that will memorialize his benefactor by financing medical education for young blacks who want to become transplant surgeons. Robert Casey was, of course, dealing with disease, not prejudice, but the origin of the gift of life that helped him cope continues to motivate him to help victims of discrimination.

It's unlikely that you will have transplanted organs to motivate you from within, but they aren't necessary. There can be an internalized spirituality driving you to "do the right thing" and setting the boundaries for appropriate action. If you are a Christian, the pattern and style of your reaction to prejudice has to be influenced by words that you might not always be anxious to hear: "But to you who hear I say, love your enemies, do good to those who hate you, bless those who curse you, pray for those who mistreat you." If you have the courage to read on, you can pick up the lesson in the Gospel of Luke 6:29.

Walk around for a while inside the skin of a prejudiced person, in or out of the workplace, and you will find evidence of all the weapons you should never use to fight prejudice: hatred, pettiness, fear, spite, and ignorance. Apparently, Samuel DeWitt Proctor's grandmother recognized in her wisdom that they were not only unworthy of her, but that they would surely be ineffective in the defense of her dignity. She had faith. So do you.

Use your faith-based resourcefulness to speak the truth in love. Act firmly and fairly to get those scales of justice back in balance. If you lose your poise in the struggle for justice, you might kill your chances of ever winning your rights. You will also have lost sight of the values that define your better self, and that would amount to handing over to prejudice a victory it should never have. Let the word of God, spoken through the prophet Amos, sink into your soul to be lifted up into consciousness whenever you're feeling the burden of prejudice:

*"Seek good and not evil,*
*that you may live;*
*Then truly will the Lord, the God of hosts,*
*be with you as you claim!*
*Hate evil and love good,*
*and let justice prevail at the gate…*
*let justice surge like water,*
*and goodness like an unfailing stream.*
(Amos 5:14, 24)

The rules of spirituality are simple and direct. Resist any impulse to return evil for evil. Go for the good, even when evil is inflicted on you. Go for the good and justice will prevail!

*Chapter 13*

# SEXUAL HARASSMENT

There's no need to take today's newspaper story on sexual harassment as a point of departure for a discussion of the subject. There will surely be another story tomorrow, and the day after tomorrow, and presumably on the day you find yourself reading this book; by then, today's story will be long gone (although not, it's fair to assume, completely forgotten).

I begin, then, with the presumption that you know, at least on an instinctive level, what sexual harassment is; that you might not be completely familiar with all the legal decisions on this issue; and that you aren't a candidate for initiating this kind of activity (self-control is, after all, one of the personal principles of spirituality you're assimilating). You could, however, find yourself some day on the receiving end of sexual harassment.

Here's the Equal Employment Opportunity Commission's (EEOC) definition:

*Unwelcome sexual advances, requests for sexual favors, and other verbal or physical conduct of a sexual nature constitute sexual harassment when submission to or rejection of this conduct explicitly or implicitly affects an individual's employment, unreasonably interferes with an individual's work performance, or creates an intimidating, hostile, or offensive work environment.*

The law recognizes that the workplace is not populated by angels or disembodied spirits; it's inhabited by sexual beings with instincts and appetites that can, of course, be controlled. Indeed, they must be controlled if human dignity is to be preserved in the workplace.

Sexual attraction is presumably present in the typical workplace every day; sexual activity is an altogether separate issue. The law, as you have seen and should review for emphasis, notes that attraction becomes harassment when it prompts conduct that, whether rejected or submitted to, affects employment status, impairs work performance, and produces an "intimidating, hostile, or offensive work environment."

# WHAT TO DO

Thousands of complaints, most of them from women, are filed with the EEOC each year. Many men and women have good reason to complain of harassment, but many more work in intimidating, hostile, and offensive environments where the reasons for those uncomfortable conditions have nothing to do with sex. Cases have to be considered on their merits, and the presumption of a sexual motivation behind unwelcome conduct must always be examined carefully. What if it happens to you, and what if you know you're innocent and it is sexual harassment? What do you do?

Register your disapproval immediately; let the harasser know that it's unwanted and unacceptable. By openly registering your reaction, you make it absolutely clear to the harasser that the moves are unwelcome, so it's best to be quite direct. Direct doesn't mean aggressive; registering disapproval takes only a word and a well-defined "stop" gesture.

It's unwise to enter into a protracted discussion about what you will or will not accept, or about what might or might not be appropriate on the job. Make it unambiguously clear that you reject nonprofessional advances, and then see what happens. If the person who caused the problem has any sense, that will be the end of the matter.

If the behavior recurs, of if you have a sense that your silence would lead to others being victimized, you should, in the interest of protecting the "environment" mentioned in the EEOC's definition, take the one-step-up approach and report the matter to a superior—preferably to the harasser's superior, but certainly to your own. In the immediate aftermath of any incident, you should also reflect on your own behavior as you run through your nine-point checklist in the evening and early morning. You want to make sure that neither your signals nor your motives were mixed in any exchanges that could have led up to the unwelcome event.

# THE "WORLD"

Sexual harassment is almost always part of a power game. Because it is, I want to discuss a spiritual matter that goes by the name of the *triple concupiscence*. If that word sounds strange, take it apart. You hear Valentine's Day references to Cupid. You know what cupidity means (and you hate to see it in anyone because it carries desire across the line to possessiveness and avarice). The prefix *con* simply means *with*, so *concupiscence* just means *with desire*. More often than not, it refers to lust or ardent sexual desire. The triple concupiscence is the lust of the flesh, the lust of the eye, and the lust for power over other persons.

This is all part of human nature. Any normal, healthy person recognizes stirrings within that reflect a desire, rooted in one's human nature, for sexual union, possession of things that attract the eye, and for power over others. These impulses, of course, have to be contained, dealt with responsibly, but there's no point in trying to deny they exist.

In the First Letter of John (2:15–17) the scriptural basis for reflection on this triple concupiscence is presented:

> Do not love the world or the things of the world. If anyone loves the world, the love of the Father is not in him. For all that is in the world, sensual lust, enticements for the eyes, and a pretentious life, is not from the Father but is from the world. Yet the world and its enticements are passing away. But whoever does the will of God remains forever.

John's use of the term *world* here requires some explanation. It's meant to signify all that is not of God. Elsewhere, for instance, in the gospel of John (3:16), the word *world* appears in a more positive sense:

> For God so loved the world that he gave his only Son, so that everyone who believes in him might not perish but might have eternal life. For God did not send his Son into the world to condemn the world, but that the world might be saved through him.

Throughout scripture, "the world" is viewed as good, as lovable, worth saving, worth working in, and worth transforming. In the quotation from 1 John 2:15–17, John warns the believer to be wary of the pull of these three drives that are so familiar to human nature. John wants the believer

**113**

to do God's will and thus live forever with God, instead of letting natural appetites, these desires for "passing" things, run wild and pull him or her away from God.

Another widely used translation of this set of three drives is "carnal allurements, enticements for the eye, the life of empty show." Sexual harassment directly relates, of course, to the first. The advertising industry plays on the second (and, in the process, reinforces selfish values that encourage sexual harassment). And the "life of empty show" or the "pretentious life" refers to a state of mind characterized by pride and the desire to dominate.

This, then, is the arena that catches up all those Interest-Excitement values, the power plays, and the drive for prestige that constitute the world's way of measuring success. These aren't the values that respect human dignity and foster the Pauline value of self-control. Rather, they are "dis-values" that your spirituality is meant to overcome.

You could easily name nine (and possibly 99) worldly values, such as fame, fortune, and power, that run directly counter to the nine Pauline pillars, which can hold your human nature up for the long haul into eternal happiness. The false values on that list support the selfishness that defines the sexual harasser.

# APPROACHING OTHERS WITH YOUR PROBLEM

If you're employed in a place that has no sexual harassment policy, you have work to do. Don't wait for an unwelcome event to occur; find out why there is no policy and when there's going to be one. If your employer has a policy, examine it for completeness and inquire about enforcement. Are accusations made public? It's understandable why they might not be. Are documented adverse findings against an accused harasser a matter of public record within the company? They should be. The time-tested principle of "punish with pitiless publicity" (even without the assistance of billboards and headlines), when applied to genuine offenders, works wonders to discourage sexual harassment.

Perhaps the strongest workplace policy statement on sexual harassment was written under a court order and put together with the assistance of the National Organization of Women. The case is *Robinson v. Jacksonville Shipyards, Inc.*, 136 L.R.R.M. (BNA) 2920 (N.D. Fla. 1991). The court found that the management of Jacksonville Shipyards, Inc. (JSI) had knowingly and systematically discriminated against women for over 10 years. With the verdict went a directive to have the National Organization of Women help the company draft a policy statement that would help JSI mend its ways. The policy in its entirety is too long and detailed to reproduce here. One part, however, a "Statement of Prohibited Conduct," provides an interesting, detailed, and unambiguous listing under each of the following headings:

◆ (A) Physical assaults of a sexual nature

◆ (B) Unwanted sexual advances, propositions or other sexual comments

◆ (C) Sexual or discriminatory displays or publications anywhere in JSI's workplace by JSI employees

◆ (D) Retaliation for sexual harassment complaints

The policy includes a schedule of penalties for misconduct and it lists "Procedures for Making, Investigating and Resolving Sexual Harassment and Retaliation Complaints," as well as "Procedures and Rules for Education and Training."

If you look for the policy, you can find it in Appendix A of Laurence Barton's *Ethics: The Enemy in the Workplace* (South-Western, 1995). If you look for the company, you will not find it. It went out of business in 1993, two years after the adverse court decision, partly because of additional legal problems stemming from sexual harassment suits, but also because of reductions in national defense spending. Had JSI not had problems with sexual harassment, however, it would surely not have had the lawsuits, and it might very well have been able to continue to win contracts.

If you look to scripture for some spiritual principle that would be helpful in the context of sexual harassment, you are likely to find yourself with the Book of Daniel, Chapter 13, where you will find the famous story of Susanna, a passage some have referred to as the first detective story!

Susanna was the wife of Joakim and the target of the lustful desire of two elders, who were also judges in the Babylonian community. They trapped Susanna in the garden of her home where they had hidden to observe her bathing. They threatened to accuse her of adultery with a young man unless she submitted to their desires. She refused, was brought to trial on the next day, and condemned to death. But Susanna cried aloud: "O Eternal God, you know what is hidden and are aware of all things before they come to be: you know that they have testified falsely against me. Here I am about to die, though I have done none of the things with which these wicked men have charged me."

The Lord heard her prayer. As she was being led to execution, God stirred up the holy spirit of a young boy named Daniel (Daniel 13:42–45). Daniel came to her defense. He chided the Israelites for condemning her "without examination and without clear evidence."

Back to court they went. Daniel separated the two elders so that he could question them individually about their charge that Susanna had dismissed her maids from the garden so she could be alone there with an unnamed young man.

"Now, then, if you were a witness," said Daniel to the first of the two elders, "tell me under what tree you saw them together." "Under a mastic tree," he replied. To the second elder, Daniel put the same question: "Tell me under what tree you surprised them." "Under an oak," he answered. Daniel's response to each was the same: "Your fine lie has cost you your head." So the judges were themselves judged; the two elders were sentenced to death. "The whole assembly cried aloud, blessing God who saves those that hope in him. They rose up against the two elders, for by their own words Daniel had convicted them of perjury. According to the law of Moses, they inflicted on them the penalty they had plotted to impose on their neighbor" (Daniel 13 60–61).

This wisdom principle, rooted in the Bible, assures the believer that innocence will be defended and malice punished. The believer knows that God "saves those that hope in him" (Daniel 13:60), as happened in the story of Susanna. This belief is, of course, underscored by the Pauline principle of faithfulness.

The reader of 1 John 2:15–17 receives fair warning against the lust (understood as uncontrolled desire) of the flesh, the eyes, and the drive to dominate. Deposit these inspired bits of wisdom into your spirituality account now, reflect on them often, and peg them to that ninth Pauline guideline, the principle of self-control.

Knowing your own human nature well enough to admit that you have the capacity for harassment and other excesses can work to your advantage. That knowledge can serve as an effective defense against excesses, including harassment, that could come your way from others who, unlike you, might be out of control.

# Chapter 14

# MISTAKES

"Nobody knows the trouble I've seen." Review your mistakes, and you might be tempted to indulge the impulse to feel sorry for yourself and sing along in the words of this old spiritual. You'll find comfort in those words only if you believe that everyone else but you lives in an all-win, never-lose world.

Whether you have reconciled yourself to the "old rockin' chair" eventually getting you, you should, nevertheless, come to terms right now with the stark fact that the human condition has had you all along right from the beginning.

Mistakes often seem pointless; they tend to reflect Linda Pastan's poetic salute to a workout on a stationary bicycle:

> ...this ride feels
> much like life itself going nowhere
> strenuously.

In time, though, most of us are willing to concede that even though you might feel put upon at times, progress is possible and most mistakes can be repaired.

Mistakes and reversals are bound to happen. There is no win-win world for everyone all the time.

Physically, unless you are quite young, you've been wearing out for years. Intellectually, you're probably active and alert, although you know that you can let yourself peak before your time by not attending to intellectual exercises, not using your mind. Psychologically, you can grow stronger every day, as long as the physical house that holds your psychological furniture keeps standing. Of course, you might have suffered a severe setback before you were old enough to know what was happening to you:

a congenital defect, an inherited disease, an accident in infancy—reversals explainable simply in terms of your location in the human condition.

It will happen sooner or later. From the start, an army of Ds is arrayed against you and all those with whom you share the human condition: disappointment, discouragement, disease, and defeat. Not all at once, not all the time, and not to the same degree, but each of those Ds will touch you sometime. Eventually and inevitably, the Big D—death—will see that you shed your "mortal coil." Neither you nor anyone else likes to think about that, but there it is: the human condition with its unavoidable end to your pursuit of happiness. That end, however, is just the beginning, your faith assures you, of a happiness that will never end. You have to believe (especially when you're reeling from a recent setback) that all the happiness you have already known, and will continue to enjoy here on earth, can serve to summon up some faint idea of how great eternal happiness will be.

## THE ALTERNATIVE

I'm always amused when, inquiring about someone's progress in recovering from serious surgery or a near-fatal accident, I receive a half-smile and the reply, "I'm doing rather well thanks, considering the alternative!" Does it take an automobile accident or serious illness to make us take some time to consider, with the eye of faith, that great alternative?

There is the story about the two elderly friends who died weeks apart and met again in heaven. One said to the other, "If I had known it was going to be like this, I would never have eaten all that oat bran!"

I do not intend to try to set forth in words what you can expect to find in the hereafter. That reality is something that "eye has not seen, and ear has not heard" (1 Cor. 2:9). I aim, instead, to help you learn to address, from a faith perspective, the terrible reality of here-and-now reversals: physical, intellectual, psychological, and financial. Why pain? Why suffering? Why me? In these pages, I want to walk you through a reflective survey of the ground that could go out from under you, sometimes through your own fault by virtue of your own mistakes, at any stage of your journey through life and work. Mistakes are an unavoidable part of life. That's reality.

It's true: Just about anything can go wrong at any time. The legendary Murphy put that into some kind of law that you might have cited in the past and are likely to repeat in the future. However, you don't have to be Irish, or paranoid, to realize that oppositional forces are arrayed against you. Not only will you make your fair share (or more) of mistakes, you already know full well that traps and pitfalls are somehow out there waiting for you. They are very much a part of what you have to deal with in the down-to-earth reality of daily life in any workplace. These traps have the potential to pull you down, or they can help you overcome the obstacles you find in your path.

You are going to have to deal with personal reversals that are neither work-defined nor necessarily work-occasioned; these reversals do, however, have direct effects on how you manage to do what you're called to do in the workplace. What follows is intended to help you cover that terrain and to keep your eye on the prize when the awareness of your mistakes weighs you down.

# COURAGE

Courage is not an explicitly stated element in the set of Pauline Criteria that define a Christian spirituality and give evidence of the presence of the Holy Spirit in the believer's soul. Explicit or not, however, courage is included in the category of love, and it is surely part of the spirituality you want to have for your journey through life.

There is no reversal that can't be met with courage. Courage is grace ("grace under pressure," in Ernest Hemingway's words). Courage is strength, strength you don't even know you have (and, without faith, would not have). Courage is your grip on the "slingshot" spirituality that allows you to hold your own and more against any reversal, even one of Goliath-like proportions. Courage, finally, is the ability to face up to your mistakes and move on in spite of them.

# FORGIVE YOURSELF

"I made a mistake once," the comedian's line goes. "I acknowledged making an error and later discovered that I was wrong." Not so with the rest of the human community. We all make mistakes and most of us have difficulty admitting it.

Mistakes can be honest, hasty, stupid, expensive, careless, critical, big or small, private or quite public. Are they always forgivable? They certainly should be, at least in the sense of self-forgiveness on the part of the one who makes them.

If you cannot forgive yourself, you raise a wall against forgiveness coming your way from anyone else. There are times when the consequences of a mistake cost you a friend, some money, your job, your reputation, or possibly your life. Even so, no mistake is beyond forgiveness. Nor are second starts ever foreclosed, as long as you live. The mistake might have removed you from the situation where you once lived or worked, but you can—you must—learn from the experience and move ahead in the hope that those who knew you in that place and at that time can forgive you and still think well of you.

# ADMITTING MISTAKES

A functioning spirituality gives you the clarity and the courage to admit your mistakes and move on. There is a Washington, D.C. saying to the effect that, when you have no one to blame but yourself, you know that you're understaffed. Even inside the Beltway, at the bureaucratic center of the universe, people have been known to own up to mistakes, however.

You don't have to take a full-page ad in the newspaper to tell the world how and why you erred. You simply have to hear yourself admit that you were wrong. You goofed. You made a mistake. Sometimes that admission requires an accompanying apology; without it, the admission of your fallibility is hollow and ineffective. Sometimes your ownership of the admission isn't complete unless you share it with someone you trust—not to seek forgiveness (when necessary, get that from God or from anyone harmed by your mistake), but to get reassurance that you were, in fact, wrong, and are now dealing with the issue honestly.

122

How often have you heard the expression "an honest mistake"? Honest mistakes happen. Honest or dishonest, your mistakes can be forgiven and forgotten, and you can get on with your life, if you have the will to do exactly that.

Perhaps this is easier said than done—but read on.

## TWO IMAGES

Imagine a sign over the entrance to your workplace that reads: "The person who never makes a mistake hardly ever makes anything." That translates to the comforting assurance that there is a place in this world, including the world of work, for you and your mistakes.

Or, if you are handcuffed psychologically to past mistakes—if, in other words, you carry them like luggage wherever you go—find a psychological equivalent of those roller suitcases you see in airports and let your past mistakes stop weighing you down.

You might need professional help, pastoral or psychological, to get your release from this kind of burden. If you need help, seek it out. One solid and sobering principle of spirituality instructs that "grace builds on nature." You can't ignore either the laws of nature or the remedies available on the natural level, if you want to keep both yourself and your career on track.

## VALUES

A writer friend of mine, whom I first met when he was well into middle age, surprised me with the disclosure that his present wife was not his first. "I made a mistake the first time," he said. "I married my first wife for her looks; I married my present wife for her values."

Forget for the moment that his (quite attractive) second wife might not be completely charmed by the comparison and that my opposition to divorce would prompt me to want to probe the possibility of living with some of one's mistakes. Think instead of the role of values in mistake prevention.

123

An internalized center for mistake control could provide effective answers from within by bringing your deeply held values to the surface in the face of important decisions. The nine Pauline principles come to mind in this regard. When you let your values decide, you are less likely to make mistakes. This, of course, presumes that you have the proper values—that what you cherish, consider worth your time and effort, and would refuse to trade or trifle away is thoroughly good.

Your values cannot rise to the surface if you haven't first permitted them to be planted in your soul. That "planting" is the work of spirituality. Nor will they rise spontaneously unless you have lifted them up in reflective awareness often, even daily, in the style of the morning and evening exercises outlined for you in Chapter One.

Think of love, joy, peace, patience, kindness, generosity, faithfulness, gentleness, and self-control as values. Use them as range-finders when you look at upcoming decisions. Frame your choices within these values; if the fit is bad, or just uncomfortable, think some more before you choose. You'll never know how many mistakes that reflective pause will help you avoid.

In Thomas Heywood's 1607 play, *A Woman Killed with Kindness*, the following lines are part prayer and part exasperation. These words deserve a place in any spirituality intended to help you live with your mistakes:

> O God, O God, that it were possible
> To undo things done, to call back yesterday,
> That Time could turn up his swift sandy glass,
> To untell the days, and to redeem the hours.

The upturned hourglass can't, alas, bring back time already spent, where your mistakes are buried. It can, however, measure the present as it makes its way into the future, where your mistakes can be overcome.

Deliver me, Lord, from "all my trumpery." I wish I could be certain that I want to make that prayer. The phrase comes from the pen of C.S. Lewis and hits me right between the eyes.

I can only hope—have the desire of the desire, at least—to mean it when I say, with Lewis, "From all my lame defeats and oh! much more/ From all the victories that I seemed to score;/ From cleverness shot forth on Thy behalf/...deliver me."

How good this poet was to see and speak of you in words that I can also use to see and speak:

> Lord of the narrow gate and the needle's eye,
> Take from me all my trumpery before I die.

Take it before I die. Otherwise, the baggage that I permit to pile up between us will surely block my way. Deliver me, Lord, from all the tripping and tricking trumpery, and bring me safely through the gate you keep ajar for those who love, and hope, and try.

# Chapter 15

# FAILURE

An old anonymous saying would have you consider that "half the failures in life arise from pulling in one's horse as he is leaping."

True enough. It can also be said that all of life's failures relate, in one way or another, to the inexorable demands of the human predicament. Pulling back the horse is an exercise of timidity, but even the courageous sometimes fail because being human means dealing with limitation, loss, and some degree of defeat.

On the page facing the title page of his book, *I Wanted to Write*, Kenneth Roberts quotes the words of another author, Oliver Wiswell: "[A]nd many a man who might have been a novelist of note has gone unproductive to his grave because he lacked the encouragement, the protection, or the help of understanding friends or of a woman." Any "might have been" male or female novelist (Wiswell would surely want to make his observation include women if he were making that statement today) will lament the absence of encouragement, protection, and understanding. However, that which "might have been" often could easily have been, if the person who failed had simply kept on trying. The Pauline principles of patience and faithfulness foster this kind of persistence.

There's a Norwegian proverb to the effect that "A hero is one who knows how to hang on one minute longer." Be a hero, and keep on trying.

## DON'T REPLAY THE FAILURE TAPES

Failures at any earlier stage of your life or career—and there have probably been many—can hurt you only if you let them. That will certainly happen if you insist on rerunning those embarrassing reels in your mind's eye and kicking yourself from here to there, instead of closing the door firmly on the past and moving on to meet new challenges. Timidity counsels you to pull back from new opportunities, courage keeps you moving ahead, and persistence keeps that forward motion on track.

Playing on the title of Paul Tillich's famous book, *The Courage to Be*, medical sociologist Reneé Fox wrote an impressive work called *The Courage to Fail* (University of Chicago Press, 1974). Her point was that, for the physician, the death of a patient is too often viewed as failure. It takes courage for doctors to resist the impulse of professional pride that drives them to go to extraordinary and unreasonable lengths to keep someone alive. In other professions and occupations, too, it could be unreasonable and unwise not to stop, not to have the courage to "fail" in a given set of circumstances. Pressing on isn't always wise. The only real failure, however, would be not to have tried at all.

Life goes on, and so do you. You simply have to move on and face up to the next challenge. Otherwise, failure will forever hold you down.

Kenneth Roberts must have kept a card file of quotations under the heading of "failure." In the foreword to his wonderful book *Northwest Passage*, he borrows these words from R.B. Cunninghame-Graham: "Those who fail after a glorious fashion, Raleigh, Cervantes, Chatterton, Camoens, Blake, Cleverhouse, Lovelace, Alcibiades, Parnell and the last unknown deckhand who, diving overboard after a comrade, sinks without saving him, these interest us, at least they interest those who, armed with imagination, are thereby doomed themselves to the same failure as their heroes were."

Even though you might consider yourself not to have all that much imagination, you should never be timid about putting yourself in a situation where you might "fail after a glorious fashion." If you take no risks, you will never give the growth side of your personal portion of the human predicament a chance to stretch. The popular slogan "no pain, no gain" is just as true when applied to the psychologically painful fear of failure as it is to the physically painful process of conditioning necessary for success in athletic contests.

# PRIDE

If it is pride, not prudence, that encourages your tendency to be completely risk-averse, you should recognize that you have a spiritual problem.

The world around you often confuses meekness with weakness; it also has a habit of dismissing humility as timidity. Humility is, to the contrary, an expression of courage, and spiritual courage brings rich rewards. If you need reassurance on this point, take another look at the Sermon on the Mount (Matthew, chapters 5–7), which says that the meek are going to inherit the earth (5:5), that lamps are not to be put under bushel baskets (5:15), that good things happen when you turn the other cheek (5:39), that care not to let the left hand know what the right is doing means dividends for the almsgiver (6:3), that forgiving your enemies wins forgiveness for you (6:14), and that if you simply have the courage to trust in God, you will be infinitely better off than the well-fed birds of the air and the handsomely-clothed lilies of the field (6:26–28).

Prudence would have you remember just enough of your past failures to avoid repeating them, and it also discourages taking foolish risks. Courage would have you set ambitious goals and forge ahead as though the failures had never happened.

# "LOST CAUSES"

The late (and truly great) U.S. Senator from Illinois, Paul Douglas, was affectionately known as a "winner of lost causes." I walked with him once from his Senate office over to the main Capitol building; when I mentioned how much I admired his integrity and courage, he stopped, pointed down to his two large and well-shod feet, and said, "Father, you're looking here at two feet of clay." Humility and courage worked side by side in Senator Douglas.

He was always there for civil rights, consumer protection, and other policy initiatives that had "no chance" of becoming law, long before the majority came around to supporting these measures. Douglas was often defeated, but he never lost heart.

Winners of lost causes don't always live to see their victories, but they have no problem in being viewed as failures by those who lack their vision. Indeed, there is a lesson in leadership for us in all of this.

As University of Notre Dame professor Dennis Goulet once remarked to me, in the Christian view of things, the leader must be "available, accountable, and vulnerable." Not all would-be leaders, even if they make themselves available and accountable to the followership, are ready to take the wounds. True leadership involves a willingness to be wide open to failure, ridicule, and unfair criticism.

"Leadership is wisdom, and courage, and a great carelessness of self," reads the inscription on the cross over an American soldier's grave outside Caen in the Normandy countryside of France. A faith-based "carelessness of self," modeled on the life of Christ, can release you from the fear of failure and equip you to meet the demands of leadership. Once released from the fear of failure—once comfortably, prudently, and confidently careless about your own image in the eyes of others—you are free to be your authentic self. You are free to lead, if that is your calling, or to follow, if you are so inclined. You are free to be and to do what your best self invites you to be or do. You are free to be open to the promptings of the Spirit, to the impulses of love, joy, peace, patience, kindness, generosity, faithfulness, gentleness, and self-control.

Without this kind of freedom, there can be no genuine spirituality.

# FEAR

An effective workplace spirituality begins, in my view, with freedom from fear. To put a finer point on this truth, I would say it all begins with a freedom from the fear of failure. To reduce this to another degree of refinement, consider that your deepest fear could be the fear that others will think you are a failure.

It has been said often that reputation is what men and women think of you, but character is what God and the angels know of you. Getting in touch with that knowledge is the work of spirituality. Once there, you are really free.

Monsignor Jack Egan (everybody calls him Jack), the Chicago priest and social activist, is a hero of mine. I've often referred to him as the most affirmative man I know; he saw the good in everyone and never stopped encouraging others. He was on the leading edge of social justice issues for four decades after suffering a heart attack; that event simply helped him put his values and his goals into sharper perspective. For his 80th birthday celebration in 1996, friends contributed $35,000 to a fledgling community organization that he wanted to assist.

Margery Frisbie's biography of this wonderful man has a title that needs some explanation: *An Alley in Chicago, The Ministry of a City Priest* (Sheed & Ward, 1995). "When it comes to a place to live," Egan often remarked, "I'd settle for an alley in Chicago over any other place in the world."

Despite being well known, well liked, much appreciated, often consulted, and successful in organizing movements that multiplied his influence, Jack Egan had to battle a nagging feeling of failure. "One of the difficulties of getting older is that you feel tired," he told Margery Frisbie in an interview. "I've done my part. I've fought against this and not much came out of it, I developed these programs and nobody seems to care. Whatever the ennui that sets in, or the laziness, or the frustration, it is a temptation. What I think I am learning as I grow older is that maybe your task, your responsibility, is changing, that you may not have to be the one to develop the programs and fight against injustice. What you have to do is find the people and encourage them, inspire them, educate them, mentor for them, train them, build bridges for them, so they will do the job. You have to pass the torch, to use a tired expression. But the torch has to be passed. You cannot just throw it in. You can't say the fight's over. It's never over. You fight injustice wherever you find it and for as long as you find it. Because you never, never stop loving, right until the very, very end…because your last breath may be your best act of love."

There it is: love, the first Pauline value. Joy, peace, and all the rest will follow. Is it possible that, when you sense that universally experienced feeling of failure, you're getting a nudge to love a little more?

Love is, after all, the source of everything positive and good. It's an impregnable defense against the downpull of failure, the antidote to fear, and the sure path to the balanced life your restless soul is seeking.

Don't even give a thought to throwing in the towel, let alone the torch. Just give your worthy goal a little more time…and a lot more love.

To keep things in the proper perspective, listen to—that's right, listen; don't simply read—these words addressed to your Creator in the *Book of Wisdom* (11:20–26):

> *But you have disposed all things by*
> *    measure and number and weight.*
> *For with you great strength abides always;*
> *    who can resist the might of your arm?*
> *Indeed, before you the whole universe is as*
> *    a grain from a balance, or a drop of morning dew*
> *    come down upon the earth.*
> *But you have mercy on all, because*
> *    you can do all things;*
> *    and you overlook the sins of men*
> *    that they may repent.*
> *For you love all things that are...*
> *Because they are yours, O Lord and*
> *    lover of souls.*

Lord, I often wonder about the value of what I do. What difference am I making now? When the final audit is in, will my receipts outweigh my donations, will my contributions offset my consumption? I care, but not all that much, about being remembered; I just want to know that I made a difference.

Our life span is measurable, but unknown to us. What we produced in goods and services for the use of others is known to us in general terms, but forgotten already by those who purchased them. If we produce offspring, there is something there of immeasurable value that is clearly identifiable; parents can live on through their children. But the other things that any of us produces, who knows?

All the while we've been keeping score in dollars and estimates of net worth, which leaves me to wonder now about the real worth of what I've done so far. I hope I've contributed my share of brightness to the lives of others, but can I claim to have given anything more, anything that will last? I sure can.

When I look back, I'm astounded by the impact of the lives of others on me. I give thanks for all those gifts and ask that you work through me, Lord, to give through me to others what will astound them someday, when they pause for a moment to take account, even though I might never know.

# Part Three

## Dealing with Personal and Family Problems

# Chapter 16

# THE SINGLE PARENT

Putting aside the circumstances that produced the condition, single parenting isn't simply a personal reversal, or some kind of wound. It's a reality, a daunting responsibility that many people take with them to work each day. I believe, however, that it can be a positive force in one's working life and in one's relationship to God.

Of course, single parenthood can be a major source of worry and distraction, and the circumstances that made one a single parent in the first place can linger on as emotional and economic burdens to be carried on a lonely walk of uncertain duration. However, the single parent has special reasons to approach both work and life with spirited commitments.

There are issues of immediacy and practicality that only a single parent can appreciate, and these issues affect his or her approach to the worlds of work and life.

## A WORKING MOTHER

I grew up in what we would today call a single-parent household, a sociological expression unknown to my brother, mother, or me. My father died when I was an infant; my mother chose not to remarry. Her first job out of college was with a newspaper, but when she returned to work in the Depression years, when my older brother and I were both in the early grades of elementary school, she opted for the security of employment with the federal government. I can recall hearing her explain her work situation to others as "going out to business" each day, and that never struck me as strange.

When I was about six, her sister came to live with us for the four years she was enrolled in a nearby medical school. We had a very happy home. Life made sense to us: good schooling, nice neighborhood, summer camp, lots of sports, close relatives, and many friends.

Years later, when my brother and I were attending college with all expenses paid under the G.I. Bill, I asked my mother whether she had set aside any money for our college education. When I learned she had not, I asked why she sent both of us, for five seasons, to a rather expensive summer camp for boys (although I knew she got discounted rates), and she replied, "I didn't have a choice. I wanted you under male influence and out of the city in the summertime. I decided to wait awhile before worrying about college."

It never occurred to me when I was a boy that those long summer months might have been lonely for her, nor did I ever give a thought to whether she had any kind of vacation of her own.

I do recall hearing adult friends and relatives refer to her occasionally as "pretty" or "beautiful," and they would speculate, ever so discreetly and not in her presence, about the possibility of remarriage. I have no memory of reacting to that prospect one way or the other; in any event, it never happened.

When she died decades later, my brother was able to open a letter she had given to him 13 years earlier. She had marked it "To be opened when I die." In the letter, she explained that she was writing on a bright, sunny Sunday afternoon, that she had recently turned 70, that she was feeling fine, and that there were a few things she wanted to jot down so my brother could attend to them after her death. One related to her wedding ring. "It's been on my finger since your father first put it there, and I want it to stay there when I'm buried."

As I read that sentence, I realized that remarriage had never been an option for her. I also realized that without ever using the word in anything she ever said to me, she had taught me a lot over the years about the true meaning of the word *commitment*.

Many single parents should and will marry or remarry and thus enrich their own lives and better manage their parenting responsibilities. After all, can you think of a more demanding job than working and raising children on your own? Regardless of their subsequent marital status, however, single parents, while they're single and balancing family and workplace responsibilities, can display a quiet dignity and strength that children absorb without knowing it. Uncomplaining single parents also bring strength to their companions in the workplace.

This quiet strength doesn't come easily to the single parent, nor does it come without the help of relatives and friends. In my view, it can't come without the support of a functioning spirituality that's broad enough and practical enough to embrace both home and workplace.

# MAKING IT HAPPEN

Love, joy, peace, patience, kindness, generosity, faithfulness, gentleness, self-control. This now very familiar list might strike you, if you are a single working parent, as a personal job description, a set of enduring value goals, a faith-bridge connecting home and work. This list also defines your personal vocation at any given moment and equips you with the invisible and indispensable means of support you need during times of challenge.

Parents, single or in pairs, are always going to be concerned about their offspring, especially when the child is very young and the parent is away from home at work. The parenting life is, almost by definition, a supremely challenging one. Taking care of children is hard work for two and harder still for one!

Listen to the following story, related by my Jesuit friend Rick Malloy, who works with the very poor of Camden, N.J. Could this ever happen in your own household?

A fellow telephoned a friend whose five-year-old son answered the phone:

*(Quietly)* *"Hello."*
*"Is your daddy there?"*
*"Yes."*
*"Well, can I speak to him?"*
*"No."*
*"Why not?"*
*"He's busy.*

*continues*

*continues*

"*Well, is your mother there?*"
"*Yes.*"
"*Could I speak to her?*"
"*No.*"
"*Why not?*"
"*She's busy.*"
"*Look, this is important; I've got to speak to one of them.*"
"*Daddy's talking to the police.*"
"*The police? What are the police doing there?*"
"*They're busy.*"
"*Well, what's your mother doing?*"
"*She's talking to the firemen.*"
"*What are the firemen doing there?*"
"*They're busy.*"
"*What's going on over there?*"
"*They're looking for me.*"

# CRISIS OF THE DAY

Single parents must learn not to bring their problems into the workplace for solution, but it's impossible not to come to work with concerns, even fears, about the safety and welfare of their children. Both the extended family and a network of friends, woven together in evening conversations and weekend planning sessions, can be rallied for support in times of difficulty—if they have been asked for support when all is clear and calm.

The enlightened workplace should encourage and assist that kind of planning; the resourceful single parent will make sure the planning happens.

# MATERIAL GIFTS, SPIRITUAL GIFTS

No single parent should be overly concerned with his or her inability to give children all the "good" things, all the advantages, and the best of everything. Better to give some thought to how to address the obstacles in life that can help form character.

Listen for a moment to the poet Robert Frost, who passed along some uncommon wisdom on this point during his annual NBC "Meet the Press" interview on March 22, 1959:

**Question:** *Mr. Frost, do you think American civilization has improved or deteriorated during your lifetime?*

**Mr. Frost:** *I think it has made its way forward, in a natural way, you know. We are so rich that we are like rich parents who wish they knew how to give their children the hardships that made them so rich.*

**Question:** *I wanted to ask you about the young people today. Do you think they are more promising? Are they harder, more alert than those of a generation or two ago? Do you think they are better than their fathers or grandfathers?*

**Mr. Frost:** *The fear is they won't be if they are made too comfortable and have their life too easy. We are like a rich father who wishes he knew how to give his son the hardships that made the father such a man. We are in that sort of position. We can't. There seems to be no answer to that.*

Perhaps the single parent has at least part of the answer. Often unable, because of tight financial constraints, to give their offspring "everything," as much as they would like to, single parents can, in fact, turn less into more. Without saying a word, simply by bearing without complaint the burdens of single parenthood, they can write into the lives of their children lasting lessons about the meaning of love, sacrifice, and commitment— what Robert Frost would have called *magnanimity.*

**Question:** *What has been the most important thing, do you think, to you in your life? Love, justice, learning, truth, faith, work; or has it been courage?*

**Mr. Frost:** *That is hard to answer. I suppose that the greatest thing of all would be magnanimity.*

That, it seems to me, is what single parents can, if they want, give by way of daily example to the children who have been entrusted by an infinitely more magnanimous God to their care.

# PARENTAL EXAMPLES

The psychological literature, both scientific and popular, is full of references to the importance of parental influence on developing children. Most single parents know that two-person parenting, other things being equal, is generally recognized as better for the child, who needs security, stability, affirmation, and both male and female nurturing on the road to development. In the practical reality of solo-flight parenting, however, men or women in that challenging situation can be resourceful in taking compensatory measures for the benefit of their children.

Uncles and aunts can offer the gift of their presence, as needed, to a child who needs a male or female role model, as can fathers and mothers of the child's closest friends. However, the single parent is best situated to introduce the child to the gift of self-denial. Robert E. Lee regarded self-denial as a blessing. Practical wisdom sees it as a necessity. Robert Frost saw its importance, but could not see how an affluent and indulgent America could find a way to offer "hardships" to its young.

Acceptance of the hardship of single parenting can equip an otherwise anxious mother or father to be an effective teacher of the essential truth that love is sacrifice and that the easy life should never be mistaken for the happy life.

Alexis Carrel once observed, "Whatever may be their length of life, the lowliness of their position, parents who have succeeded in bringing up children of good quality, experience at the end of their life the feeling of having fulfilled their destiny."

Whether alone or in partnership, the faithful parent exhibits the fidelity of God to the child. For parents who have no alternative but to go it alone, this witness can be compelling in the eyes of all.

Those who benefit most from this example of daily spiritual commitment are the children of single parents, if those parents can bring themselves to accept Isaiah's direction: "Trust in the Lord forever! For the Lord is an eternal rock" (Isaiah 26:4). Then, with Isaiah, the single parent can say: "O Lord, you mete out peace to us, for it is you who have accomplished all we have done."

If you're in this special situation, you have done far more good than you realize as a single parent, and no one can take that away from you. You will, however, deepen both your faith and your personal satisfaction if you can bring yourself to admit, with Isaiah, that it's God who has accomplished all you have done. That's a partnership of which you can always be proud!

# Chapter 17

# ACCIDENTS

Do accidents really just "happen"? Some accidents, it appears, are the result of unconscious, self-defensive choice, a reflection of an unconscious desire to punish oneself or dodge personal responsibility. Some people have what appears to be a "mysterious" built-in tendency toward personal injury. Please understand: This chapter is not about helping the accident-prone, those whose propensity toward physical fractures and internal knots has psychological explanations, to understand how medical problems might be used to cover failure (actual or anticipated) in facing up to deadlines or job-related goals. Those problems are best addressed by medical and psychological professionals.

It is worth noting, however, that any reflective person confronting a cycle of repetitive injury or illness might want to consider the possibility that something internal, which he or she isn't aware of, is causing the accident patterns. In Mental Health in the Workplace: A Practical Psychiatric Guide, Jeffrey Kahn, M.D., editor (Van Nostrand Reinhold, 1993, pp. 83–105), Brian L. Grant, and David B. Robbins, two psychiatrists, offer their essay "Disability, Worker's Compensation, and Fitness for Duty." In it, they point to a "misattribution" tactic that some workers might need to explore with a qualified professional. "[I]t is not uncommon," Grant and Robbins write, "for an employee to pursue a disability claim out of a psychological need to misattribute an actual psychiatric disorder. For example, an employee with panic disorder might be unable to see his or her anxiety and social avoidance as internally derived. Instead, that person might be more comfortable seeing an external cause of impairment and resulting disability." This misattribution, the authors point out, can lead to a workplace lifestyle of dependency on playing the "sick role," making the person "still more resistant to insight and treatment."

Instead, the aim here is to discuss the sense of engaged presence that's enough for most of us to avoid injury in the first place and to help instill dignity and purpose in workplace situations after accidents happen.

# BOREDOM

Boredom is often the poison at the bottom of the workplace well that's responsible for accidents and a lot of strange behavior in the workplace, such as sexual harassment on an automobile assembly line. Strategies aimed at overcoming boredom, or eliminating it altogether, are worth careful consideration by anyone who hopes to bring positive change to a blue- or white-collar workplace.

Effective strategies to reduce boredom have one thing in common: They try to engage an individual's mind in performing job-related tasks not on a repetitive or rote basis, but as an active part of planning both process and product in workplace activities. If you feel your ideas have an ongoing effect on what you do all day, you are more stimulated, more alert...and a lot less likely to get hurt.

Baseball players "talk it up" in the infield to keep themselves awake and on their toes, ready for anything, including a screaming line drive headed straight for their faces. The moral? Simply staying alert is a good defensive mechanism on the ballfield and on the job. Detachment from a team approach to a task, however, makes staying alert harder. Good communications skills among team members in the workplace is an organizational advantage for many reasons, not the least of which is that communicating well with others on the job is a good defense against accident and injury.

Exposure to the risk of physical injury is declining in both goods-producing and service-rendering workplace settings. The office of the future is likely to have fewer risks of physical injury (allowing for corrective measures to the damage done by repetitive, keyboard-based motions and elimination of radiation exposure associated with some office equipment). But psychological disengagement (your teacher called it "daydreaming" when you were in elementary school) could be on the rise in a work environment made more "private" by socially atomizing workplace equipment. You can click on "Help" or call an 800 number instead of turning to a workplace companion when you have a problem. A workforce increasingly attached to monitors is increasingly detached from helping human hands and from the stay-alert signals that human interaction provides. Daydreamers don't see the line drives coming at them.

These are considerations to be woven in and out of your daily reflection on the nine Pauline Criteria. Your workplace spirituality should heighten your sensitivity to the problem of boredom, not only in your own working life, but also in the lives of those in whose company (a word, you will recall, that's intimately related to the idea of "companionship") you work. Your efforts to transform the workplace, starting, of course, with the transformation of yourself, should address the challenge of helping to reduce the boredom of others.

# AFTER THE ACCIDENT

Preventing injury is one thing; returning to the workplace after an injury (either on or off the job) is quite another.

When the injured person returns to work, or when a person with a disability comes on the job, the issue of human dignity comes to the fore. There has been a revolution in the workplace in recent years on the rights of people with long- and short-term disabilities. Quite properly, they don't like to be referred to as "disabled people" because they are perfectly capable of a full life that involves intelligent and resourceful management of one or more physical limitations not shared by the majority of other employable people. "You manage your problems," these workers seem to be saying, "and I'll manage mine, and by the way, let's agree to respect and help one another in meeting our shared responsibilities in the workplace."

Those who manage disabling physical limitations along with all their other responsibilities are often sustained by a spirituality that reflects wisdom principles, the type of spirituality needed by anyone seeking to come to terms with the aftermath of physical injury. In my experience, I've noticed that many disabled people bring virtue (the word literally means *strength*) to the workplace; their example lifts the spirits of those around them. Without speaking about it, they tell the rest of us something about working our way through the human predicament. Without preaching, they

**147**

communicate, in their day-to-day interactions with others, something of the practical meaning of love, joy, peace, patience, kindness, generosity, faithfulness, gentleness, and self-control.

# PERSPECTIVE

On any given day in America, 14 workers are killed on the job and 9,589 become disabled at work, according to the *1996 Statistical Abstract of the United States*. All told, there are 247 accidental deaths every day. Confronted with statistics like these and aware that an accident could happen to you at any time, you might easily become fatalistic, even sad. In the face of such large numbers, you could conclude that you're just a tiny cog in a big machine, that you don't really count or amount to much. Spirituality, however, has a way of putting small cogs in proper perspective—God's perspective—where there is full and everlasting awareness of your unique and infinite value.

During times of trouble and challenge, your spirituality lets you look to God as the creating and sustaining source of all you are and have and ever will be. Without that perspective, you could qualify as the object of an imaginary conversation found on a leaflet distributed in England's Salisbury Cathedral:

*Said the robin to the sparrow,*
*"I would really like to know,*
*Why these human beings rush about and worry so."*
*Said the sparrow to the robin,*
*"I don't know, but it could be,*
*That they have no Heavenly Father*
*Such as cares for you and me."*

Do accidents happen? They certainly do, and they offer you daily reminders to be sure to take care. Your spirituality gives you another more important reminder—that there is a loving God who can never stop caring for you.

Trust him.

*Lord, why am I here? I keep searching, running, working, worrying, hoping, helping, loving. What's behind it all? What makes me keep putting one foot in front of the other? Where am I going?*

*As a child, I was told that I was created by you, made to know, love, and serve you and thus make it into heaven, where I could live happily with you forever. I wasn't told much about my relationship to others, except that I should obey them if they were older (especially parents), that I should not hit them if they were around my age (especially playmates, brothers, and sisters), and that I should always tell the truth to everyone.*

*Now that I am fully grown—getting older and still running—the world is filled with people running in front, behind, and all around me. Not all of them always tell the truth; not everyone plays fair. I worry about myself. I don't want to run with the pack.*

*So help me, Lord; keep me on course. Let me see where I fit in now, and how I can run even harder and faster, if necessary, to help make this place a better world.*

# Chapter 18

# AGING GRACEFULLY

Although most of us know that aging makes wine better, few of us are completely free of the cultural bias that sees aging not as achievement, but as failure.

I'm not talking about the way we regard someone who is frail and elderly as failing. No, the cultural bias I refer to regards any physical sign of less than optimal acuity, mobility, or performance as a personal failure. Absurd as it sounds—and it does sound absurd, which is probably why those who think that way don't say it out loud—the youth-worshiping contemporary culture in America judges you to have somehow failed simply because you have grown old. This, of course, is a form of prejudice.

Thoughts about graceful aging provide a transition to the set of topics in the following chapters, reversals that occur outside the workplace or independently of the work environment, but that nevertheless have a profound impact on your workplace activities.

Everyone is aging every day. You grow older by the minute. There was a time when the elderly were, for practical reasons, held in higher esteem and consulted much more frequently than they are today. This was during a stage of economic development when there was "classic" repetition of both technique and trade, generation after generation, in the process of making a living. The young depended on the declining elderly to learn the "tricks of the trade" and the time-tested methods of making a living, regardless of occupation.

The Industrial Revolution began to change that relationship between the young and the elderly; the late twentieth-century revolution in science and technology broke that dependency forever. Now the knowledge and wisdom of their elders is of little practical value to the young, who would not understand what Emerson meant when he wrote, "The years teach much which the days never know."

The young all too often consider older folks not worth consulting, and, sad to say, sometimes conclude that they aren't worth much. This need not and should not be the case.

# THE VALUE OF AGING

There is an unnoticed spiritual value in aging that can serve the veteran employee well. That value, which can also serve as pace- and pattern-setter for those less practiced in the ways of work and life, is an amalgam of the Pauline Criteria mentioned throughout this book. If I were to reduce the value to one word, that word would be *wisdom*.

Within this book's set of nine spiritual principles, there is one virtue that can have a remarkably positive impact on both workplace and worker (young or old). That virtue is generosity.

In Galatians 5:22–23, Paul identified this set of nine values as the "fruit of the Spirit," the Holy Spirit, the life-giving Spirit revered as the Spirit of truth, wisdom, unity, and love. If this "fruit" is evident in a believer's life, you can safely conclude that the Holy Spirit exists in and with that person. By definition, the presence of the nine Pauline values in one's everyday life is evidence of a functioning spirituality.

I single out the virtue of generosity as important because usually the issue for the workplace community is not aging; it's generational in nature, a generation gap. There's nothing like generosity to close that gap. The generous person quite literally opens up to another; he or she can't remain closed and also be generous. Those around a truly generous person (one who also exhibits love, joy, peace, patience, kindness, faithfulness, gentleness, and self-control) can't remain closed for long, either. Openness meets openness wherever generosity is practiced.

# GENEROSITY AND VISION

The generous person is always an outward-looking person and often a person of vision. The practice of generosity, when adopted as a rebound-and-recovery strategy, demonstrates its power to sustain the seasoned survivor of workplace wounds and reversals.

Generosity helps the giver as it eases the burdens and brightens the workplace for others. It might not seem likely to result in long-term personal advantage, but survivors can attest that it does. You won't understand this unless you try acting generously.

The prophet Joel issued a call to repentance in anticipation of the "Day of the Lord." Having freed the people of Judah from an invasion of locusts and then blessed their land with peace and prosperity, the Lord, speaking through the prophet (3:1–2), said:

> *...I will pour out my spirit upon all mankind.*
> *Your sons and daughters shall prophesy,*
> *your old men shall dream dreams,*
> *your young men shall see visions;*
> *Even upon the servants and the handmaids,*
> *in those days I will pour out my spirit.*

Young workers, those on the short side of the generational divide, aren't going to have those exciting "visions" about the future of the organization, if the elders in their midst aren't decorating the place with "dreams." The "spirit" that this prophecy promises has been, and will continue to be, poured out. It can make its appearance now in the workplace in the form of generosity. This spirit can, of course, take other forms, too; any list of virtues would suggest the possibilities. However, generosity, a practical possibility for anyone, is worthy of special consideration by those concerned with spirituality in the workplace.

I would argue that generosity is a necessity for those on the long side of the generation gap who want to feel good about themselves as they are growing old. Particularly if they have been hit with wounds and reversals, they need the practice of generosity to rebuild their confidence and to avoid getting lost (and becoming irrelevant) in reveries about the "good old days."

Talk about the "way we used to do it" when that way is obsolete, and you will be talking to yourself, making others see you as peculiar. Talk about exciting possibilities in a future you don't fear, and you will have not only attentive listeners, but also enthusiastic partners, genuine companions in the enterprise.

# "JACK"

Everyone refers to John F. Welch, Jr., who became CEO of General Electric in 1981, as Jack. His success at GE, the success of the managerial revolution he achieved there, rests on a new relationship he established between employer and employee. Jack Welch built an organization based on shared vision and values. He forced employees to face reality, which meant seeing the world as it really is. In the new global world of business, he noticed, control from the top was a liability. Here are his own words:

> *The old organization was built on control, but the world has changed. The world is moving at such a pace that control has become a limitation. It slows you down. You've got to balance freedom with some control, but you've got to have more freedom than you ever dreamt of. To measure value, we're trying to look at what you contribute instead of what you control. (Quoted in Noel M. Tichy and Stratford Sherman, Control Your Destiny or Someone Else Will, Doubleday, 1993, p. 229)*

You might see these words as having little to do with generosity and nothing to do with aging gracefully, but you would be wrong. A CEO's lifespan as CEO is relatively short. Jack Welch aged in the job gracefully. Why? He was willing to share control. He moved to the long side of the generation gap with speed, but in a way that left behind only those who chose not to follow his pace. "Understand today fast. Shape tomorrow in your mind, and then leap to tomorrow" (Tichy and Sherman, p. 260).

> *My view of the 1990s is based on the liberation of the workplace. If you want to get the benefit of everything employees have, you've got to free them, make everybody a participant. Everybody has to know everything so they can make the right decision by themselves.*
>
> *In the old culture, managers got their power from secret knowledge: profit margins, market share, and all that. Once you share that information with everyone, however, it often turns out that the emperor has no clothes.*
>
> *In the new culture, the role of the leader is to express a vision, get buy-in, and carry it out. That role calls for open, caring relations with every employee and face-to-face communication. People who can't convincingly articulate a vision won't be successful, but those who can will*

*become even more open because success breeds self-confidence (Tichy
and Sherman, pp. 203–204).*

You might wonder about the organization's "caring relations" with the
thousands of GE employees who lost their jobs when the Welch revolution
began. Jack Welch accounted for the lay-offs as an inevitable part of reality.
He told employees that customers are their only source of job security. If he
and they can work together in participatory freedom and open communication to keep and enlarge the customer base, jobs will be safe.

Welch has been quoted as follows on this issue: "You've got to be hard
to be soft. You have to demonstrate the ability to make the hard, tough
decisions—closing plants, divesting, delayering—if you want to have any
credibility when you try to promote soft values. We reduced employment
and cut the bureaucracy and picked up some unpleasant nicknames, but
when we spoke of soft values—things like candor, fairness, facing reality—
people listened" (Tichy and Sherman, p. 245).

Welch's goal is to engage the mind—the thinking and the imagination—of every employee in the life of the company. I think that can be
viewed as an organizational form of generosity. I also think it reflects a non-
paternalistic style of a powerful CEO who, as he finds himself on the long
side of the generation gap, sees the wisdom of keeping close touch with the
other side.

## COPING WITH AGE AND CONSTANT CHANGE

Wherever you are in your career, both you and your workplace are aging
gradually. It's up to you to straddle both sides of any generation gap if you
want to help yourself and your workplace to age gracefully.

Perhaps you're thinking to yourself, "I'm no Jack Welch." You think
of yourself as an average man or woman who's getting on in years and not
all that delighted with the message you get from the date on your birth
certificate. A functioning spirituality tells you that you can turn that downer
into an upper simply by being generous.

Stop to think how you have probably always thought of older people
as having always been old. Sure, you yourself were aging, in a growing,

blooming, breaking-through-the-teens-and-twenties sort of way. Even through your forties and fifties, perhaps, you found ways to see the aging process as expansive and exciting. The "really" older folk were, well, old—the way they've always been. On the job, your impatience might have been a problem as you waited for the elders to "pack it in" so you could move up a notch. Now that there are far more notches (measured horizontally in calendar years, if not vertically in status and prestige) behind you than ahead, you might notice that younger folks are wondering when you're going to step aside or down.

Be generous to them. That's precisely what a solid, time-honored spiritual principle would have you do. Generosity invariably rewards the generous. Others are beneficiaries too, of course, but the generous person soon learns that generosity is its own reward.

What a difference a generous person makes in the workplace. Burdens are lightened, smiles multiply, and courtesy and civility gain breathing space. If you want to change things for the better, in life or work, and don't know what to do, just be generous. The results will astound you. Strange, isn't it—or maybe not so strange—that this simple truth is never grasped by many and that it's more easily grasped when you're older. The Pennsylvania Dutch have a proverb that offers an explanation: "We grow too soon old and too late wise."

It is never, however, too late for generosity.

Consider whether God might be trying to speak to you now in these words from the Book of Proverbs (3:36):

> *Let not kindness and fidelity leave you;*
> *bind them around your neck;*
> *Then will you win favor and good esteem*
> *before God and man.*
> *Trust in the Lord with all your heart,*
> *on your own intelligence rely not;*
> *In all your ways be mindful of him,*
> *and he will make straight your paths.*

# Chapter 19

# ILLNESS

Several years ago, a manager I know found himself burdened with worries over illness at home; both his wife and his elderly mother were seriously ill. During one of our visits together, he said to me, "The Book of Job has my name on it." I laughed, but he wasn't trying to be funny.

Illness has a way of making those who have it, or who have to deal with it in those they love, feel put upon. This is exactly the expression Robert Frost used in his verse play, "Masque of Reason," to let Job describe his feelings. In the play, God says to Job:

*Oh, I remember well: you're Job, my Patient.*
*How are you now? I trust you're quite recovered*
*And feel no ill effects from what I gave you.*

Job replies:
*Gave me in truth: I like the frank admission.*
*I am a name for being put upon.*

And yet that "frank admission" and the unspoken notion that God directly attacks humans with physical misfortune aren't necessarily accurate. God far more often permits illness to touch a human life, to be part of the human predicament, instead of positively willing to inflict illness on a person.

Your spirituality has to wrap itself around the problem of human suffering, the coexistence of an all-good and loving God with the pain and suffering that accompany the human condition. Your practical spirituality must come up with some reasonably satisfying answers to the questions: Why pain? Why suffering? Why me? Otherwise, you will be tempted simply to give up on life. For the moment, view illness as a teaching riddle, a means of learning more about yourself and life.

I want to use the riddle of illness as a way to open up an extended reflection on this dimension of the human predicament. Your struggle to cope with illness is related to your faith-based strategy to deal with any other kind of reversal.

# WHY?

My attempt to answer the triple-why question—why pain? why suffering? why me?—begins with a quotation from the opening prayer in a Mass Roman Catholics offer "For the Sick." This beautiful prayer says simply: "Father, your Son accepted our sufferings to teach us the virtue of patience in human illness. Hear the prayers we offer for our sick brothers and sisters. May all who suffer pain, illness or disease realize that they are chosen to be saints, and know that they are joined to Christ in his suffering for the salvation of the world...."

There is a famous text in the Letter of Paul to the Colossians: "Even now I find my joy in the suffering I endure for you. In my own flesh I fill up what is lacking in the sufferings of Christ for the sake of his body, the Church" (Col. 1:24). The body metaphor is an important part of Paul's theology of the church. All of the baptized are somehow incorporated into the body of Christ. Through baptism (the word means *plunge*), the Christian is not only incorporated into the body of Christ, but also plunged symbolically and sacramentally into his death. Recall the death-dealing potential of water. People can drown in water; hence the death symbolism of baptismal waters. The Christian is plunged sacramentally into the death of Christ at baptism so that he or she can rise (that is, experience resurrection) with Christ to newness of life, the life of grace. To dismiss the death and rebirth elements of this experience as mere symbolism is to miss a vitally important point in the Christian faith: The eternal life to be enjoyed in heaven differs only in degree, not in kind, from the grace-life available to the believer here on earth.

# "FILLING UP"

Christians believe that this grace-life was made possible and available through the sufferings and death, as well as the resurrection, of Jesus. Paul's instructions in the Letter to the Colossians, as well as the point made so plainly in the prayer from the Roman Catholic Mass for the Sick, suggest that a person can, through illness, suffering, setbacks, disappointments, and defeats, "fill up" in some mysterious way "what is lacking in the sufferings of Christ for the sake of his body, the church"—that is, for the community, the people of God.

This is a powerful point, one worth considering closely and weaving into your practical workplace spirituality. This reflection isn't an exercise in feel-good theology, nor is it some kind of cotton-candy spirituality— sweet, soft, and short-lived. What I am proposing is as serious as sickness itself, and it takes you into the heart of the Christian revelation.

A Christian might ask: How can there be anything "lacking" in the sufferings of Christ? Weren't his sufferings and death on the cross enough for the salvation of the entire human race? Yes, they were. But God in his infinite wisdom and generous providence seems to make the salvation of some dependent on the ministry of others. He needs, in some mysterious way, the ministry of men and women to work with Jesus for the salvation of the world. God could choose, of course, to do it all without the ministry of human hands and hearts, but clearly he chooses not to. He presents himself as a God in need of help. He looks for helpers not only among those who are ready to deny themselves and take up their cross to follow Jesus, but also among those who suffer illnesses and other setbacks not of their own choosing. It is in this way that you can participate in filling up the sufferings of Christ.

# REVERSALS

Reversals are an unavoidable part of being human. Everyone has to deal with them. Those who choose to accept Jesus can also freely choose to contribute their pain, suffering, frustrations, impatience, and all the other downside disappointments that come to them in the workplace and in life, to "fill up what is lacking in the sufferings of Christ."

**159**

Saint Paul was called—had a vocation—to be an apostle, to bring the "good news" to places Jesus had been unable to reach during his years on earth. Of course, wherever Jesus brought the good news, which included a call to repentance, to a radical change of heart, he met with resistance. Paul caused division among the men and women who heard him preach in each new locality he visited.

Paul knew something about reversals. He had the experience common to all apostles: Some people happily accept the proclamation of the good news, but others not only reject the message, but persecute those who proclaim it. In this sense, scholars suggest, the "sufferings of Christ" referred to in the Letter to the Colossians are the apostolic sufferings endured as the gospel is brought to new places and new people. There will always be something lacking until the gospel of Christ is proclaimed in all times and places and accepted by all who hear that proclamation.

This means there's a lot of apostolic work to do in every new day of every new age. The good news of salvation still has to be proclaimed by word and, especially, by example. My point is that the sick and those burdened with other setbacks have a privileged way of participating in that work. Reversals—certainly physical illnesses—constitute a calling, I believe, that awaits a full, free response in faith.

# YOUR CALLING

Those burdened with illness or reeling from reversals can preach the gospel by acting as a witness to spiritual values. They can exhibit trust in God. They can offer the example of patience, kindness, and the other virtues Jesus urged his followers to adopt. Their simple acceptance, in faith, of God loving and caring for them, together with their acceptance of God's will for them, serve as powerful and persuasive preaching to others. This preaching can be done today in places where Jesus obviously never walked, including the place where you work.

Acting as a witness in this way reflects what St. Teresa of Avila must have had in mind when she said: "Christ has no body on earth but yours, no hands on earth but your hands. Yours are the eyes through which he looks out with compassion on the world. Yours the feet with which he chooses to go about doing good. For as he is the head, so you are the members, and we are all one in Christ Jesus."

This line of reflection opens the door to a deeper exploration of the implications of what it means for a Christian to be a member of the body of Christ. As I mentioned, baptism incorporates a person into the body of Christ, into the church, the community of believers. One of the images Jesus chose to use in explaining this fundamental reality is that of the vine and branches. You will find that expression in the portion of John's gospel (especially Chapter 15) where he constructs from the sayings of Jesus a farewell discourse given to the apostles at the Last Supper: "I am the vine, you are the branches. Whoever remains in me, with me in him, bears abundant fruit."

When you look at a tree, or bush, or vine, could you say precisely where the stem or trunk ends and the branch begins? John's vine-and-branch imagery conveys the point that you are enlivened, energized, and activated by the life of Christ within you, once you have been "grafted onto" the body of Christ through baptism. To continue the analogy, grace is like the sap that enlivens both branch and vine.

The word *grace* means *gift*. The substance of this grace, this gift, is divine love. It remains within you, sustains you, and gives infinite value to all you do.

## "THE FRUITS OF THE REDEMPTION"

Back in 1961, Pope John XXIII sent an encyclical letter out to the whole world under the title "Mater et Magistra" ("Mother and Teacher," his characterization of the church). Toward the end of that encyclical, he wrote:

> We invite with paternal urgency all our sons [and daughters] belonging to either the clergy or the laity to be deeply conscious of their dignity and nobility based on their oneness with Christ as branches with a vine, 'I am the vine and you are the branches' (John 15:5), and on their ability to share his divine life. Hence, when Christians do their normal work, even if it be work of a temporal nature in union with the divine

*continues*

**161**

*continued*

> *Redeemer, every effort becomes a continuation of the effort of Jesus Christ and is penetrated with redemptive power: 'He who abides in me and I in him, he bears much fruit' (John 15:5). It thus becomes a work which contributes to one's personal supernatural perfection and helps to extend to others the fruits of the redemption. It also leavens with the ferment of the Gospel the civilization within which one lives and works.*

Give some thought for a few moments to the immense possibilities for good that are open to you because you, by grace, are alive in Christ. By simply asking God to let it happen, your medical problems, your business losses, your psychological defeats, your discouragement, disappointments, frustrations, and all the other negatives associated with the human condition, can participate in the same redemptive power that gave meaning to Jesus' suffering and death. This is not to suggest that physical suffering vanishes when you hand yours over, so to speak, to God. By bearing pain, suffering, and discouragement in union with Christ (made easier for you, perhaps, if you recall the deeper meaning of those Pauline values of patience and faithfulness), you enjoy the great privilege of continuing and extending into your own day Christ's redemptive work, the work of saving the world.

# ACCEPTANCE

No one can explain adequately why God, in his infinite wisdom, chose suffering as the instrument of salvation, but he did. Similarly, no one can adequately explain why human illness and suffering can have redemptive power, but they do. No attempt to explain any of this is even possible, however, without some reference to the virtue that tops the list of the Pauline Criteria: love.

Perhaps when sickness or disappointment is accepted gracefully, that acceptance empties people of any pretension to autonomy and opens them up to be filled by God with his powerful love—love not only for the sick or disappointed, but for others whom God chooses to help through another's pain. By "letting go and letting God," as the saying goes, you become a loving instrument of God's healing grace.

Think about illness as a calling, and pray about it. See it as an opportunity to experience and extend God's love. As you do, ponder the "why me?" question in the context of that opening prayer from the Mass for the Sick, which might just as well be a Mass for the Discouraged, the Disappointed, and Those Dealing with Downside Reversals. Here it is again: "May all who suffer pain, illness or disease realize that they are chosen to be saints, and know that they are joined to Christ in his suffering for the salvation of the world."

Why you? Why not you? You have been called to sanctity. You have a challenge in what you've been mistaking all along as a burden or even a curse. Your reversal is an opportunity to work with Christ for the salvation of the world.

The wonder of it all is this: Your faith assures you that the human condition that weighs you down is redeemed, indeed transformed, by the incarnation (the enfleshment) of Jesus, who took upon himself the human condition. If you are a Christian, you are incorporated, by baptism, into the body of Christ, as a branch is connected to a vine. Simply by willing it, therefore, you can convert what weighs you down—your illness, discouragement, defeats, and disappointments—into a spiritual force that lifts up a tired world.

Dorothy Day, founder of the Catholic Worker movement, put it this way: "The consolation is this and this our faith too: By our suffering and our failures, by our acceptance of the Cross, we unleash forces that help to overcome the evil in the world."

*The task is mine; the power is yours. Why is it so hard for me to get that straight, Lord? I keep looking to you to do my work by miraculous intervention—a rescue operation when things are going badly. I keep thinking that the power to perform is all mine when things are going well. Without you, I could not do anything; I would not even exist…but I keep forgetting that.*

*I also forget that there are tasks you have assigned to me that you haven't given to anyone else. I forget (probably because I just can't understand) that you have chosen to be, however mysteriously, a God in need of help. You invite laborers to work in the harvest; if the laborer turns down the opportunity, some of that harvest will not be brought in. That's a frightening prospect, so I bring it before you, Lord, in prayer and ask that you shake my complacency and instruct me clearly on the rules of the road that leads to eternal life.*

# Chapter 20

# INSECURITY

I know a successful executive who claims that the first principle of effective management is "Don't get everyone mad at you all at once." The reason he is successful, however, is his commitment to another management principle: "You'll never make any employee more productive by making him or her feel less secure."

By way of contrast, let me tell you about an unsuccessful executive who began his first (and, as it turned out, only) university presidency by requesting all managers from directors on up through deans and vice presidents to submit letters of resignation for his consideration upon taking office. This step, of course, thoroughly destabilized the place and made not only the targeted administrators, but also everyone who worked for them, feel insecure. "They call me Jaws," he told me, with no small amount of satisfaction, shortly after he took over his new responsibilities. (At the time, the film of the same name was frightening audiences across the country.) Although he accepted only a few of the proffered "resignations," this academic executive, who had come from the opposite coast to take this new job, faced the virtually impossible tasks of finding good replacements for those employees he let go and eliciting good performance from everyone else. Having succeeded in creating an environment of uncertainty and insecurity, he lasted as president only eight months.

## INSECURITY AS A WORKPLACE CONSTANT

Something is in the air these days, something that communicates subliminally, but nonetheless effectively, a deep sense of insecurity in the workplace. It's not just the fragility of employment arrangements and the stagnation of middle-level incomes, nor is it simply the dawning realization that today's young adults are likely to constitute the first generation in the nation's history that will be less well off economically than their parents' generation (even though Bill Gates is doing all he can to pull the average up!). Neither is it the whole array of anxieties about healthcare finance or the fear of AIDS among the young and Alzheimer's among the elderly.

This something in the air has to do with all the preceding factors but it also has to do, I believe, with something less obvious and, therefore, less discussed. I'm thinking about information and the powerful new technologies that move it around with lightening-like speed.

Information technology is racing forward, aided by "chips" that are for the most part neither seen nor understood by most of us. Yet they are our depository of essential facts and figures; they have become our memory. We rely on them to keep our accounts in order, our automobiles running, and our planes on course and safe for takeoff and landing. Can they crack or break? What if one of those millions of grooves gets clogged? What if they just wear out? Now that it is common to find computer networks in the workplace, we have recurring frustration and chronic apprehension over a possible systems crash, not to mention the spread of a crippling computer virus. "When the network goes down, the business goes down with it" is the fatalistic comment heard in offices where, not all that long ago, the business ran on hand-cranked adding machines.

And what about those tiny batteries that keep time for us and promise to warn us if fire strikes? What about whatever it is that we depend on whenever we throw a switch, push a button, or make a call? What if the power fails? Where and how can you get your hands on whatever you need to reassure you that your home, files, documents, money, medical monitoring equipment, life-support systems, and automated production processes are safe, sound, dependable, reliable, and will be there for you tomorrow? We are becoming a hesitant, dependent society at the very time we're accelerating the rate of what we call, in our less reflective moments, progress.

Is it any wonder we're uneasy and culturally insecure? The technology that was meant to make life easier has instead, in all too many instances, left us feeling frustrated, helpless, and disconnected.

You carry this dependency, this hesitancy, this insecurity with you when you go to work. You carry it home again, of course. You simply have to realize that the uneasiness technology brings can originate either at home or on the job, and it can be aggravated in either domain and in almost any dimension of your existence. I say "almost any" because I hope that spirituality can be a special preserve where stability and security can be achieved by those who seek it in faith.

# FAITHFULNESS AND SECURITY

Security is an achievement, not just a passive benefit for those lucky enough to receive it. It's also a grace and, therefore, a gift whose worth can't be measured. You have to cooperate with grace, however; by that, I mean you have some work to do to achieve it. In other words, you have some responsibility for making a functioning spirituality function. When it functions, you derive a deep sense of personal security.

The one Pauline criterion that comes into play here in a special way is faithfulness. That is what God expects you to be: faithful. It's really all that God expects of you—to be faithful to God, to your responsibilities to other persons, and to yourself.

This Pauline value leads to an important ethical principle, that of keeping commitments; this means dependability, reliability, and fidelity. If we are less and less confident that we will find these qualities in our machines and our written agreements in the workplace, perhaps it's time to start looking for them in each other.

You can't, of course, guarantee that commitments will be kept by others, but if you focus in on faithfulness as you make the Pauline Criteria part of your personal spirituality, you can offer yourself, your character, as a pledge that you'll uphold your end of any commitments you make on or off the job. Too few people today are capable of making that pledge, which says a lot about the condition of character in our time.

## COMMITMENT AND A SENSE OF SELF

In the preface to the American edition of his play *A Man for All Seasons* (Vintage Books, 1960), Robert Bolt explains that Thomas More, "as I wrote about him, became for me a man with an adamantine sense of his own self. He knew where he began and left off, what area of himself he could yield to the encroachments of his enemies, and what to the encroachments of those he loved…but [he would not] retreat from that final area where he located his self. And there this supple, humorous, unassuming and sophisticated person set like metal, was overtaken by an absolutely primitive rigor, and could no more be budged than a cliff."

Bolt goes on to note that More "found something in himself without which life was valueless and when that was denied him was able to grasp his death." "Why," asks Bolt, "do I take as my hero a man who brings about his own death because he can't put his hand on an old black book and tell an ordinary lie? For this reason: A man takes an oath only when he wants to commit himself quite exceptionally to the statement, when he wants to make an identity between the truth of it and his own virtue; he offers himself as a guarantee. And it worked. There is a special kind of shrug for a perjurer; we feel that the man has no self to commit, no guarantee to offer." For Robert Bolt, Thomas More was a hero of selfhood.

Selfhood is altogether different from self-centeredness, or selfishness; it's character, the bedrock of personal commitment and the precondition of personal and societal security. In an age of insecurity like ours, all the blame can't be assigned to the permanent possibility of technological failure. Your own character has to become the basis of your response to the instability of the times. Search for answers from within when you want to assess or address the condition of insecurity, that which makes you anxious now.

That spiritual bank account that I've encouraged you to establish will eventually be filled with what you need to stand tall against feelings of insecurity: divine grace, first and foremost, but also maxims, memories, and convictions that give you ground for reassurance. "Fixed as he was in the things of eternity," Douglas Horton said of the late Gustav Weigel, "he could sit loose to the things of time." Most of us have difficulty in "sitting loose" when a sense of insecurity closes in. With practice, however, this protective posture can be developed.

# ASKING GOD FOR HELP

Give a moment's reflection to the following spiritual security-builder. It is of anonymous authorship. I once read that it was found on the dead body of a soldier who lost his life in the Civil War. I can't vouch for that. I simply offer it as a perspective-setter, a balancing factor for anyone who is troubled by insecurity:

*I asked God for strength, that I might achieve.*
*I was made weak, that I might learn to obey.*
*I asked for health, that I might do greater things.*
*I was given infirmity, that I might do better things.*
*I asked for riches, that I might be happy.*
*I was given poverty, that I might be wise.*
*I asked for power, that I might have the praise of men.*
*I was given weakness, that I might feel the need of God.*
*I asked for all things, that I might enjoy life.*
*I was given life, that I might enjoy all things.*
*I got nothing that I asked for but everything I had hoped for.*
*Almost despite myself, my unspoken prayers were answered.*
*I am, among all men, most richly blessed.*

At the end of the day, you are faced with a question of faith. Where is yours? If you're putting your faith in money and the things money can buy, you will always be insecure. On the other hand, total reliance on the God you cannot see will bring total security in ways you can never explain. Pray for it today, and act everyday as if that prayer were answered.

*"Know that the Lord works wonders for the faithful"* (Psalm 4:4).

Lord, I love the beach, the ocean coast; east or west, it draws me
to you. I love to walk the shore; it puts me in your presence. There
is something that happens to us, Thoreau said, "walking along the
shore of the resounding sea, determined to get in into us."

What gets into me walking on the beach is a deep-down sense of
your fidelity—yours, not mine. You are faithful; you can't be
otherwise. I can always count on that. I am fickle, often faithless.
I am always restless (like the sea!) and sometimes fearful, but your
fidelity comes pounding home to my consciousness like the always
present, ever dependable rolling in of the waves that say to me:
"God is with you." "God forgives you." "God loves you." "God
cannot be anything but faithful to you."

So, Lord, I keep on walking, and I look out at the ocean of your
mercy, and up to the heavens where I know you have prepared a
place somewhere for me.

# Chapter 21

# ADDICTION

In the medical vocabulary, *behavioral health* is a relatively new category that embraces mental illness and all forms of alcohol and chemical abuse. The arrival and acceptance of the new terminology in the human resources community represents a positive development for human progress in the workplace.

Realism requires the admission that addiction is a disease. Alcoholism and drug dependency are diseases that have spread to almost every workplace; their carriers are free human beings (although their freedom is impaired by disease), many of whom are in denial and struggling to disguise their dependencies. These people are ill, so they are qualified to apply the material in the previous chapter on illness to themselves.

People with substance abuse problems, then, are actually "called to be saints." They need, however, to adopt the spirituality embodied in the 12-step program of Alcoholics Anonymous or to try other dependency-breaking strategies to regain their freedom. They can't rely on miracles. They have to take all necessary human means. They have to decide, to act, to take however many "steps" are needed to gain their full freedom.

## THE TWELVE STEPS

Here are the twelve steps that originated in the experience of an Akron, Ohio physician and a New York stockbroker, both alcoholics, who had a conversation in 1935 that led to the founding of Alcoholics Anonymous. These steps have proved to be immeasurably helpful to countless men and women over the years:

1. We admitted we were powerless over alcohol—that our lives had become unmanageable.

2. We came to believe that a power greater than ourselves could restore us to sanity.

3. We made a decision to turn our will and our lives over to the care of God as we understood Him.

4. We made a searching and fearless inventory of ourselves.

5. We admitted to God, to ourselves and to another human being the exact nature of our wrongs.

6. We were entirely ready to have God remove all these defects of character.

7. We humbly asked Him to remove all our shortcomings.

8. We made a list of all people we had harmed, and became willing to make amends to them all.

9. We made direct amends to such people, wherever possible, except when to do so would injure them or others.

10. We continued to take personal inventory, and when we were wrong, promptly admitted it.

11. We sought through prayer and meditation to improve our conscious contact with God as we understood Him, praying only for knowledge of His will for us and the power to carry that out.

12. Having had a spiritual awakening as the result of these steps, we tried to carry this message to alcoholics and to practice these principles in all our affairs.

These twelve steps are wisdom principles for any person in any stage of life. They have more than addiction-breaking power; they have the potential to put a person on a high road of spirituality yet remain fully and firmly grounded in the human condition. To the extent that the break from addiction can be said to be up to you, it begins with self-control.

The last of the nine Pauline Criteria is self-control. It can come to anyone, but it doesn't come easily. Perhaps the underlying problem that most of us struggling with the human predicament have to face up to is that we foolishly think that to live easily is to live happily.

Addiction is an illness with origins outside the workplace. On-the-job stress can aggravate the problem, and the work environment might encourage alcohol or substance abuse. The problem, however, almost always has roots that predate the employment contract. To trace the etiology in any given case would be to follow a complex trail across complicated psychological and physiological terrain.

Consider what we know about drug addiction. Deep down on the demand side of the drug problem lie three causal considerations. First is the natural desire to experience some exhilaration—what is often called a *high*. Second is the desire to avoid pain. The third causal consideration is a biological or physiological predisposition toward addiction that could be operative in any given case.

The first two of these demand-pulls can be handled by just about anyone; you can choose legitimate, non-addictive means of experiencing exhilaration and managing pain. The third pull, fortunately, never takes the form of a sudden attack. Warnings of a physiological predisposition come early enough so that, if heeded, they can save a person from subsequent addiction. But hard work, responsibility, and self-discipline are required if your defense mechanisms are to function well on all three fronts. To say all this is possible is not to say that it's easy.

No one is immune to the risk of addiction. You might have a dependency problem that you haven't yet noticed, so be alert for signals that people who care about you might be trying to send. You could be having a problem with alcohol even though you're not physiologically or psychologically predisposed to alcoholism; the abuse without the addiction could still make you a danger to yourself or others. Or you might be happily free of any burden along these lines—something to be thankful for during your morning and evening periods of self-assessment. If you want to be in a position to send a necessary signal or offer help to friends, you should take some time now to learn what to look for as signs of unhealthy dependency in others.

# FIGHTING DENIAL

If you do have a problem and know it, fight the impulse toward denial. Have a healthy distrust of your judgment in your own case. Talk to several trusted people in and out of the workplace. Overcome your fear of a breach of confidentiality and take advantage of your organization's employee assistance program. This might be the time to test the provision that belongs in any Christian faith-based spirituality: You must lose your life, if you want to find it (see Matthew 10:39).

If you have a dependency problem, admit it. Like a thief with homicidal tendencies, your addiction is taking your life right now. Your courage (read: humility) can save you. Give your life over to the care of a therapist, a counselor, a spiritual director, or a support group (or a combination of all of them) to find it.

# AGGRESSIVE WORKPLACE INTERVENTION

The *Wall Street Journal* had a wake-up headline on September 9, 1996 in these words: "In Leaner, Meaner Workplace, Bosses Get Tough on Addiction." The story suggested that policing the office for substance abuse is now part of the job description of middle managers. The "leaner, meaner" characterization refers, of course, to workplaces in the aftermath of downsizing. Problem drinkers would presumably be more readily detectable in today's thinner employment ranks, although the *Journal* points out that a small but significant percentage of cut-back survivors are now spending more time as telecommuters working at home or with laptops on the road, so they are more difficult to observe. The problems will out sooner rather than later, however, and aggressive interventions are now commonplace.

Supervisors are instructed to keep an eye on job performance and limit their remarks to that one observable and costly dimension of the problem: impaired performance. Although the Alcoholics Anonymous saying remains true—that problem drinkers have to first "hit bottom" before recovery strategies can work—employers are beginning to realize that they can raise the bottom to the level where the substance abuser is now. How? By

174

expecting decisive, aggressive, no-holds-barred intervention by supervisors who insist on referral to the helping professionals.

No help sought means no job held. Both those who deliver and receive that message will be fuller human beings if they can process it in terms of a functioning spirituality. On the delivery side, the message should be regarded not as a threat, but as a promise of restored health for a suffering human being and renewed productivity for the firm. Not to deliver this ultimatum could be cowardice or a blindness to tolerant kindness toward addiction being a form of cruelty.

Those who hear this tough message directed at themselves and who receive it through the ear of faith as though it were coming to them from God have a spirituality that rests on humility. As those who have been through it all ask, "What more do you need?"

## THE ROAD AHEAD

Answers to the question of what you're going to do about your addiction can come only from within. Those answers will prove to be false if there is nothing of God, and grace, and faith residing within; the empty center simply can't produce a solution. Why? Because it's empty!

Professionals who deal with problem drinkers and drug abusers offer a uniform warning: "They will lie to you." I'm not sure they're always telling lies in the technical sense—expressing outwardly information or intentions they know inwardly to be contrary to the truth. I think people with dependency problems are often saying what they desperately want to be true. That's the hopeful indicator: their desperation.

If the desperation is real and acknowledged as such, it can help the desperate open their bodies and minds to professional help; it can also open their souls to grace.

They want to stop, but unless they confront their desperation, unless they stare into its bloodshot eye long enough to see clearly that it can, if they let it, become the foundation of hope, change won't happen. Until they admit their powerlessness to change, there will be no change.

How then, you might ask, will change come about? Spirituality has an answer. By God's action within the soul, a believer can build a new life on the ruins of the old. Is this a miracle? Not really; it's simply grace building upon nature. On the natural ruins of humility and the acknowledgment of human dependency (not on drugs or alcohol, but on God), the human spirit can find its vital center, its fundamental sense of self. From that base, it can soar because, like all others who are burdened with sickness, substance abusers are, in the eyes of the believer and the prayer of the church, "called to be saints."

## "THAT YOUR LOVED ONES MAY ESCAPE"

Psalm 60 is a lament after defeat in battle. It offers a vocabulary to sub-stance abusers who are moved to pray for help. The petition in verse 6, "Help with your right hand and answer us, that your loved ones may escape," is exactly what alcoholics and addicts who are unconvinced of their lovableness have to say. The assertion in verse 13 is what every problem drinker and drug abuser must believe: "We will triumph with the help of God."

Lord, let me follow a five-point check list in approaching you in prayer. First, of course, I want to give you thanks for your presence to me always and for your action in my life this very day. It's good for me to meet you here in gratitude.

Next, I ask for your light. I ask you to put your searchlight on my soul so that I can feel your presence there and let that presence illuminate my selfishness and expose my sinfulness. Your light does away with my darkness. It allows me to know my inauthenticity; it encourages me to clear up the clutter in the dark corners of my soul.

Third, Lord, I want, in your presence, to face up to my failings: I resist your grace, I refuse to love others you put within my reach, I leave so many tasks undone, I neglect to stretch out my hand in help, I am insincere, and I am timid about taking on the challenges you place before me every day.

So please forgive me, Lord. With this fresh awareness of your gifts to me and with the illumination your presence in me provides, I find a need deep within me that only you can fill. It's the need for your forgiveness. It's not a mechanical guilt-displacing forgiveness that you give, but a release, by your presence within, of my unattended potential for action. My inaction is forgiven by you. My wrong actions are overcome by you. My next actions will, I hope, be more faithful representations of you in my small corner of the globe.

Fifth and finally, Lord, I promise to make amends. For me this means re-enlisting in your service, declaring again my availability to work with you, which means, I know, to let you work in me. Give me, Lord, the gift of accepting that I am a loved sinner. That's really all I want or need.

# Chapter 22

# INDECISION

Regarded by many as the greatest trial lawyer of his time, Edward Bennett Williams had a reputation for thorough preparation, undistracted focus, and intense self-discipline throughout a trial. While trying a case in New York City, Williams reportedly took a telephone call in his hotel room from one of Eleanor Roosevelt's sons, who said Mrs. Roosevelt would like to have a conference with him. Williams politely declined; the trial required his total attention.

Later, according to a friend of the attorney who told me this story, Mrs. Roosevelt herself called back to press the request. "I understand your position," she supposedly said. "I appreciate the value of time. And I learned long ago that the two great culprits in the theft of time are regret and indecision."

I don't know whether Ed Williams ever agreed to see her, but I do know, from personal dealings with him, that he incorporated Mrs. Roosevelt's counsel into his working life and normal way of proceeding. He never lost a minute to regret or indecision, especially during the 11-year battle with cancer that eventually took his life.

Recall the Pauline value of faithfulness as you think about the related problems of indecision and uncertainty in the workplace. Absolute, unshakable certainty is admirable and possible in the order of faith (where you rely, after all, on God's own word rather than on your own abilities), but absolute certainty is just not going to be there to help you make earthbound choices as you work your way through the human predicament. Moreover, at this very practical level, not to decide is to decide. You can't escape the necessity of making choices.

# WHO YOU ARE

The indecision that can cripple career progress is always rooted in fear, which often takes the form of fear of failure, although it could be fear of success, fear of authority, or a complicated fear that has you caught in the opposing forces of attachment and separation. Sometimes career and workplace hesitation is explained by an unrealistic aspiration for the best that can become the enemy of the attainable good. This hesitancy to decide could be a vestige of whatever troubled you as a child standing at the ice-cream counter, when you didn't know how to deal with the problem of wanting all the flavors at once. In your adult years, you might have discovered a label for that indecision in the existentialist expression "the tragedy of the excluded alternative." The insight in that expression isn't new; Cicero saw grief as part of indecision: "In indecision itself, grief is present" (*De Officiis*, book iii, chapter 8).

You, too, might have noticed that regret and indecision have a lot in common. As poet Sam Hazo says so well, "Regretting/ what you did or did not do/ or always wished to do adds up/ to who you are." You are, then, the sum of your choices, so make them. Don't keep putting them off. You surely don't want to become the sum of your regrets. In the face of all the alternatives about to be excluded by an imminent choice, you can be paralyzed. Just go ahead.

# THE OPEN DOOR

Don't misunderstand. I'm not trying to induct you into an army of ready-fire-aim decision makers, but there are times when further analysis is just too much analysis. After due consideration and reflection, you should just go ahead and do it. Decide…and then see what happens.

Read Goethe's *Faust* (in Auster's translation) and you'll find this bit of common sense: "Lose this day loitering, 'twill be the same story/ Tomorrow, and the next, more dilatory;/ Each indecision brings its own delays,/ and days are lost lamenting o'er lost days." Indecision has a way of multiplying, building up, and piling on. Don't let it do that to you.

Indecision is a self-imposed paralysis—not to be confused with waiting for a promotion, for the next job, for a response to your proposal, for a decision that can be made only by someone else. Waiting is a form of suffering (recall the relationship of patience to suffering). While you are waiting, you are suffering. As business consultant John Fontana remarked to me, "Colleges today are, in effect, selling careers. Graduates expect career satisfaction. They don't expect that they are going to have to suffer."

Suffering because of the indecision of another is one thing, and you might not be able to do much about it. Suffering as a result of your own failure to decide is another matter; you can dispose of that problem by simply deciding to decide. You can, in other words, stop pushing against an open door.

# LEARNING

Margaret Mason, a *Washington Post* Style-section columnist ("Body and Soul") added to her column on September 18, 1989, a reflection she received from one of her readers. It is titled "Comes the Dawn" and is shared, the reader noted, "courtesy of an Al-Anon meeting." It can aid your reflection on those dimensions of the human predicament that relate to addiction, regret, and indecision, and prepare you for the material that awaits your consideration in chapters that lie ahead on broken promises, divorce, the death of someone dear, and layoff from employment.

*After a while you learn the subtle difference*
*Between holding a hand and chaining a soul,*
*And you learn that love doesn't mean leaning,*
*And company doesn't mean security.*
*And you begin to understand that*
    *kisses aren't contracts,*
*And presents aren't promises,*
*And you begin to accept your defeats*
*With your head held high and your eyes open,*
*With the grace of a woman or man,*
    *not the grief of a child.*
*You learn to build your roads*
*On today because tomorrow's ground*

*continues*

181

*continued*

> Is too uncertain for plans, and futures have
> A way of falling down in mid-flight.
> After a while you learn that even
> > sunshine burns if you get too much.
> So you plant your own garden and decorate
> Your own soul, instead of waiting
> For someone to bring you flowers.
> And you learn that you really can endure.
> That you really are strong.
> And you really do have worth
> And you learn and learn…and you learn
> With every good-bye you learn.

But first you have to say good-bye. You have to cut loose, move on, stop pondering, and decide. This process is going to be unusually difficult for some people who shouldn't even attempt it without professional help. That won't work for everyone. It would require a personality transplant for some indecisive people to overcome the paralysis, but most procrastinators don't procrastinate forever. They just need to be nudged to do what they know they should do, want to do, and eventually would have done without the nudge. You can, with practice, learn to provide your own nudge.

The fulcrum that can move you forward could be as simple as a sheet of paper used to write a to-do list. It's your list, so put the things you ought to do, but want to defer, at the top of the list. If, at the end of the day, there are important items not yet done, give them top billing on tomorrow's list.

Keep a pad of paper handy and make notes to yourself as the day unfolds. Notes like these should record reminders, ask questions, and prompt answers from within, deep within. These notes can tell you a lot about yourself. They can help you better understand what you fear and what your genuine likes and dislikes are; they can, if you let them, trace out your personal pattern of deferral. Take that pattern as a prescription for action, the kind of action that cuts through indecision. With or without your athletic shoes on, "Just do it!"

## INFORMED DECISIVENESS

Informed decisiveness is a universally attractive trait. You hope to find it in those you want to trust. How would you react to a surgeon with a shaky hand? How would you feel about advice from a broker who has no firm views on a portfolio composition suited to your needs? How, when in your car and lost in unfamiliar territory, would you appreciate directions from a stranger who qualifies every suggested turn with "maybe," and estimates every distance with wide allowances of "more or less"? What do you think of a shopper who can never decide?

As I mentioned earlier, not to decide is, in fact, a decision. Typically, it's a decision to remain in place, off balance, apprehensive, and even miserable. You can do a whole lot better than that. You can choose to move forward.

## MISTAKES

What if you make the wrong choice? First ask yourself, wrong in relation to what?

Who ever said you have to be right all the time? Of course, you don't want to choose what you clearly know is morally wrong, and normally you won't. Even if you did, you would surely know it and face up to your responsibility to make amends. The issue here isn't choosing between vice and virtue, however; it's typically about the choice between the good and the better, between no risk and some risk, between standing still and moving ahead. There's more: Overcoming indecisiveness is about reinstating yourself in the human community, at work or at home. It's about getting back into the game, being a participant, and engaging yourself with life. There is no life without some risk.

Look around at the people and the tasks that await the impact of your presence and say, only to yourself, "These are my circumstances; these are the people with whom I must connect." Then do it. Otherwise, your life will be an echo of the heavy words of the German poet Hebbel:

*The one I am sadly salutes the one I could have been.*

Let the one you are now gladly, not sadly, salute the circumstances that surround you. Then step lively, and without regret, into an unknown future.

**183**

# Chapter 23

# BROKEN PROMISES

"Double dealing" is, unfortunately, a common occurrence in and out of the typical workplace. I chose *broken promises* as the more appropriate category for this chapter because it's a broader term. (It can also help to make this chapter function as preamble to the next, which deals with the unhappy reversal of divorce.)

Consider a memorable passage from Thornton Wilder's play *The Skin of Our Teeth*. In the middle of act 2, Mrs. Antrobus stares straight out into the audience as her errant husband is pacing back and forth, off to the side. The stage directions instruct her to say her lines "calmly, almost dreamily."

*I didn't marry you because you were perfect. I didn't even marry you because I loved you. I married you because you gave me a promise.*

Then the stage directions have her remove her wedding ring and look at it. She continues:

*That promise made up for all your faults. And the promise I gave you made up for mine. Two imperfect people got married, and it was the promise that made the marriage.*

Promises are contracts of a sort, although they are almost always personal, oral, and unwritten. We tend to sit up straight and get more serious when we talk about contracts. Contracts, written or unwritten, are part of everyday life. They are the way we contextualize and formalize trust. We agree. Sometimes we're perfectly content to secure the agreement with a handshake; in such cases, we readily accept each other's word as bond.

At other times, we get everything down on paper. We have witnesses; we sign the documents, get the signatures notarized, and bind the agreement with a seal. The trust is still there, only now it's framed in proper language and formalized according to relevant law. If formal contracts are broken, any related complaint is adjudicated according to the principles of interpretation of contract law. This means examination of the contract's fracture in light of whatever can be established as the reasonable expectations of reasonable people on entering into the contract now under dispute. However, we can't rely on legalistic remedies to heal the emotional wounds associated with a double-cross.

Any broken promise is a violated trust. A host of painful emotions familiar to anyone who has ever been betrayed roil up to bother victims of broken promises that were made in (or out of) the workplace. Again, the question is how to leave at the workplace door the anger and hurt inflicted on you by the person in whom you placed your trust when you got his or her promise.

# FAMILY PROBLEMS, WORK PROBLEMS

David E. Morrison and his colleague David A. Deacon co-authored a chapter on "Organizational Consequences of Family Problems" for *Mental Health in the Workplace*, edited by Jeffrey P. Kahn, M.D. (Van Nostrand Reinhold, 1993). They examine problems that move from the family into the workplace and see the family as "the place where one gets ready to go to work." If all is not well in the family, things can hardly go well at work, "the arena of discipline, performance, and accountability." It would be foolish if an employee who is depressed over the situation at home expected not to be depressed on the job (although the diversion of work is often used to bring some relief in trying circumstances).

On the point of broken promises, Morrison and Deacon write: "Employees boiling over in anger after discovering a spouse's affair will certainly have moments of distraction, and diminished clarity of thought and expression." Ordinarily, it's best to keep that problem out of workplace conversations, even though others will notice that something is wrong. It's essential, however, to talk the problem out with trusted friends or counselors away from work and to take special care not to let it interfere with job performance.

One lesson to be learned from the distress that broken promises might have caused you is to be aware of the distress your own failure to deliver on a promise can cause others. Never make a promise you can't keep. Recall the Pauline value of faithfulness.

Words are important. "You can count on it," is equivalent to saying, "It is guaranteed." "I'll do my best," is always understood as referring to something short of a sure thing. Similarly, when you're on the receiving end of work-related commitments, don't let anyone overpromise to you. Tone down their "absolutely," "without a doubt," "you can bank on it" assurances to a level of reasonable and prudent expectation. Modesty is a protective shield for integrity, and your integrity is on the line when you make a promise.

# INTEGRITY

Integrity is your center of gravity, the force that allows you to lead a balanced life. This means maintaining a balance between and among your commitments to God, family, work, community.

You can strengthen your integrity by conviction and practice. If your spirituality convinces you that God cannot be anything but faithful to you, no matter what your mistakes or failures might be, you can stand firm, by God's grace, on the ground of your own integrity. This relationship of firmness-to-firmness is a God-to-you relationship. You strengthen your integrity by gaining a deeper appreciation for God's faithful firmness toward you, and you have to take quiet time to deepen that appreciation.

Take the time, too, to check up on the promises you make to yourself. They can be quite unrealistic and often unattainable. There can be a tyranny in the promises you make to yourself. Why do you make them? Are you (consciously or unconsciously) trying to fill in some holes in your own integrity? Are you, for instance, making firm, specific, and thoroughly unrealistic promises to yourself about becoming the person you think you ought to be?

This lack of realism is often nothing more than a wishing-well maneuver. You can't improve yourself (or address an issue effectively) solely by means of a promise. No one can. It's like trying to let a long list of New

187

Year's resolutions extend your lease on self-esteem. You have to own self-esteem; you can't rent it by making payments of empty promises.

Can you think of a situation in which you might have attended to tasks by assigning them to your promise bin, and then feeling good that they had somehow been taken care of? If you can, you have that much more evidence of your membership in the human race. Everyone is fully capable of doing exactly that, and someone might have done that to you. Perhaps you've been let down simply because someone else made feel-good promises that had more to do with ordering his or her personal life than with holding up their end of any commitment to you. Some painful letdowns should not be taken personally.

# THE HEART KNOWS

We human beings are a whole lot more complicated than we generally care to admit. We're always capable of fooling ourselves; in that seldom acknowledged foolishness, we all too often disappoint others. So when you're disappointed, feeling let down, holding the short end of any promise stick at work or at home, recognize that the problem could well lie within the other's heart, just as the potential for that problem lies within your own. It isn't your business to attend to another's empty center; you've got enough to do attending to your own. As you do, notice how important all those promises made and kept have been to you over the years.

# TRUE FAITHFULNESS

The way our excesses express themselves in broken promises is worth taking note of, too. The arrogant person is often a promise breaker. So is the greedy, lustful, intemperate person, the one whose outlook on life can be summed up in two words: "me first." The absence of self-control and the presence of self-centeredness combine to practically guarantee that a person so enclosed will be insensitive to the rights and dignity of others; other people will be viewed as disposable parts, as means to ends.

You might have been on the receiving end of this kind of treatment. If you think yourself incapable of treating others this way, think again, especially if you look within and find an insufficient supply of self-control. That last item on the long, and by now familiar, list of Pauline Criteria is an anchor your spirituality can provide. It will be there for you in times of betrayal.

That list begins with love. Just as you can't love without having experienced love (typically the dependable, reliable love that parents confer), you can't be faithful without first having experienced fidelity. You will have trouble keeping promises if promises made to you, especially those that were implied or made by inference early in your developing years, were broken. If that's the case, it's much more important for you to reconnect reflectively (perhaps through the Psalms) with the God who has been, and cannot ever be anything but, faithful to you all along.

The 119th Psalm invites you to say to your God, "In my heart I treasure your promise." God's promise is to be with you always wherever you are, to never abandon you. Think of the immeasurable value of that promise, its everlasting character, its pledge to you of eternal security. Let your soul savor other portions of this same psalm as you pray, "Lead me from the way of deceit...The way of loyalty I have chosen.... This is my comfort in affliction, your promise that gives me life...Steady my feet in accord with your promise; ...rescue me according to your promise."

You know how important promises kept have been in your own life, how crucial they are to helping you maintain your personal balance; think of how essential they are to the stability and security of the larger society in which you live. By keeping your promises, you can encourage others to keep theirs.

You and others encouraged by your promise-keeping example will, therefore, be doing what you can to help your community—civic, political, social, economic, and family—keep itself together. No small contribution that!

*Every now and then, Lord, I find myself wondering about the "it," the ubiquitous, ever recurring "it" in my thoughts and conversations. The "it" that rains, snows, or simply happens, and usually works out all right in the end; the one that "seems to me" is "just one of those things," that is always "later than you think." I find myself wondering, from time to time, about every "it" I encounter as I move through life.*

*Are you behind the "it" that keeps appearing in my thoughts and conversations, Lord? I know somehow you are. Could every undefined "it" in daily experience reflect your presence, your power, your will? Is that what "it" is all about? Is it a hint that no ordinary thing is really ordinary?*

*All of creation is an "it," but certainly you're not. You're a person, and so am I. So I must be somehow different from all the "its" of your creation, and in that difference, I can find meaning in my existence and a measure of my likeness to you. I'm not only not ordinary, because I'm not an "it"; I'm quite extraordinary because I'm a person who images you.*

*So let me simply say (and pray), Lord, that I realize you are above, and behind, and somehow within all the "its" that are good, and that you are somehow absent from all the other kinds. Let me believe deep down in the core of my being that I am no "it" and never will be. I'm yours. Now there's an "it" that's more than I will ever understand.*

*Chapter 24*

# DIVORCE

One day in 1967, I asked an executive of the Bendix Field Engineering Corporation what his company produced. "We produce divorces," was the unexpected reply.

The company, which is now a division of the corporate giant Allied Signal, was then active in manning the tracking stations around the globe for this nation's new space exploration program. Work that separates spouses for long periods of time, as the executive knew, is work that contributes to an unbalanced life, and that's the kind of work many people were doing at Bendix Field Engineering. Even commuter marriages with briefer separations over shorter distances can be considerably more than inconvenient; they can be downright risky.

## A SURPRISING ANSWER

I remember an evening in the late 1970s, when I was serving as president of the University of Scranton. We had been able to separate the department of business and economics from its base in the College of Arts and Sciences and set it up as a free-standing School of Management; we also established in that school (where enrollment was then one-third female) a Women in Business Club. As one of its early activities, the club invited a top-level female executive from a major broadcasting network to be guest speaker at an annual awards dinner.

In her after-dinner talk, this executive described her career and current responsibilities. She mentioned that she had a lawyer-husband and toddler child (over whom, she remarked, the elevator starters always made a big fuss when the child appeared for a visit to mom's office). In the course of her remarks, this woman mentioned several times how willing she would be to leave her company's corporate headquarters in New York to take full-time responsibility for managing one of the network's half-dozen O-and-O (owned and operated) stations. "What would you do," one of the students asked, "if they offered you the job of running your O-and-O station in Los Angeles and your husband was unwilling to leave New York?" "I'd get a divorce," was her immediate, no-nonsense (and absolutely no-kidding) reply.

This answer shocked a crop of future female executives and gave them something to ponder later among themselves, with professors, and with their male friends who were also future executives and professionals. When I heard the statement and observed the reaction of the students, it occurred to me that preparation for marriage should include general prenegotiation of such matters as whose career is going to follow whose.

If that discussion doesn't happen until years after the marriage, and only moments after the attractive new job offer is made, the probability of having a crisis in the marriage is very high.

Divorce is sometimes simply not preventable. In some cases, it's best for all concerned, including the children. In most cases, however, it is preventable, if only the right steps are taken before the marriage and after the wedding at the first signs of marital stress. Although some separations clearly leave children in a better situation, almost every divorce leaves scars of some kind on the youngsters involved—sometimes very serious scars indeed.

# THE AFTERMATH

Some years ago, a well-known professional football player was asked, moments before his 9:00 p.m. nuptials, why the ceremony was scheduled for so late an hour. His response: "Well, if it doesn't work out, you haven't lost a day." He was joking, of course. Divorce is no one's idea of a good time, and it's difficult to imagine how anyone could enter a marriage with no hope or desire of making it permanent.

Whatever the reasons and circumstances, and no matter how the blame is divided, either party to a divorce is going to have adjustment problems.

The Pauline Criteria of love, joy, peace, patience, kindness, generosity, faithfulness, gentleness, and self-control still apply. They can help the adjustment, even if they seem to be remotely abstract and irrelevant. During and immediately after a divorce proceeding, you should use these criteria as a mirror for self-analysis—and also as a window on your continuing relationships with others on and off the job.

If your marriage failed, there was probably an antecedent failure of communication within that marriage. Your adjustment might be helped by honest, sympathetic communication with someone you trust about issues you know are important.

If value disagreements were the fault line in your marriage, spend time identifying, clarifying, and taking fuller possession of those deeply held values that you want always to be a part of you. Disclosure to another, perhaps wiser, person of what your values are is a prudent measure that can help you verify and confirm those values in your heart. It is from that heart, and from the values stored there, that you hope to draw answers from within during stressful times.

If infidelity on your part contributed to the split, face up to that fact now and take careful stock of your integrity and basic honesty. These qualities could be in short supply and in need of replenishment and revitalization. If you, on the other hand, were a victim of your partner's infidelity, realize that others see you as "wronged," and opportunists might, therefore, presume you're vulnerable.

Here, as in so many of the situations discussed in this book, keeping your sense of humor is important. The absence of a sense of humor reveals the presence of an imbalance. Whatever the stresses and strains that troubled your partnership were, perhaps two senses of humor living as happily (and as cheaply) as one might have been able to protect and preserve the marriage. Who can say? Let your sense of humor surface to help sustain you now.

The late Kim Williams was a naturalist, a writer, and a guest commentator on National Public Radio's "All Things Considered." Shortly before she died she published a book titled *Kim Williams' Book of Uncommon Sense: A Practical Guide with Ten Rules for Nearly Everything*. Her "uncommon sense" on staying married was simply this: "At 9:00 p.m., say to your spouse, 'Hey, did I make you laugh today? Did you make me laugh? Well, now's the time." Maybe you were never the class comedian, but just about anyone has enough wit to comment humorously on life's incongruities and to respond with a laugh to humor expressed by others.

If it's too late to try this strategy in an effort to revive your marriage (and I hope it isn't), it's definitely not too late to use humor as a tool for managing stress. Humor can be a fulcrum that lifts you out of the despondency of divorce. In fact, humor can help pull you through just about any of the reversals covered in this book. Perhaps that explains why joy is right up there next to love at the head of the Pauline Criteria list.

## MOVING FORWARD

Humor can emerge as an essential survival tool. At the same time, divorce is no laughing matter. In nearly every case, it's a sad and difficult experience, and often tragic. In his play *King Henry VIII*, Shakespeare used it as a metaphor for death by the sword—the "long divorce of steel."

Divorce is not just dreams deferred, but dreams destroyed. Standing on the ruins of a marriage you once hoped would last forever, you might wonder where the Holy Spirit can be. Look within for your answer; that is where the Spirit is. If your attitude, your words, and your actions match up positively against the nine criteria that define your spirituality, you know that the Spirit is there within you. The absence of the principles represented by the criteria signal the absence of the Spirit and serve as a reminder of progress to be made.

Despite any deep-down sadness and fears you might have about your future, you know these deeper-down pillars of support are sure signs that God is also there with you. You might say that you don't feel loving, joyful, peaceful, or patient; you might have no feeling of kindness or generosity toward your former spouse. Perhaps you can't ignore the fact that faithfulness is, by definition, gone, at least the mutual, lasting fidelity you had hoped to find in marriage. The loss of these values in your marriage, however, doesn't mean the departure of the Pauline principles from your life as a whole. Look closely at yourself and at the God who cannot be anything but faithful to you; take careful inventory of all the positives that remain in your heart, and resolve to build again on that foundation. Gentleness might still be there; it could become a saving strategy as you begin to reconstruct your life. Self-control, already severely tested, is probably still there. It, too, can become an important element in your reconstruction strategy.

# STARTING OVER

The spirituality you've been considering throughout this book is surely a spirituality of second starts. God is, after all, both creator and sustainer. Working in and through your life, God can re-create, reconstruct, renew. You might think you have spent all your capital and depleted your resources, but God, who is infinite in both mercy and love for you, goes on making deposits into your account. Grace is there to be drawn out as needed. It can, if withdrawn in faith, replace your sadness, anger, and fear with the values embodied in the principles the Apostle Paul laid out for you.

You might feel silly, at first, admitting your dependency before God. Being something of a sophisticate and always wanting to be in control, you feel awkward in your nakedness. Unaccustomed as you are to admitting, even to yourself, that you are all need (and unable to see that your posturing to the contrary is all bluff), you effectively keep yourself outside the reach of God's helping hand…but help is there, and it's there for you.

Out of your nothingness, ask. Never forget that Jesus said, "Ask and you shall receive." Out of God's infinite love, you will indeed receive. Just ask, but don't be surprised or disappointed if you have to wait. That seems to be the way God works. You ask, and wait, and the waiting expands your capacity to receive.

The only way you will ever know whether this is true is to give it a try. You can't just stand there doing nothing. You've got to make some choices and get on with your life.

Remember that gentleness is a helpful element in your reconstruction strategy. If you move gently, speak gently, and walk and drive gently, you will avoid rushing into second mistakes. The Spirit is there in your gentleness.

*Lord of all gentleness, let me follow the advice I found one time in
the Book of Proverbs (2:9–11). You wanted me to find it,
otherwise the message would not be there waiting to be found by
anyone who opens that book.*

*The words are encouraging: "Then you will understand rectitude
and justice,/ honesty, every good path;/ For wisdom will enter your
heart, knowledge will please your soul,/ Discretion will watch over
you, understanding will guard you."*

*Pondering those words again, Lord, I find myself asking: When is
the "then" after which I will understand every good path, possess
wisdom, and enjoy the protection you promise? The words of the
first several verses of that second chapter in the Book of Proverbs
supply the answer. There I hear you telling me that if I receive your
words; if I treasure your commands; if I turn my ear, incline my
heart; if I call, and seek, and search; then I will understand. "For
the Lord gives wisdom," says your inspired word to my prayerful
inquiry about the thens and whens surrounding the gift of wisdom.*

*It is a gift, Lord, I know. All I can do is ask. Put me on the good
path, Lord, and let me grow wiser by the day.*

*Chapter 25*

# DEATH OF SOMEONE
# CLOSE TO YOU

*You don't get to choose how you're going to die. Or when. You can only
decide how you're going to live.*

This handwritten message was pasted on the refrigerator door in her
kitchen by a mother who was dying of cancer. It remained there throughout her illness. It is now engraved on the memories of the dear ones she
reluctantly left behind, the ones who, she knew, would have to choose how
they were going to live without her. They are also the ones through whom
she will, in a genuine spiritual sense, continue to live in this world.

We all know, as Norbert Wiener put it, that "we are not the stuff that
abides, but patterns that perpetuate themselves; whirlpools of water in an
ever-flowing river." Faith says we will live forever, but not here. The stones
of our present surroundings will outlast us, but they can never outlive us.

## PASSING THROUGH

We are all passing through, and the unevenness to it all is simply part of the
human predicament. We come and go at different times. Even twins are
born moments apart, and they almost never die together. As groom and
bride become husband and wife, neither gives a thought to the virtual
certainty that one will bury the other.

The death of any person reaffirms the unrepeatable oneness of that
person's life. Nonetheless, people can be perpetuated in the memory of
others, in the lives of their children, and in the influence of those they

influenced. Unless the living, those who are left behind, re-engage themselves with life, the dear ones who have died are deprived of the opportunity to have their influence continue to flow and their spirit continue to live in the world they have left behind.

This is not to be dismissed as sentiment or confused with even so beautifully expressed a sentiment as the one that "The Civil War" television documentary producer Ken Burns retrieved from a letter written on July 14, 1861, by Major Sullivan Ballou, a Union officer in the Second Rhode Island Regiment, to his wife, Sarah. Major Ballou felt "impelled to write a few lines that may fall into your eye when I shall be no more." All who saw the Ken Burns documentary on public television were moved by Major Ballou's beautifully written letter that ended with these words:

> But oh, Sarah, if the dead can come back to this earth and flit unseen around those they loved, I shall always be near you in the gladdest days and in the darkest nights, always, and if there be a soft breeze upon your cheek, this shall be my breath as the cool air fans your throbbing temple. It shall be my spirit passing by.

Major Ballou died several days later in the Battle of Bull Run.

Sentimentality is not to be mistaken for spirituality. Your faith-based spirituality lets you entrust a dear one, who has been separated from you by death, to the care and company of the Lord. The spirituality you bring back with you from bereavement to the busy-ness of workplace life can accommodate the conviction that it's not only God who chooses to work through you, wherever you are, but also that the dead can "rise" to continuing influence because of you.

Your involvement—not with grief, but with life—somehow brings those who have died back to life. Although their death does not release you from the bonds of affection, the obligation to remember, and the need to mourn, you are now not only free, but obligated, to follow your vocation, your calling from the God who never stops calling, into the next phase of your life. You honor the memory of those dear ones who have died, and you perpetuate their influence in this world, by getting on with your own life and work.

# DEATH OF A CHILD, GRIEF OF A FATHER

The death of a child figures prominently in a case that came Dr. David Morrison's way. A member of an executive group was referred to Morrison Associates because he was annoying colleagues and disrupting meetings by talking too much. Ten minutes into an interview with David Morrison, the man mentioned the death, a year or so earlier, of his 10-year-old son. After playing soccer, the child returned home, began vomiting, collapsed, and died. The event was violent only in its suddenness; there had been absolutely no warning that anything like this was possible.

Throughout the whole session with Morrison, the man spoke of nothing but his son's life and death. At the end of the interview, he said to Dr. Morrison, "No one has listened to me in the past year as you have today." The problem at work was that this team member was talking too much; the issue, however, was that no one was listening to him! Several weeks later, the boss who had referred him called and asked Dr. Morrison, "What did you do to this guy? You wouldn't believe the change." Morrison replied, "All I did was listen; what he needed was someone to talk to." Clearly, it was the death of his son that produced that need.

# COMING TO TERMS

There is no way you can deal with the fact of death—your own yet to come or the death now of someone dear—without faith. Spirituality helps you understand that faith is the act by which you entrust yourself to God. As some contemporary believers like to put it, in faith you just "let go and let God."

Faith is also a form of knowledge, a higher knowledge than what comes at the conclusion of any natural reasoning process. St. Paul, the author of the criteria that keep reappearing in these pages, was aware that faith is knowledge; happily for us, he let that awareness shine through as a beacon of hope in these words concerning death: "For we know that if our earthly dwelling, a tent, should be destroyed, we have a building from God, a dwelling not made with hands, eternal in heaven…. [W]e know that while we are at home in the body we are away from the Lord, for we walk by faith, not by sight. Yet we are courageous, and we would rather leave the body and go home to the Lord" (2 Cor. 5:1, 6–8).

We know, but how? By faith. That knowledge fills us with confidence (*confide* means, literally, *with faith*). Filled with confidence, we can better deal with the fact of death.

Will there be moments of doubt? Certainly, but doubt doesn't really disqualify you from membership in the community of believers. You might have your doubts; they help explain your own lack of enthusiasm about the prospect of leaving your own body to "go home to the Lord." That's understandable. Doubts and fears afflict us all. Not so readily understandable, however, is your mournful wish to have a loved one back in the body, given your belief that his or her death meant going home to the Lord.

If long illness and physical pain preceded the death of a loved one, you normally would take no offense when those who offer sympathies say it was "a blessing." In that case, you and those who want to comfort you are genuinely sorry for the sufferings the loved one had to bear, but grateful that those sufferings have passed now. That passing is a "blessing" that leaves you with a question: Is the understandable impulse to wish a loved one back to life on earth poignant testimony to your love for that person, or is it, perhaps, evidence that you're simply feeling sorry for yourself? Who doesn't know that feeling after the death of a loved one? But who would say that feeling should control your life?

## RHYTHMS OF DEATH AND REBIRTH

Back in the early 1970s, Bread for the World (BFW), a national movement of political advocacy for the hungry poor, began in New York City. Faith-based and ecumenical, BFW attracted generous, creative, and idealistic young people who wanted to do something about world hunger by lobbying the U.S. Congress and the executive branch on behalf of the voiceless poor. One of the early supporters of this movement, Dan Sendzik, offered hope to the organizers in a death-resurrection reflection that he literally wove into a banner that hung on a wall in the organization's modest headquarters in lower Manhattan (BFW has long since relocated to Washington, D.C.). Here are Dan Sendzik's words:

*The rhythm of life is one of death and rebirth,*
*burial and resurrection,*
*of ending and beginning,*
*of closing down and opening up,*
*of bringing things to a halt and*
*of starting over again.*
*We stop being reborn only when we*
*stop wanting to.*
*Resurrection is impossible without enthusiasm,*
*and it is the possibility of resurrection*
*that excites enthusiasm.*
*To quit, to give up, is to die.*
*To try again, to start over, is to live.*
*We rise from the dead because we*
*want to. And the only barrier to*
*resurrection is quitting.*

As a board member of Bread for the World, I often sat looking at those words during meetings focused on finding ways to keep the fragile organization afloat. I remember admiring the thoughts but questioning the theology. Once dead, I used to say to myself, no one can rise again by simply willing it. Resurrection, I told myself, is all God's work. Then I came to realize that Dan's words could help not only lift the spirits of social-justice advocates (as they surely did from their place on that meeting-room wall), but also help a survivor rise from the death of a loved one.

The death of a loved one, of someone really dear to you, is a diminishment of yourself; you "die a little," as you might have found yourself saying. Well, now it's resurrection time; you can rise a little every day. You can open up, start over again, just by wanting to. That "wanting to" is your new and beautiful expression of your love for the one whose influence your re-engagement with work and life perpetuates.

Every spirituality addresses the fact of death in its own unique way. The essence of the Christian answer to the question posed by death found its way onto a banner I saw displayed at the funeral of a believer: "As the bird freed from its cage seeks the heights, so the Christian soul in death goes home to God." Believing that, you can stop looking vacantly up to the heavens that have received you dear one's soul, and start looking ahead for opportunities to keep your dear one's spirit alive on earth.

*I walk and wonder, Lord; I wonder as I walk through the woods, on city streets or country roads, along the shore, in the early morning or after dark. Even though I keep putting one foot in front of the other and the surface beneath my feet is real, I forget about the reality of this particular time, and place, and pace, and wonder where I'm going, when I'll get there, and whether I'm making progress or falling back. I often wonder as I walk what the world would be like if all of us obeyed the law of love under which you expect us to live.*

*I've been taught to love my neighbor as I love myself, and I sometimes wonder, in those moments of self-doubt bordering on self-hate, how sound a deal that is for my neighbor. I know there is "no greater love" that anyone could have than to lay down his or her life for a friend, but I keep wondering what's in it for me if I try to measure up to that ideal.*

*I know I've got a lot more walking and wondering to do on the road to understanding the many truths you want me to grasp, Lord. Please walk along with me and let me see!*

# Chapter 26

# LAYOFF

Anyone who has been through it will tell you that a layoff is a kind of death, or that it's like getting cancer when you lose your job.

Typically, news of the layoff is broken (usually awkwardly) in the workplace, but the wound inflicted by that news is nursed at home. The vocabulary of job loss says you're "out of work," "beached," "streeted," "on the bricks," but you're usually hiding out at home. You are trying to find your way back into another workplace somewhere, yet all too often you're on your own and lonely, hopeful of plugging your wound with a good job before the lifeblood of your self-esteem drains all the way out.

Right up there next to death and divorce, and on equal status with cancer or cardiac arrest, you find mid-career job loss on anyone's list of stress-producing personal reversals.

The familiar expression "I could write a book" is doubly applicable here. This reflection on layoffs could easily take on book-length proportions. I did, in fact, write a book about the experiences of 150 men and women who were separated from their jobs in the wake of corporate downsizing. It was published by Adams (Holbrook, Massachusetts) in 1995 under the title *Finding Work without Losing Heart: Bouncing Back from Mid-Career Job Loss.*

As part of the research that resulted in that publication, I learned that some discouraged job seekers found comfort in the Psalms. To make the psalter more available and user-friendly for Christians and Jews who are struggling with the stress of unemployment, I edited a prayer book of psalms for discouraged job seekers. It was published by Sheed & Ward (Kansas City, Missouri) in 1995 as *Take Courage: Psalms of Support and*

*Encouragement.* I recommend it frequently for use on a psalm-a-day basis by those struggling with their faith and their job search. From the psalter, you might want to select encouraging phrases that can give voice to your needs and feelings as you begin the new job of reconnecting with meaningful employment.

*But you, Lord, are a shield around me. (Ps. 3:4)*

*Restore again our fortunes, Lord. (Ps. 126:4)*

*And now, Lord, what future do I have?*
*You are my only hope. (Ps. 39:8)*

*You are my help and deliverer.*
*Lord, do not delay! (Ps. 70:6)*

*Show me the path I should walk,*
*for to you I entrust my life. (Ps. 143:8)*

# RELIGIOUS FAITH AND PHYSICAL AND MENTAL HEALTH

At the 1996 annual meeting of the American Association for the Advancement of Science, Dr. Dale A. Matthews, of the Georgetown University Medical Center, reported on the outcome of a study he and others conducted on the relationship of religion to health. In three fourths of the 212 cases they studied, the researchers found a positive effect of religious commitment on health. It proved to be helpful in dealing with drug abuse, alcoholism, depression, cancer, high blood pressure, and heart disease. Dr. Harold G. Koenig, of Duke University Medical Center, reported that "people who attend church are both physically healthier and less depressed."

Precisely how religion works to make people healthier is not at all clear, but the studies can at least encourage people to let religion and spirituality shore up their sinking spirits and offset the discouragement, and occasional depression, associated with the typical job search.

If you're out of work, you have to realize that you have a self to serve during your transition to your next job. You are your sole client, your chief concern. As I put it in *Finding Work without Losing Heart*:

*Throughout the transition, you are the center of a process of personal self-assessment and self-renewal; you must be or become the object of your own self-esteem and self-respect. You are the one who has to guard against self-pity and loss of self-confidence. You are the agent of change. If you are to find new employment, you have to take the initiative. The process is fundamentally self-serving, and there is absolutely nothing to apologize for in acknowledging that it is. Ultimately, the job search is a test of character. And character, as both history and literature attest, is proved in action.*

During counseling sessions, I've often said to job seekers, "Your job search is your character in motion." If spirituality is, as it should be, part of your character, you can expect your spirituality—your prayer elevated to a lifestyle—to work for you during this transition.

## CHARACTER AND FAITH

No doubt you are frustrated and tense during a job search because you're not in control of your employment destiny. Dependent, as your faith tells you you always are, on the sustaining grace of your creator-God, you have to wonder how you ever got the idea that you were independently "in control" in those glory days when you were fully employed.

Perhaps, like many others who have encountered personal or career reversals, you have convinced yourself that the Book of Job has your name on it. Yet it would be a misreading of Job (and a disservice to yourself) to blame God. Reflect on these words from the Introduction to the Book of Job in *The Jerusalem Bible*: "In his anguish [Job] reaches out for God; God eludes him, but Job still trusts in his goodness.... This is the book's lesson: faith must remain even when understanding fails." The faith that remains will have you trusting in and reaching out for God, which is spirituality at work.

One job seeker, who came to me for help as I was writing this book, told me he had been laid off several times over the years. Earlier in his career, he returned to the U.S. after working overseas for an international relief agency where, as administrator of the feeding programs in an impoverished part of the world, he had been "handling millions of pounds of foodstuffs every year." He thought, he said, that with his experience it would be easy to find a challenging job back in Washington, D.C. He was wrong. He found himself "chronically unemployed, on welfare, and reduced to using food stamps." One day, someone from his parish community, whom he did not know at all well, appeared on his doorstep to present him with four bags of groceries and a $50 bill. "I just thought," the benefactor said, "that you might appreciate a little help."

The beneficiary of this gift, reflecting on the event years later, told me how he had been struck with the irony of the situation. When employed, he had given away millions of dollars worth of food, and now he found himself unemployed and on the receiving end of food relief. He also recalled how hard it was for him to accept help. "We don't accept things easily," he said. "We think we always have to reciprocate."

To his credit, he recognized this experience for what it was: a spiritual problem of false pride and an exaggerated sense of independence. This spiritual problem must be dealt with immediately when you're separated from a job. That doesn't mean you should demean yourself in preparation for encounters with potential employers. Far from it! It does mean, however, that it's going to take a lot of humility to get yourself back in gear and on the road to re-employment.

# HANDLING THE BAD NEWS

An outplacement firm I know of is hired by major corporations to train executives in the "art of laying people off": what to do and what not to do in breaking the bad news. After a manager, appropriately trained, fires a person, that person is taken, along with other displaced employees, to a room where a counselor from the outplacement firm is there to help.

John Fontana, who once did this kind of work, recalled a day when he was the consultant in a room with about a dozen managers who had just received the bad news. There was shocked disbelief. Tears flowed freely. One woman, who had been through it twice before in her career, offered the hopeful observation that after each of her previous layoffs, she found a better job. Another refugee to the "crying room," a 30-something gentleman who always had ambitions of becoming a comedian, tried to lighten the atmosphere by asking the others to imagine they had a gun with just two bullets and found themselves in a room with three others: two notorious human rights violators (he named two well-known dictators) and their own CEO (also mentioned by name) who had just made the downsizing decision. "What would you do?" After a pause, he answered his own question: "You would, of course, shoot the CEO twice!" Their laughter encouraged the would-be comedian to begin his new career right there. He told more jokes and the whole group got into it as they all went out to lunch together.

# PATIENCE

Laughter belongs in the medicine cabinet of anyone who has to deal with the terrible pain a layoff inevitably brings. Job loss is, of course, no laughing matter, in either the short- or long-term view. The only satisfying solution to a mid-career layoff is a 360-degree turnaround back to meaningful employment. You have to make that happen through persistence, prayer, and, yes, some laughs, through a search process of uncertain duration that will surely test one of those nine Pauline Criteria that you might not regard as part of your strong suit: the virtue of patience. Your spirituality can make a virtue out of patient persistence; it can put patience to work for you in your campaign to return to work.

Patience shows total respect for the facts. Romano Guardini called it "the deepest possible acceptance of things as they are." This is not to suggest that things cannot change. It simply acknowledges that it takes time to produce more favorable circumstances.

Your impatience is a protest against the facts; your patience is a tacit commitment to participate in a process that will overcome unfavorable facts. Recall again Othello (act 2, scene 3): "How poor are they that have not patience!/ What wound did ever heal but by degrees?" The wound of layoff is no exception to this rule.

*Chapter 27*

# CARING FOR A PARENT WHO IS FRAIL AND ELDERLY

If this particularly sensitive outside source of workplace stress were to be described in one word, that word would be *pietas*, a Latin word referring to the reverence and respect that a child of any age should have for a parent. The English *piety* just doesn't catch this meaning, so the loving care that any son or daughter should give to a frail elderly parent has to be described in words that convey the special circumstances becoming more common as the lifespan in America lengthens.

## DIFFICULT DECISIONS

Not infrequently, caring for a frail elderly parent generates tension among siblings who argue over relative shares of the responsibility. Economic considerations loom large, compounded by emotional stress associated with the nursing-home decision to go or not to go, to go now or later, and the never easy decision of whether and when to sell the house and dispose of furniture and accumulated family belongings. The older generation's "treasures" are often of little value to the eyes of the able-bodied young.

Having the elderly parent move in with one of the children is an option. Which one of the children and on what terms of occupancy are questions that rarely find easy answers. What if such an arrangement in a two-income marriage leads to the frail, elderly parent being at home alone during the day, in need of help?

In the workplace, the effects of trying to manage this issue can be seen in absenteeism, arriving late, leaving early, extended non-business phone calls, distracting anxiety, and conscious or unconscious guilt that can keep a person off-balance. What was said earlier about indecision would, by and large, apply here. The decision to be made is rarely a unilateral one, however; the family has to come together to decide in such important matters.

# TALK IT OUT

As in so many instances of reversals that might be work-related, the best thing to do at the outset is talk about the issue in the workplace with a sympathetic superior and then with a set of two or three trusted associates, permitting them, if you want, to let others know. Not only is this approach likely to rally some emotional support for you during working hours, it can also generate suggestions, open the door to possible solutions, and free others to come to your assistance when productivity and job-related results might otherwise suffer.

What if your superior isn't sympathetic? What if your commitment to the well-being and advancement of the organization and your loyalty are questioned? What if you are denied a promotion and you know that your concern for your aging parent is the reason?

Keep on talking, and try to frame the conversation in the context of justice and fairness to all parties concerned, notably to your employer and associates in the workplace. You want to be fair to them, just as you hope they will be fair to you. You might have to direct this conversation to someone higher up than your immediate superior. The parent-care concern is, of course, the kind of issue that could be brought to the attention of an ombudsperson, if you're fortunate enough to be in an organization that has one.

All these conversations will go better if you can document the amount of company time you might have lost by attending to the responsibilities of parent care. Documenting work time diverted to parent care might help you manage that time more efficiently, keep it at a minimum, and have a basis for offering compensatory time back to the company at a later date. In any case, be open to talking about the problem.

Curiously, this openness will also allow you to separate the personal problem from your professional responsibilities. Your associates will know about your problem. They will recognize and probably respect any "conversation zones" you might want to set up to discuss the issue with them after work or during a lunch break. With sympathy and sensitivity, they will almost certainly work along with you during the hours of business, offering you (at least with respect to the personal problem) silent support. This openness frees you of wondering whether and how much they know and what they might be thinking.

In this and all the other family or personal challenges that accompany you to work, it's as though the world in which you have to manage your affairs were one grand hotel. As the popular song by the Eagles puts it, "You can check out anytime you like, but you can never leave." What would be the point of checking out or giving up? You carry the reversals or challenges with you at some level of consciousness wherever you go.

## SPIRITUALITY ENDURES

This is also the way it works with spirituality: Once you have it, it accompanies you wherever you go. You can compare your faith-based spirituality with the embers of a fire—they are simply there. You can fan them with what anyone would acknowledge to be prayer, regardless of the language, audibility, or length of your conscious outreach to God for assistance. The conscious "flames" of your call for help can recede to ember form at any time, but as long as faith is there, the embers (not ashes) of your spirituality are also there, awaiting your summons for support. The Book of Sirach offers encouragement to those who want to face up to this responsibility: "He who reveres his father will live a long life; he obeys the Lord who brings comfort to his mother" (3:6).

## "NOTHING'S ANY DIFFERENT"

Try slipping inside your elderly parent's head and seeing things from his or her perspective. "Nothing's any different from my point of view," remarked an aging mother to her son when she turned 80. "Things are still the same hue of blue, green, and red; shapes haven't changed. I know I look different to folks who haven't seen me for decades, but the world still looks the same to me."

The son wondered, however, about her inner world. He told me that he took the imaginative climb inside her head to try to see what he would feel or fear at her age, even though external shapes and colors might still look just the same when viewed through his own aging eyes.

In going through that exercise, he said, he learned something about hope. He knew his mother to be a hopeful person; he realized that hope in a God who promised her a better life to come made this life, even as it diminished, continue to be seen by her as a gift to be thankful for. He assumed that there was a mixture of discouragement with the hope, but he just knew that for her, hope would prevail. He also experienced a shock of recognition: Someday he would be frail and elderly, too. He wondered how he would cope.

Her hope affected him. What he came to realize was that hope in God, in her, and in himself could help him be a cheerful presence to his elderly parent. Her hope anchored her in God's providence; his hope in the same God let him see through all the limits and the decline that surrounded her, to the better life ahead that she would soon enjoy.

## FAITHFULNESS

What if there is no hope for anything positive as this life, like sand in the hourglass, is running out? What if hope has no place in the heart of the frail elderly parent? Then there's nothing left but faith, however thin and fragile your faith or your parent's might be. If there's enough faith to support a prayer, let that prayer be for more faith. Faith is a gift; you can't earn it.

All—literally all—you can do is ask!

## A MORE FLEXIBLE WORKPLACE

On a practical note, you often hear the phrase *family-friendly* in descriptions and assessments of the contemporary workplace. Typically, the friendliness relates to the organization's attitude toward parents of children in need of day care and parents of newborns or just-adopted children, but the same principles can be extended to other family needs. "Work-family managers" is a new title on organizational charts of many corporations, flextime to accommodate attending to aging parents is now neither an unusual request nor an extraordinary concession.

Not to be missed in this developing family-friendly workplace environment is that caring for a parent with a serious health condition is included in the provisions of the 1993 Family and Medical Leave Act (FMLA). Up to 12 weeks of unpaid leave must be given to employees who request it for any of the reasons specified in the law. Although it's unpaid leave, employees keep their health benefits and are entitled to reinstatement in their old jobs or comparable employment elsewhere in the organization, after attending to their family responsibilities.

The FMLA is not without its difficulties: What constitutes a serious health condition? What satisfies the need for medical certification? What is an appropriate time frame for reasonable prior notice? How do you measure an "equivalent position" when the leave is over? Although these are all important questions, it isn't the law that should interest you at the moment. It's enough for now to recognize that the spirit behind this law can be woven into any workplace's procedures.

It's less of a challenge to do this in workplaces where the employee with the problem (in this instance, the need to care for an elderly parent) and the employer (with whom any solution must be worked out) agree that the principles of their respective spiritualities should influence what they do Monday through Friday, nine to five. Is this too much to expect in a secular workplace? Perhaps, but it's not too much to hope that shared values can shape a workplace culture. That happens all the time. The challenge is to get conversations going across the employer-employee hyphen that raise value questions and identify mutually agreeable principles, which, when left to follow their own laws of growth, eventually influence the way solutions to problems like this one eventually emerge.

*My son, take care of your father when he is old;*
*grieve him not as long as he lives.*
*Even if his mind fail, be considerate with him;*
*Revile him not in the fulness of your strength.*
*(Sirach 3:12–13)*

# FACING THE CHALLENGE

Caring for the frail, elderly parent is a challenge to be met by every generation. No generation has ever had more than 24 hours to distribute over one day's duties; no generation has had enough time, money, and patience to meet all parent-care responsibilities with ease. Your generation, like all that have gone before you, can't keep "the fulness of your strength" for long, and you know that some day in the not too distant future, you will be on the receiving end of the need for care from the next generation. So think and pray about intergenerational relationships now, and look for ways to put your thoughts and prayers into action.

> *With your whole heart honor your father;*
> *your mother's birthpangs forget not.*
> *Remember, of these parents you were born;*
> *what can you give them for all they gave you?*
> *(Sirach 7:27–28)*

*Who's afraid, Lord? I am; I really am.*

*I know I'm fooling myself when I try to explain away that admission by recalling the biblical instruction that fear of the Lord is the beginning of wisdom. I know that fear in this context really means reverence, and that reverence is the road I should wisely take toward you. It is the irreverent fears that bother and burden me: the sweat ringing my neck when I awake in the middle of the night, the stomach knots I can't untie, the ground-down teeth, the skin rash, the worry wheel between my ears. No reverence in any of that—just fear.*

*Help me, Lord, to turn my fears into reverence. Reverence is awe, and I surely prefer awe to anxiety. I stand in awe before your power, your providence, and your love for me. I know by faith that you are there, calling me to walk through my fears and into the security of your embrace. I know that if I want to cling to you, I can do so only by the embrace of faith. I also know that I will always be free to take the foolish route and go on clinging to my fears. Help me to use my freedom wisely, trade in my fears for reverence, and attach myself in faith to you.*

# PART FOUR

## SPIRITUAL PILLARS FOR THE WORLD OF WORK

*Chapter 28*

# SECOND STARTS

I once heard an ever-so-earnest executive make the following pronouncement (spoken, of course, over a stiff upper lip): "Yesterday we stood on the brink of disaster, and today we took a great step forward!" Anyone who has made it this far in this book might recall one or two personal experiences with the "brink of disaster" in a cursory review of his or her own past reversals.

It would be a healthy exercise if such a review were accompanied by a sober anticipation of future setbacks. But any review, retrospective or prospective, should be made in light of a well-thought-out strategy for recovery. You certainly don't want your resolute "step forward" to take you over the cliff!

## PREVENTION AND RECOVERY

It's time now to reflect on a positive strategy of prevention and recovery for all the reversals outlined in this book, one that's reinforced by a faith-based spirituality. Rebound strategies are yours to plan.

The objective of this chapter, and the remaining ones in this book, is to encourage the conviction that you can rebound from virtually all the reversals you meet in the workplace or other circumstances of life. It's largely up to you. The Pauline Criteria, sketched out for you in "scorecard" form for your daily use in Chapter One can, if assimilated, propel you along the strategic path these final few chapters outline for you. Let me emphasize: These steps are yours to take on the road to recovery from any—and I mean any—reversal.

You can learn wisdom by just observing what happened to you in those unguarded moments when you weren't wise. The consequences of your foolishness might last a lifetime, but you're always free (and always able) to start again.

# STARTING OVER

Christianity is a religion of second starts. Anyone who tries to push nature too far—attempting, for example, to defy the law of gravity—discovers how unforgiving nature can be. Anyone imbued with the principles of Christian spirituality, however, is convinced of the availability at any time of mercy and the readiness of God to grant forgiveness whenever you ask for it honestly. That's the disposition you need to set yourself up again for a fresh start.

The early morning and late evening reflection exercise recommended for your consideration and outlined in Chapter One is an invitation to begin again every day. Understand, though, that it's not a "forget what's behind and be prepared for anything that comes" approach. It's a strategic new beginning in light of past mistakes; *strategic* in this case means being grounded in a sense of purpose (your personal mission statement), a purpose that gives you a clear sense of direction. It's strategic also in the sense of laying out a step-by-step recovery plan.

How do you begin your new beginning? Consider whether forgiveness (of yourself or of others who might have injured you) should be the first step in your recovery strategy from a workplace reversal. If you refuse to forgive yourself for past mistakes, large or small, you will never get off to a fresh start. If you refuse to forgive others, your feet could become encased in the cement of hatred. Chapter Thirty, "Forgiveness," helps you reflect on the importance of forgiveness.

No, you can't undo the past. Yes, it's impossible to upend the hourglass of events and run them through again. However, a future is beginning now, and a new stream of events can start any time you're willing to let them begin.

Second starts (which, over time, can be multiplied as long as life lasts) always look to the future. If initiated under the impulse of a faith-based spirituality, these new beginnings do not represent a fuzzy faith in the future; they represent a faith in God who owns the future and who holds the human planner's destiny in his hands.

## IDENTIFYING PROBLEMS

The success of any second start depends on how accurately you identify the issue that prompted a rebound or recovery. In other words, you have to frame the issue correctly.

Take, for example, the case of a small subsidiary of a large corporation that I heard about recently. A management team of four or five peers, all talented people in their late 30s and early 40s, was functioning well under the informal leadership of a woman regarded as "first among equals." She was, for all practical purposes, head of the subsidiary because she also served on the board of the parent corporation. Suddenly, one of her peers was formally appointed to head the subsidiary.

Stress fueled by anger, resentment, jealousy, and hurt feelings set in. Management group harmony and productivity in the subsidiary suffered, until outside intervention, in the form of professional consultants, helped those adversely affected by the decision to "reframe" the issue and identify it for what it truly was. This wasn't an issue of ambition on the part of another or unfair advantage taken by another; it turned out to be an issue of personal loss. Once a formal leader was named, the members of the management team each had to come to terms with not being selected to lead the subsidiary.

The others came to recognize their discontent as the experience of loss, a loss of their respective dreams or fantasies of personal achievement. Their hopes had been dashed. The recovery strategy had to begin with a focus on human hope in each member (and in the team as a whole). Reframing in this way—discovering the real issue rather than being distracted by buzzwords or technicalities—is a good way to gain insight and clarity in identifying an appropriate first step in a second start.

# TALKING AND LISTENING

Successful second starts often require having someone to talk to before setting out on a new course. If you talk and the right person listens, you can release stress and gain clarity.

Here is a description, written in his own words in a letter to me, of how a faith-committed entrepreneur, a successful CEO in the recycling industry, worked through a stressful situation in making a good second start for a troubled company:

> When I took over as CEO of my company in 1988, it was in serious trouble. Gross revenues had fallen by one-third; we were losing serious money (in the hundreds of thousands of dollars), and backlog (signed contracts for future business) was barely one year's sales rather than the more than two years we consider comfortable.
>
> I began to feel the stress almost immediately. In the early days after I took over, we had to lay off staff that had been with us for a long time, stretch out payments wherever we could, renegotiate our bank loan. In the first few months, things got worse before they got better and I suspect some staff had doubts whether we would survive.
>
> Of the many ways I tried to reduce the stress, four worked. For some years, I had a routine of praying and meditating at 5:30 each morning. To this I added journaling three or four times a week. I also was much more conscientious about seeing my spiritual director. The prospect of such meetings kept me from abandoning journaling at times when it seemed stale or when I encountered lots of internal resistance, or apathy, or whatever. She also provided me with someone besides my wife to whom I could pour out my frustration, fears, resentments, etc. Lastly, I was very fortunate to have a protégé (now CEO) in whom I knew I could confide and who shared my conviction that we could turn things around.
>
> I do not know which of these was more important, but I do believe that I might not have pulled it off had I not had another male, in this case someone from within the company, in whom I could confide with total candor. I say this because in my experience most men in the business

224

*world have good friends but not really confidants in the same way that, judging from my wife, women do. Men seem much more reluctant totally to let go of their "successful businessman" masks or whatever masks they are wearing.*

*We were able to bring in new business within a few months, and fortunately we kept the confidence and trust of our clients and Board throughout. But it took close to two years before we could climb back to profitability and even longer to convince our bankers and others that things really had turned around for good."*

# WILL IS NOT ENOUGH

Reframing the issue was necessary in the case of the disillusioned management group dealing with the elevation of a peer; there the second-start strategy began with a re-examination of the subject of personal hope. A four-point strategy of prayer, keeping a journal, seeking spiritual counseling, and talking things out with a business confidant worked well in the case of the CEO who faced a serious decline in his company's performance.

A solid second start requires more than just the will to begin again. It takes faith in yourself and in your ability (with the help of friends) to get back on your feet, crank up, and move forward.

The unbeliever might say that's all it takes. However, the believer knows it also takes faith in God, the God with whom you connect through a functioning spirituality, the God who holds your destiny in all-powerful, all-loving hands that are reaching out toward you at every moment of your existence, in good times and in bad. More often than not, simply because this is the way God wills to work, it takes a human intermediary through whom God chooses to work to touch you in your personal corner of the human predicament.

This point is worth considering closely. You won't be touched unless you reach out for help, unless you take that first step and give another human being a chance to help you.

# ASKING FOR HELP

Why is it that most of us find it so hard to ask for help? The first (and almost always accurate) answer to that question is simple: pride.

Pride is a tricky trait. It is, to some degree, necessary for the proper maintenance of self-esteem, but pride can easily get out of hand. When it does, it sometimes moves in deceptive ways.

Open yourself up to a moment of honest reflection. You normally think of pride in others in association with power, even arrogance, and you expect pride to manifest itself in bluster and aggressive action. But pride often borrows humility's garb and becomes harder to identify.

When pride withdraws from the front rank, it does so as a protective measure. What is being protected is, of course, your proud estimate of your own superiority and independence. Perhaps you know from personal experience that unless you're willing to "come off it," acknowledge that you have two flat feet of clay, and ask for help, your second start could be deferred indefinitely, possibly forever.

If spirituality has anything at all to teach you, the lesson is that you are not independent. Acting as though you were completely independent is an exercise in practical atheism; it gives the lie to whatever pious proclamations you might make on Sunday when you go to church.

The remarkably practical Book of Proverbs can serve up a working principle to guide your reflection at just about any step in a strategic second start: "Pride goes before disaster, and a haughty spirit before a fall" (16:18). You often hear this familiar verse collapsed into the saying "pride goeth before the fall." Heed that "haughty spirit" warning always, and rest your second start on the solid spiritual foundation offered in an earlier verse of Proverbs: "Entrust your works to the Lord, and your plans will succeed" (16:3).

226

# Chapter 29

# FAITH AT WORK

Faith at work within you is one thing; faith in you at work is something else again.

There can be a gap between practicing one's religious faith (being an observant Jew or a practicing Catholic) and living it. What does it mean to practice your religion, if you don't live it every day? Having it, so to speak, but not living it, seems to reduce faith to some kind of label for social identification, instead of making faith the content of a committed life.

The split between the faith that good people profess before God and the horizonless lives they live in their respective workplaces contributes to the joyless approach so many people take to their jobs. Anyone who succeeds in closing that gap can begin to better understand what the balanced believer I quoted earlier meant when he remarked, "If you really feel called to what you do, you'll never work a day in your life!" Now that's a man who is well aware of the importance of having a day-in, day-out sense of vocation.

## NO TIME-OUTS

If you are a believer, a person whose faith commitment is real, free, and rooted in God, something of great spiritual significance is going on within you all the time.

Faith works wonders within you in all situations. It gives you a share in God's own life and love that you wouldn't otherwise have. It promises you eternal security, salvation that you could never under any circumstances gain on your own. "We carry this treasure," writes St. Paul, speaking of grace, "in earthen vessels." Earthen vessels can drop and break.

We are free to reject God's gifts, so we are always at risk of dropping the vessel and losing both faith and grace. Far too many believers live with a dualistic mindset that separates "otherworldly" considerations, like faith and grace, from this world's workplace realities of give and take, of getting and spending in the human community.

An African proverb says, "This world is a marketplace; the other world is home," but even the marketplace can be a place of grace. The whole purpose of the practical workplace spirituality presented in this book is to help you close that dualistic gap and bridge the this-world/other-world attitudinal divide.

A healthy spirituality doesn't encourage you to hate or flee the world; it doesn't reward any attempt to bury your treasure for safekeeping. It encourages your involvement with the world of work for the service of others and the glory of God, who created it all and wants your help in developing the gift of creation to the fullest. Only a balanced person need apply for this kind of work.

## BALANCE AND THE PAULINE VALUES

Balance begins with an awareness that faith is at work within you and that you are, therefore, alive in the Spirit. This knowledge sets you apart as one who is in balance, on target, and at peace. The less apart you find yourself to be—or, to put it in positive terms, the more you find yourself to be just one among many who are balanced, on target, and at peace with themselves in their transit through life—so much the better the workplace will be!

Faith in you at work represents transformative potential for the workplace. There's no room for pulpits, pamphlets, sermons, or proselytizing in your place of employment (unless you work for a church, synagogue, shrine, or mosque!). Such activity would be inappropriate, unfair, and unwise. The transformation that faith can bring to the office, factory, store, laboratory, construction site, transportation system, or any other place where daily bread is earned (including church-related employment) is in the form of human love, joy, peace, patience, kindness, generosity, faithfulness, gentleness, and self-control.

If you think your're incapable of bringing these nine Pauline values to birth in the workplace, you aren't giving your own human potential a fair chance. If you recognize your capability, but say that, although your spirit is willing, your flesh (that is, your capacity to activate these values) is weak, I would argue that you aren't giving faith and grace a fair chance to get to work within you. I'd suggest that you spend some time with the morning-and-evening checklist outlined in Chapter One and prayerfully consider the relevance of the nine Pauline Criteria in your life.

## ENTRUSTING YOURSELF

Faith is the act by which you entrust yourself to God. It is not, however, purely volitional; it's a matter of both will and intellect.

I have a friend whose single favorite Shakespeare line of all time is King Henry's response to a report that the French are poised for battle against him at Agincourt and ready to charge. Having just made his soul-stirring, confidence-building Saint Crispin's Day speech to his outnumbered soldiers, Henry responds to the news of imminent attack by saying: "All things are ready, if our minds be so" (*The Life of King Henry the Fifth*, act iv, scene 3). The Earl of Westmoreland responds: "Perish the man whose mind is backward now!"

All things are ready, if your mind is ready.

Henry seems to rejoice in the overwhelming odds (five to one against him) in the face of a powerful enemy. Logic says flee; faith (assuming, of course, that your cause is just) says trust, and give full credit to God for the victory that faith assures you is on its way. Practical faith means having your mind in the right place.

You should know your faith. That means putting yourself in touch with the sources of God's revelation to you: scripture (which you probably have on a bookshelf at home) and tradition (referring to the understanding of God's revelation, which the church has been handing down generation to generation in doctrine, practice, sermons, ritual, and memory). Make the effort and take the time to put yourself in touch with scripture and tradition.

The relationship of the word *tradition* to the verb *trade* is worth exploring here. The Latin verb *tradere* means to *hand over*. Trade moves items from one hand to another; tradition hands down, generation to generation, something considered worth preserving in the lives of like-minded people.

In the words of the Second Vatican Council, "Sacred Scripture is the speech of God as it is put down in writing under the breath of the Holy Spirit" (*Dei Verbum*, No. 9). If you are a believer, such a characterization should remind you that you can listen to that "speech of God" simply by taking the Bible off the shelf and setting some time aside for reflective reading. You don't have to set up camp in a church or surround yourself with scholarly books to get in touch with tradition, but it would seem wise to put yourself closer to this second source of revelation, both through some exposure to history, theology, and social teaching, and through participation in liturgical worship.

If you find yourself wincing at the thought of these formal observances, or saying, "Not for me," you might want to ask yourself: How are you going to feed the faith-based spirituality that you need to sustain yourself in the workplace?

## "CAMPAIGN HEADQUARTERS"

I know a man of considerable depth in both faith and wealth who exercises responsible stewardship, is eminently practical, and devoutly religious. He once told me that he thinks of the place of worship called "church" as a "campaign headquarters." "You go there for inspiration, nourishment, and strategy," he said, "but you go there in order to go out again, not to devote time, talent, and treasure to building a bigger campaign headquarters." You go there, in other words, so that you can be sufficiently energized to put your faith to work, and you should leave there to return to work on Monday morning with a prayer like this in your heart:

*Lord, God, work is your gift to us, a call to reach new heights by using our talents for the good of all.*

*Guide us as we work and teach us to live in the spirit that has made us your sons and daughters, in the love that has made us brothers and sisters.*

230

You can find that in "Daytime Prayer for Midmorning on Monday," *Christian Prayer: The Liturgy of the Hours* (New York: Catholic Book Publishing Co., 1976, pp. 1001–1002)

If love is a reality not normally associated with your return to work on Monday morning, perhaps you should consider closely the next chapter on forgiveness. Your inability to accept yourself as a loved sinner, one who is both forgiven and loved, could be impeding your ability to forgive others and find them lovable. Or, you might consider it impractical, even silly, to make a place for love ("the love that has made us brothers and sisters") in the workplace.

The same St. Paul who passed along the nine wisdom principles you've been pondering on your way through these pages had a practical, down-to-earth explanation of the meaning of love. He spelled it out in the 13th chapter of his First Letter to the Corinthians:

*Love is always patient and kind; it is never jealous; love is never boastful or conceited; it is never rude or selfish; it does not take offense, and is not resentful.*

*Love takes no pleasure in other people's sins but delights in the truth; it is always ready to excuse, to trust, to hope, and to endure whatever comes.*

*Love does not come to an end.*

The late Rabbi Abraham Joshua Heschel had the workplace in mind when he said, "Our concern is not how to worship in the catacombs, but how to remain human in the skyscrapers." Faith at work can humanize the workplace; it can also guarantee a place for love in the most secular nine-to-five surroundings.

Clear water reminds me of your love, and your grace, Lord. As a youngster, I used to love to water the lawn with a garden hose. I also liked to water the flower beds with a sprinkling can. With water came growth, and growth was always proof of life. The greening of plots beneath my feet gave promise of the sustainability of life on the whole of planet earth. This is the seeping, soaking promise of rain; this is the mystery of water, which always rises to seek its own level.

Water reminds me of your grace, Lord. Without water, the earth is parched and lifeless, dry and infertile. Without divine grace, my soul is arid, and my spirit produces no growth. Your grace follows me through life, Lord; it sustains me. Like water, your grace keeps me spiritually alive and afloat.

Rain on me, Lord. I know that whatever water can do for my body, grace can do for my soul. So let your grace, a gift like rain to me here on earth, irrigate my parched spirit.

Salt water has less appeal. I feel its stormy assaults and hate the bitter taste. Those crashing waves remind me, though, that your grace can sometimes present a challenge. The ocean also reminds me of your fidelity and the vast expanse of your mercy.

So, I open myself up to your grace, Lord, to the water of my spiritual life. Pour it out to keep me green and growing and alive in your love.

*Chapter 30*

# FORGIVENESS

The healing power of forgiveness cannot be overemphasized. Whether given or received, forgiveness heals. Regardless of whether it comes from God or another human being, forgiveness is a matchless gift.

## REFUSING TO FORGIVE

In a book called *Hearts That We Broke Long Ago* (Bantam, 1983), the Canadian writer Merle Shain wrote:

> *Until one forgives, life is governed by an endless cycle of resentments and retaliations, and we spend our days scratching at the scabs of the wounds that we sustained long ago instead of letting them dry up and disappear. There is no way to hate another that does not cost the hater, no way to remain unforgiving without maiming yourself, because undissolved anger stutters through the body of the person who cannot forgive.*

That "undissolved anger" can be the source of deep depression. If you feel depressed right now, you could be, in Shain's words, "maiming yourself" by your refusal to forgive others. You might also be refusing to forgive yourself, permitting you to be your own worst enemy.

Again, talking things over with others whom you respect and trust is important. Like any other mortal, you aren't the best judge in your own case. In opening up to others who have no axe to grind, you might discover your persistent (and perhaps initially unconscious) refusal to forgive yourself. If the people in whom you confide are true friends, and if you give them the opportunity to do so, they can help you realize that you're acting destructively toward others...and even toward yourself.

Jim Wallis, the pastor of Sojourners Community in Washington, D.C., and longtime editor of *Sojourners* magazine, says that "the idea of forgiveness often seems abstract and 'religious' in an otherworldly kind of way. But in fact forgiveness is very practical and necessary for human life on the planet to survive.... When we refuse to forgive, the cycle of vengeance, retaliation, and violence just escalates.... It's only genuine forgiveness that breaks the cycle of destruction and opens up new possibilities."

# RECONCILIATION

The Sermon on the Mount, which has firm instructions against retaliation, addressed the issue of forgiveness in the context of worship. Your refusal to forgive would make you unworthy to stand before the altar. "If you bring your gift to the altar and there recall that your brother or sister has anything against you, leave your gift at the altar, go first to be reconciled with your brother or sister, and then come and offer your gift" (Matthew 5:23–24).

I believe that one of the best ways to face up to your responsibility to forgive another is to offer a gift to that person. There is no parallel, of course, between your gift to God, as mentioned in the Sermon on the Mount, and any gift you might offer to someone who has injured you. All the same, Jesus' radical teaching on forgiveness could be taken as encouragement not only to leave your gift at the altar, but also to put another gift, one that symbolizes your forgiveness, into the hand of the one who hurt you.

A practical spirituality has you measure your performance against the standard embodied in the Lord's Prayer: "Forgive us our trespasses, as we forgive those who trespass against us." Realize that, in making this prayer, you're asking to be forgiven on a contingent basis. You are declaring yourself willing to be forgiven only if you forgive others. This is a remarkable standard. No one is perfect, of course, but no one can dodge that standard; it will be there to challenge you every day of your life.

The stakes are always high, but the choice is always yours.

# OPENING UP

A great humanist, Maynard Mack, once remarked that if you could reduce everything Shakespeare ever wrote to one word, that word would be *forgiveness*. I don't know enough about Shakespeare's works to comment on that, except to say that anyone who understands human nature as well as Shakespeare did certainly respects the power of forgiveness in helping you find your way through the human predicament.

Add to all this the bonus promised in an ancient spiritual maxim: "If you do not close your ear to others, you open God's ear to yourself." When someone seeks your forgiveness, you are being given an opportunity. Pay attention and respond appropriately; realize, too, that you are giving others the chance to grow in grace when you ask forgiveness of them.

# THE NEED TO FORGIVE

In the following example, an unmet need to forgive almost crippled a promising career.

Not long ago, a rising star in a large insurance company was sent by his employer to a distant city to reinvigorate a troubled branch of the organization. Described as a "charger with a great analytical mind," this man was nevertheless losing some of his "charge" in this new assignment. He found himself unable to think things through as easily and clearly as he had done before. He found the situation to be a lot worse than he had been led to believe.

The worse it looked to him, the more distressed he got. Heavy layoffs were necessary, so workplace morale plummeted. In the face of these challenges, the "superstar" manager became volatile and showed evidence of increasing disorganization.

Were these heavy workplace demands all that were troubling him? The answer, it turned out, was no. While consulting with John Fontana and David Deacon of Morrison Associates, he disclosed that his wife was ill and incapacitated; there was no support from his relocated family as he tried to meet his mounting and more challenging workplace demands. He was also operating without the support of his church. In his youth he was educated at an Episcopal boarding school, where he was helped a lot by a clergyman he admired. He even considered a career in the ministry at that time. Before taking on his new assignment, this manager had long been active in the church. When he presented himself at a church in his new location, he was asked "to send his references" from the former pastor; this soured him on the new congregation, and he never went back.

Even so, the consulting psychologist, David Deacon, told him, "I think the issue in your not going to church is your anger with God." Together, the manager and the psychologist focused on the issue of anger. They noticed that although his boss thought relationships between them were smooth, things were not all that smooth on the side of this manager, who thought he had been misled into thinking it was really a "little fix," not a "monster turnaround" that was called for when he was transferred. He was, in fact, angry with the boss for less than full disclosure, with his wife for being ill and non-supportive, and with God for letting it all happen.

But he was afraid to admit to being angry with God. The way out for him, according to David Deacon, was forgiveness. "He had to forgive himself for getting angry with God and for being so grandiose that he thought he could judge God," said Deacon. "He also had to forgive God for 'doing' whatever it was that he thought God had done to him, and he had to forgive his boss for putting him out on a limb, and his wife for getting sick."

"Grace is necessary for forgiveness; there is no way you can earn grace." These insightful words from David Deacon underscore the need for a functioning spirituality on the rebound and recovery route.

In commenting on his role in this case, John Fontana noted that another issue was this man's need for support structures. He went into a new environment without familiar structures or old friends. The social support he previously got from church connections vanished. Family support was withheld and, once he was in the distant city, there was noticeably less support from the company. Before the change, when support structures were in place, he had become "overly self-reliant," said Fontana, "and he didn't have to use power and authority." In the new setting, where he needed cooperation and support, he fell back on a power-and-authority device—namely, volatile behavior. "Disruptions cause stress," commented Fontana. "The more you ask people to change, the more affect is an issue."

In other words, feelings surface with the stress; you have to watch that the horse doesn't throw the rider.

Once he assimilated all this feedback from the consultation, the manager settled down and turned the operation and himself around. He extended a measure of forgiveness to himself so that he could learn from this experience and move ahead. In time, he returned the branch to profitability and regained control of his life.

# No Way to Hate Without Diminishing

It would be difficult to exaggerate the power of forgiveness at home or on the job. It takes a large-hearted person to decide to forgive; by the act of forgiving, the heart of the forgiver becomes even larger.

Forgiveness fastens friendships; anyone interested in contributing to the return of loyalty to the workplace might simply look for opportunities to forgive. Anyone who can count should take a moment to calculate in measurable, practical workplace terms the value of the lesson in the words of Merle Shain: "There is no way to hate another that does not cost the hater, no way to remain unforgiving without maiming yourself."

Try to build forgiveness into your life. This is a project with two dimensions and countless manifestations. The upward dimension, so to speak, is your need to seek God's forgiveness for yourself. Nobody is perfect. You know that, but how deeply in your heart can you locate that knowledge? Acting as though you stand in no need at all of forgiveness is blind arrogance. Factor a simple request for forgiveness into your evening review of the day just ended. You are in God's presence. You will notice that there have been failures during the day; acknowledge them and ask your Creator to make you whole.

The other dimension of forgiveness in your life is outward, to those who have ignored you, offended you, and injured you. This dimension has innumerable manifestations. Do all that's in your power to make those broken relationships whole. At least you can build the bridge from your side as far out as you can, hoping in the best of faith for a connection from the other side.

All you can do is try. You have to try, or else you give the lie to a spirituality rooted in love, peace, and generosity. Your effort requires you to do more than simply keep the door open; it's clearly not enough simply "to live and let live."

# Nothing

Genuine creativity involves making something out of nothing. From the "nothing" of your evacuated pride, from your humility, your forgiveness can create strong new relationships. You will never know unless you try!

You're familiar with Alexander Pope's saying "To err is human, to forgive, divine." You have often heard that it's wise to "forgive and forget," although Shakespeare put that proposition the other way around on the lips of King Lear: "Pray you now, forget and forgive."

You will never be divine, but you can imitate divinity in forgiving. You might never be able to forget, but you can act as if you have when you forgive from the heart. In either case, true forgiveness is the restorative measure, the transforming decision that puts you on a brand new page.

*Turn away your face from my sins;*
*blot out all my guilt.*
*A clean heart create for me, God;*
*renew in me a steadfast spirit.*
*(Psalm 51:11–12)*

Chapter 31

# HONESTY

Truth-telling is a healthy, wonderfully restorative character trait that carries with it significant practical benefits. Anyone who makes a regular habit of telling the truth finds life simpler and considerably less complicated than a person who lies as a matter of course.

The lives of those who always have to remember how they altered or distorted the facts in past statements, or how they spun out stories totally unrelated to the truth, are anything but worry free. As a general rule, their own duplicity divides their hearts. Their memories as well as their morals are strained, and people notice. (You might have known someone for whom the old joke was applicable: "He doesn't murder the truth; he doesn't even get close enough to do it bodily harm.")

From your own experience, you would probably agree that people who exhibit calm, enjoy peace of heart, and know what it means to lead a balanced life are, as a general rule, people who can be relied on to tell the truth. This isn't the philosophy portrayed in the old cartoon that pictures a harried secretary standing by the desk of a boss who lectures her as follows: "Yes, Miss Jones, honesty is the best policy, but it just isn't company policy."

## FREEDOM

Over the entrance to the Lauinger Library on the campus of Georgetown University, these famous words from the gospel of John are inscribed: "You will know the truth and the truth will set you free" (8:32). That's why students (and others) use libraries: to search out the truth and gain their freedom from ignorance.

Truth is liberating. In a theological sense, it frees you from sin. In a practical, day-to-day, workplace sense, the truth-teller is a free person, recognized as a person of integrity who has not just something to say, but a self to commit—a self that's out there on the line—with any statement he or she makes.

Instinctively, you dismiss the prevaricator, the perjurer, the liar, as unreliable, not to be trusted, and as being shallow in a fundamental way. You trust the truth-teller as a person of depth and genuine character. You know there is something there, deep within.

Thomas Wolfe, writing with an anti-capitalist bias in his 1934 novel *You Can't Go Home Again,* let his own prejudices show through in his protagonist's description of that "type look" he had come to recognize "as belonging to the race of small business men."

> *It was a look which he had discovered to be common to all members of this race whether they lived in Holland, England, Germany, France, the United States, Sweden, or Japan. There was a hardness and grasping quality in it that showed in the prognathous jaw. There was something a little sly and tricky about the eyes, something a little amoral in the sleekness of the flesh, something about the dry concavity of the face and its vacuous expression in repose which indicated a grasping self-interest and a limited intellectual life.*

My own intellectual life was one notch less limited after I consulted a dictionary to discover the meaning of *prognathous.* (It means having jaws that protrude.) This unflattering portrayal of a sadly familiar business type might encourage some men and women in business to take steps to make sure the caricature can never be applied to them.

What is the point of quoting Thomas Wolfe's depressing (and Depression-conditioned) characterization here? I use it to highlight an element of truth about the absence of truthfulness. I think it's fair to say that "grasping self-interest" is usually all that's needed to explain the motive at work when the truth is bent or broken in the workplace.

Take the opposite tack to set the direction of your personal style. Use nothing "sly or tricky" in your approach to others; exercise your own tight control over the "hardness and grasping quality" that the business culture can encourage, adopting for yourself a "countercultural" attitude over and against the excesses of the business culture.

## SELF-CONTROL AND THE HONEST SELF

The ninth of the Pauline Criteria—self-control—has as much relevance to the way you conduct yourself in the office as it does to your behavior at the bar or dinner table. Success, in the sense of balance and contentment, in the workplace depends in no small measure on your ability to tell the truth (at least to yourself) about yourself. That certainly requires a measure of disciplined self-control.

David Morrison tells an interesting story about a 35-year-old female business executive whose effectiveness was hindered by her inability to expose her vulnerability to ask for help. She was painfully shy, and she had trouble admitting her shyness even to herself.

In high school, this bright, energetic, and attractive person had decided to adapt to her shyness as she searched out a place for herself in the adolescent social scene. She adopted what Morrison calls a "masculine" achievement strategy. She didn't realize, however, that the boys were shy. The more she achieved, the more she removed herself from the boys she hoped to attract. She was unaware, says Morrison, that her presence, her apparent poise and self-assurance, made the adolescent boys feel vulnerable and uncomfortable. At age 35 she was still doing this. The "script" she worked out of in business was tilted toward achievement instead of attachment (that is, cooperative participation with a team). She didn't understand that to get the productive business relationships she wanted (as well as a meaningful personal relationship), she had to expose her vulnerability. She needed to acknowledge exactly where she was, accept her vulnerability, and ask for help. This truth would set her free for success in business and, indeed, in other areas of life.

## CANDOR

Another issue in the matter of truth-telling in the workplace (as well as in interpersonal relationships) might best be categorized under the heading of "candor," which should never be confused with rudeness or aggressiveness for the sake of being aggressive. You hear different opinions expressed on the value of bluntness in on-the-job discussions that are expected to produce decisions. Some appreciate it; others resent it. If a person wants, for the good of the decision-making process, to be candid—making sure that all the facts, pleasant and unpleasant, are on the table—he or she runs the risk of having candor mistaken for rudeness, blunt arrogance, or an opinionated attempt to dominate the conversation. If you're convinced that being candid is important, it's your duty to be so, diplomatically.

You should welcome, even invite, assistance from the person chairing the discussion by having that person ask the others at the table, "How does that strike you? Do you agree with that?" This questioning opens the door to immediate clarification or qualification from others on what's been said, thus encouraging your candor and not letting social pressure muzzle your desire to speak the truth.

It shows good leadership skills if the person chairing the meeting gets all the pros and cons on the table and urges all participants in the decision-making process to speak to both sides of the question before it's resolved. This technique requires freedom; perhaps it's the freedom associated with veracity in the scriptural saying "the truth will set you free." To point to the "something good" in an option you don't favor could diminish the chances of winning the argument for the option you prefer. The question, however, is do you prefer that option for the right reasons? Is it right from the perspective of the whole organization's greater good?

It's also good leadership if the manager of the meeting can get participants to reveal how they feel about both sides of the issue. Seeing something good on both sides of a question is not insincerity or make-believe; any question important enough to be on the table and under review for eventual resolution certainly has two sides. But honesty, the search for truth, requires a willingness to determine why you feel one way or another about a proposed option, and it requires that you express your ease or unease about accepting a given possible outcome.

Your feelings can function as windows on your motives, and your motives can, as you well know, be elevated or base, narrowly self-interested or rooted in the common good. Veracity implies vulnerability, a willingness

242

to be open to full disclosure of the true origin of the answer emerging from within.

This is not just tricky terrain that I have you walking through at the moment (it's always difficult to understand your true motives); it's also sacred ground. You are much more than the sum of your feelings, of course, but it helps to recognize that your feelings connect you to the presence or absence of the Spirit within. The feeling alone, the affect, is not enough to provide an answer. You have to know why you feel as you do in the face of a decision to be made. A feeling of fear, for example, could be there because you understand your limits in facing up to a challenge the Spirit would have you meet; it could also be there because you know the decision will involve the loss of something you have and want to keep for purely selfish reasons (thus influencing you to resist the call the Spirit wants you to heed).

All that would apply to candor in workplace meetings applies to candor in those "meetings" that take place between your ears when you're alone and trying to decide. You are a complicated person, precisely because you are a person (not because you happen to be you). Personhood is complicated. So is life. You, as a person, can't make it through life without dealing with the complications. Your compass on this journey is your veracity.

## SEEKING THE TRUTH

Being a truth-seeker, a truth-teller, and a truth-lover is your assurance that you're in balance and on target as you travel on a journey of unknown duration, through intermediate goals you can't always clearly identify, toward an eternal goal of security in the God of all truthfulness, who you can see now only through the eyes of faith.

Spirituality has a wonderful potential for keeping you on course. It also keeps you grounded in humility, which is the special soil of sacred ground. From the depths of your humility, you will find veracity and you will see the truth. You will also, if you're like me, add an "Amen" to this poetic wisdom from George Herbert: "Dare to be true: nothing can need a lie;/ A fault, which needs it most, grows two thereby."

Consider, too, these words from the psalter:

*Good and upright is the Lord,*
*who shows sinners the way,*
*Guides the humble rightly,*
*and teaches the humble the way....*
*Who are those who fear the Lord?*
*God shows them the way to choose.*
*They live well and prosper....*
*(Psalm 25: 8–9, 12–13)*

"Anyone home?" "Is anyone home?" I lean forward just a bit, hunch my shoulders, lift my eyebrows, and perk up my ears whenever I ask that question. The door was open, and I just walked in. Here I am inside. "Is anyone at home?"

The trouble is, Lord, I don't ask that question often enough of myself. I suppose I presume that simply because I'm here, someone is home inside. The deeper down I search, however, the more reason I have to wonder (and worry) about vacancies, about empty space within.

The further I drift from an awareness of you as creator and sustainer within me, the higher the risk I run of a value-vacant existence. That frightens me.

So let me pray: Be present to me, Lord, in your life-giving grace and your life-enhancing virtues. Your gifts to me of love, joy, peace, patience, kindness, generosity, faithfulness, gentleness, and self-control can fill what would otherwise be an empty center within. If they are there, you are there, and I am present: the me you want me to be.

# Chapter 32

# CREATIVITY

Creativity is a form of generativity. Who has ever experienced the thrill of becoming a parent and not known something akin to the psychological surge produced by rebound and recovery from past setbacks? It is all there: the freshness of a new beginning, the expectant hope, the conviction that something all-powerful is at work in this blessed event. You just know that an abundance of good things is on its way. You are upbeat; you are smiling. The setbacks, like labor pains, are all behind you.

Recovery through creativity is a wonderful way to rebound from reversals in or out of the workplace. Creativity involves both mind and heart, and it requires sensitivity. Whatever metaphor you choose to describe it, your engines are running, your juices are flowing, and your eye in on the future. Creativity is your best weapon against the limitations that hem you in. Creativity allows you to "run away" without ever leaving home.

## HOW TO DO IT

Now, of course, no one can command you to "be creative," and you can't just make up your mind that you're going to be creative. You have to work, and work hard, at being creative.

How? Imitation is one route, quite literally a free way that's open to all. Study the creative achievements of others. Read as much as you can; find out about the accomplishments and exploits chronicled in history books or reported in newspapers. Be alert to unusual ways of doing things; take note of the original and unconventional in what unobservant others might regard as ordinary surroundings. Learn how inventions and innovations first came to light. Read biographies of creative people. Try to figure out how things work.

Some lights will go on in your mind; no need to apologize for enjoying the fruits of "derivative" thinking. In the face of something new and interesting—an idea, a product or service, a slogan, a process—ask yourself: "Why didn't I think of that? What could I think of now that's just as impressive?" Then wait for an answer!

This is not a preamble to your new career as inventor-entrepreneur, or writer-producer, or composer-director. You don't have to change your occupation or place of employment. The point is simply to get invovled with your work again in a creative way.

There are undiscovered opportunities for you at work and new directions to explore in approaching old problems. There are potential collaborators whose creative potential you haven't yet recognized. There might also be subordinates just waiting for you to take General George S. Patton's words to heart: "Never tell people how to do things. Tell them what to do and they will surprise you with their ingenuity."

Here's another thought on creativity as it might unfold in the workplace: How many times have you nodded assent to the old saying that there's no limit to the good results you can produce, as long as you're unconcerned about who gets the credit? How often have you failed to act accordingly?

## WORKING WITH OTHERS

Having spent all of my adult life in the academic workplace, I've noticed different approaches to work in different divisions or departments of a typical university. Some are intensely competitive: students trying to outpoint others for grades, for example, or faculty trying to outpace and outdistance colleagues on the research-and-publication track. I have also noticed others who are genuinely (and generously) cooperative. The competitors sometimes resort to forms of academic sabotage, but the collaborators freely share ideas and criticism.

Architecture is one discipline in which both students and faculty seem to be characteristically collaborative; I will leave it to the reader to speculate on where competition typically gets out of control in other areas of academic life. The point is that you can also apply the collaboration-competition framework to your own workplace setting. What aspects of your work lend themselves particularly well to cooperation?

Spirituality, as you have noticed in previous chapters of this book, recommends the integration of *com-panionship* (*cum-pane*) into workplace life. The collaborative cultivation of new ideas is just one manifestation of companionship.

I suspect that creativity and collaboration work well together. The opposite could be argued in the case of isolated writers and researchers who emerge after years of relative seclusion with genuinely creative results to show for their solitary labors. All the same, it seems reasonable to suggest that sensitive people of open mind and generous heart can, working together in conscious collaboration, produce wonderfully creative outcomes and, in the process, become closer friends. Hence the collaborative—not just participative—workplace will, I would argue, be a happier, more productive place, a better place to work. Consciously taking this route back from your reversals will, I believe, help put you firmly on a higher, better road.

## COLLABORATION AND FEELING

Collaboration fosters outcomes that are more than the sum of the producing parts. In the practice of collaboration, a bonding process develops that brings the collaborators closer together as friends. Collaborating friends in the workplace, who are in touch with their feelings (their affects), can change the organization's functioning and atmosphere.

Creativity is always an exercise of intelligence. Before you conclude that only geniuses can be creative, recall that derivative thinking can lead to creative outcomes. Even attempting to mimic the style or approach of another can lead you to positive, and distinctive, new initiatives.

The point is to believe that the exercise of intelligence is within your power on or off the job. It is your birthright, yours to do at any time. In fact, it's your obligation to exercise your capacity to think, if you want to measure up to your full human potential.

Thinking, then, is your task. Just remember that although the task is yours, the power is the Lord's.

Thinking is also immaterial—not in the sense of being insignificant, but in the sense of not being a material substance. There's always enough for everyone. The more you think, the more there is for everyone else in the world of ideas. Creative thinking belongs in the realm of spirituality, where the arithmetic is all addition and multiplication, where, as if by divine command, you and your ideas "increase and multiply."

# EFFORT AND VISION

None of this creative thinking simply happens, though. Creativity demands your effort and often your cooperation with others. The effort will have you searching out the history of persons, ideas, innovations, successes, and failures that explain how the place where you work, the product or service you produce, and the environment in which it all happens, got to be the way they are today. Your effort will have you looking to other settings where other products and services are produced and wondering what can be learned there.

If, for example, you're employed in healthcare and are looking for creative ways to reduce errors and increase the quality of patient care, a review of cockpit procedures for ensuring airline passenger safety might prove instructive. Your effort to make creative comparisons between the two areas is an exercise of intelligence. Whenever comparisons are being made, the opportunity for collaboration (with all due regard for avoiding anti-competitive activity) increases.

Creativity is indeed a spiritual pillar for you as a believing person in the world of work. Your belief looks ultimately toward an intelligent God, the God of all intelligence, the source of your intelligence. You believe you are created in God's image and likeness, and although you can't see God directly, you know that you can know God in the effects of his creation.

You can also know God from the sense you have of divine presence within you. There is probably an emotional dimension to your sense of that presence within you, but there is an even more enduring and pronounced intellectual dimension. By that, I mean you might feel awkward and uncomfortable saying that God talks to you, and you are properly skeptical of those who "hear voices." Faith, however, assures you that God communicates with you, works through you, cares for you, and is present to you. That faith-knowledge should encourage, and will certainly support, your creative energies.

# THE ALTERNATIVE

Not to be creative—choosing not to make any effort or participate in any collaborative search for new ways and new ideas—is, as strange (and sad) as it sounds, to choose not to be spiritual. To let the senses alone decide your uses of time, your choices of right or wrong, better or worse, is to abdicate the higher side of your humanity. To leave your mind at home when you go to work, or your mind at work when you come back home, is to disengage yourself from the source of spiritual life and lead only half of your human life.

Creativity is an ignition key to spirituality. Turn it on and you ignite your mind. Your mind is then involved with the countless other minds you find in print, in artistic imagination, and in the voices of those around you. Creativity ignites countless conversations, endless adventures in reading, and, if you let it happen, it can lead you, through a sense of wonder, to God.

It's not only regrettable, but tragic, that so many intelligent people live hemmed-in, self-centered lives, never really looking out or up, but only toward themselves. They failed along the way to gather up their share of enduring values for storage within their souls. Once again, you have the problem of the empty center. Preoccupation with weight loss and muscle tone, accompanied by an enormous capacity for absorbing entertaining images, conditions self-enclosed people for passive spectatorship and consigns them to unfulfillment in a world where progress depends on creative contributions.

Where might you look for creativity in your set of Pauline Criteria? Try generosity (where the decision to make the effort resides), and don't forget that deep-down joy is part of every creative moment and the reward for every creative act. If generosity and joy are part of creativity, it goes without saying that the Spirit is also there!

"In the beginning, when God created the heavens and the earth, the earth was a formless wasteland, and darkness covered the abyss..."

(Genesis 1:1). Ever since then, there has been a great deal of work to do. Human creativity participates in this work, and it's an ongoing project. You are equipped to participate because God created man and woman in his image. Your creativity is rooted there; your creative roots run back to where it all began. In creativity, you can find the origin, the Source, of your being.

# Chapter 33

# HELPING OTHERS

I like to think of service, or helping others, as turning your talents inside out. When you're on the rebound from serious personal or career reversals, it's a wise strategy to do things that help you get out of yourself. There's no better way to do this than to become intent on helping others.

So many seemingly intractable personal problems take care of themselves if you simply fix your attention on helping others. Once you become more concerned about easing the burdens of others than with having your own load lightened, you will experience a new sense of freedom and feel a whole lot better. Many people doubt that this principle will really work for them, but that doubt dissolves after they've given this approach an honest try.

An old African proverb advises, "God gives nothing to those who keep their arms crossed." So open up your arms and reach out to others with a helping hand, and be prepared to receive more of the spiritual gifts God is always ready to share with you.

## THE BENEFITS OF REACHING OUT

In work I've done over the years with job seekers (mid-career managers involuntarily separated from their jobs), I've noticed that those who had been involved as volunteers with outside organizations had a ready-made network of contacts to help them when they were out of work and looking. Those whose workaholic tendencies kept them tied up in their own places of employment found, when ousted, that their former workplace contacts weren't so eager to help.

With the rise of affluence in America, there has been a proliferation of socially atomizing appliances. You probably don't think it's unusual to have a private car, a single-family home, a personal phone (on your desk, in your car, and in your pocket), and a stationary or portable fax, computer, radio, and television set. You have ready access to a freezer, a microwave oven, and a host of other appliances. Your automatic washer and dryer are ready when you are. You rarely have to borrow from or ask anyone for anything to meet your daily needs. Without a conscious choice on your part, you are, for all practical purposes, sealed off from the human interaction previous generations enjoyed at the village well, the general store, the daily food market, the bus or train depot, and the public gathering places for recreation, worship, and communication. Not so very long ago, these points of contact were routine, even indispensable, parts of ordinary life. Now, in their increasing absence, a commercially sanctioned culture of loneliness, isolation and alienation has set in.

You have to deal with this isolation first in yourself; the best way to do that is through service to others. You have daily opportunities to assist neighbors and others as they make their way through their similarly isolated lives. Just as a change of pace, why not shock someone by taking advantage of such an opportunity? Help carry up the groceries. Give up the cab you just hailed. Bring in the mail. See what happens.

# CONNECTIONS

Tom Mahon, a technology-marketing consultant in the San Francisco Bay area has written:

> *Science and technology deal with things: atoms and galaxies, levers and microprocessors. The life of the spirit, on the other hand, deals with the connections between things: mercy, justice, and love. We have become very good in the age of science and technology at knowing about things, but we're not really as wise as we should be at making connections (TIMELINE, May/June 1996, p. 11).*

Your workplace spirituality might prompt you not only to be grateful for life, family, job, and so many other gifts, but also to raise your head above the short-term chaos to notice that there are connections waiting to be made. You can make them. Helping others is the way to make those connections real.

Voluntary community service, whether spiritually motivated or not, is a civic responsibility. Someone has called it the "rent" we have to pay for our citizenship. I've often thought that judges in this country have, without intending it, given community service a bad name.

Since the mid-1960s, offenders in some cases have been sentenced to a particular number of hours (usually in the thousands) of community service. I find it curious that we assign as a punishment in a judicial sentencing category an obligation that every good citizen was once expected to meet voluntarily. Perhaps *compensatory service* would be a better term for courts to use when imposing a civil or criminal penalty to offset damage done to the community by a lawbreaker.

Your voluntary community service, rendered in the spirit of generosity, will have many benefits for you and for those you help. Biblical spirituality tells you that it's better to give than to receive. Helping others will convince you of the solid practical truth of that proposition.

In some instances, you might find yourself helping others overcome one of the setbacks you have experienced. This experience might let you see, at long last, a reason for the reversal you suffered. Perhaps your unhappy experience prepared you to assist others. Of course, you don't have to set yourself up as a specialist in helping others over a specific hump. Your best approach might be to keep yourself free and flexible to respond to opportunities to be of service whenever they arise.

# INITIATIVES

Let me caution you to be your own center of initiative in any recovery situation. By this, I mean that you need the experience of being the one taking initiatives, not the person acted upon by others. When others give you welcome assistance, you should take it, but you should never let them, however innocently and unwittingly, take control. You can never afford to substitute outside help or helpers for yourself as the center of initiative in your life, nor should you ever permit yourself to occupy that center in the life of someone you hope to help.

# BEYOND SERVILITY

Contrary to the impression given by rugged individualists in fact or fiction, service (in all its forms) is not servility, nor are service workers in any way intended to be second-class citizens. They are persons of unique value whose dignity is enlarged precisely because their vocation allows them to serve others. The focus of this chapter, however, is not on service employment, but on voluntary service.

Private voluntary service is a special opportunity to enhance your sense of your own human dignity as it expands your appreciation of the dignity of those you serve. As with so many other suggestions offered in this book, you will never know that service works to your advantage, as well as to the advantage of those you serve, unless you give it a try.

There are impressive statistics on the number of hours of volunteer service being offered by men and women of all ages in America's communities today. Some are at the intersections of life where the needs are urgent; most are farther out on the periphery. All are necessary. Helping others can, of course, happen at home or at work; it doesn't have to be extra help out in the community.

# BEYOND DEAL-MAKING

Unhappiness at home or work often relates to a refusal to be voluntarily helpful to others there. When an unwritten law of reciprocity ("I'll help you, if you help me," "You go first and then I'll do my part") rules the home or workplace, all moves are measured and generosity is squeezed dry. Some people, I've observed, seem far more ready to be helpful out in the community than they are at home or work. They are hiding, not serving.

# BEYOND FEAR

Overcoming some fear might be necessary before you are free enough to help. The fear of rejection is always there, and the fear of bodily harm is sometimes associated with efforts to help impoverished people in very poor communities. The fear of not knowing what to say holds some people back from volunteering to help the very ill.

Just as there is security in numbers, there is reassuring encouragement for the would-be volunteer if the work can be done with other volunteers. At least the going-there and coming-back part of the experience can be structured in such a way that connects you to others and helps lower the level of fear.

I was impressed when college students who volunteered as tutors in a low-income, high-crime neighborhood in Washington, D.C., told me they had no problem at all getting to and from their assignments on city buses because they were always met at the bus stop by the illiterate men they were teaching how to read and write, and escorted back safely by these same appreciative pupils once the sessions were over.

I served for several years on the board of directors of what was originally called the Commission on National and Community Service (now the Corporation on National Service), a federal initiative begun in 1990 to encourage volunteer activity in America. Once, at the urging of another board member, Richard F. ( Digger) Phelps, former basketball coach at Notre Dame, the commission members went "across the street," as Digger liked to put it, into a storefront church in a poor neighborhood in the District of Columbia. Our aim was to see some of the problems that service initiatives there and around the country would, we hoped, be addressing.

Two women, members of a support group for mothers of youths killed in the drug wars, described the conditions that brought their sons to early graves and themselves to unrelenting grief. A street-smart young man explained his willingness to risk arrest by dealing in drugs ("in order to get money, to get clothes, to get girls") and to use firepower in the street to defend himself whenever he and his supply were attacked ("I'd rather be tried by twelve than carried by six"). That was in 1992, when Malcom X came back to life on movie screens and the words of Martin Luther King, Jr., were being widely quoted in many discussions (including ours) on community service as a neighborhood rescue strategy. The youth who had expressed a preference for a jury over pallbearers also remarked, "Any community that has to look to dead men for role models is in real trouble." Of course, he was right.

An older gentleman from that same neighborhood, a participant in this same discussion and the father of two sons who had met violent

257

deaths in the drug wars, commented: "I'd rather be dead than be 18 or 19 today."

The 18- and 19-year-olds in poor neighborhoods, as well as countless people in lower and higher age brackets, in neighborhoods rich or poor, need the kind of help that generous, open-minded, and, yes, brave community service volunteers can provide. The spiritual principle of generosity, one of the Pauline Criteria, will point you in the direction of those who need your help. It's up to you to take the step.

The Book of Proverbs advises: "He who has compassion on the poor lends to the Lord, and he will repay him for his good deed" (19:17). You have been encouraged previously in this book to think of your spirituality as a savings account from which you can draw the strength you need to meet your day-to-day responsibilities. The help you freely give to others is a form of compassion. When you do this for the poor and needy, you are assured by the Book of Proverbs that you are "lending" to God, who will repay this loan to your account at exponential rates of interest.

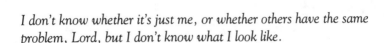

I don't know whether it's just me, or whether others have the same problem, Lord, but I don't know what I look like.

Oh, I recognize myself in pictures, of course, and I could offer a description of myself, if I had to. I see the same face in the mirror every day. It's just that when I walk away from the mirror and look out at the rest of the world, I'm not sure how the rest of the world sees me. What do I look like? What do they see before they evaluate or judge me?

You see me, of course, and I'm tempted to ask, "What do you see when you look at me?" I'm not sure I want to think about the answer.

No one sees the gradual changes that come with each new day. Some changes are, we like to say, "imperceptible." They are not, however, imperceptible to you. Nothing about me is imperceptible to your eye.

Give me, please, the grace of perception. What you perceive in me might be perceptible only to you. If, by your grace, I become more perceptive, I might begin to see myself from your point of view. Let that happen, Lord, only to the degree that I can manage it. Let me manage what I see for your glory and for the good of others. If I can see as I am seen, I might then become grateful for all the good that only you can see in me.

# Chapter 34

# HOPE

The poet George Herbert expressed the encouraging idea that anyone "who walks in hope dances without music."

Most of us have to make it through life without the benefit of background music. Whether you walk or dance, you make your way each day by even-paced measures, without the tempo-enhancing encouragement of violins and trumpets. For many years, you have probably been absorbing from the movie screen lessons about life that are cleverly (and often deceptively) wrapped in background music. Characters in the films have music to intensify their emotional highs, warn them (and the audience) of impending danger, or accelerate their slide into deeper despair. In those rare moments of emotional intensity when the music stops, you, the viewer, are left in a suspended state of watching and waiting, trying (often uncomfortably) to figure things out for yourself.

Real life is different. You can make your own movies, so to speak, by imagining what, and why, and how you will do what you're going to do today and in all your tomorrows. But you have to choose the attitude, the inner silent state of mind, that will accompany you (and serve as your "accompaniment") along the way. If you want to walk in hope, you have to choose to do so.

## THREE VIRTUES

Hope is one of three "theological virtues," so named because each has God for its direct object. The other two are faith and charity. The object of each is God. Your faith is directed toward God, your hope is grounded in God, and your charity (love) is aimed directly at God.

Your practice of these three virtues will have indirect effects on many other people. In consequence of your firm faith in God, you know how to be faithful to others. Full of unshakeable hope that God's promises to you will be fulfilled, you can present yourself to others as a hopeful person, an anchor, a rock. Your unconditional love of God, for God's own goodness and not for what he has to give to you, lets you convey something of the divine goodness to others in your own (by definition, limited) acts of charity and love.

The one-act play title *Hope is the Thing with Feathers* has intrigued me since I first came across it in my college years. The play is a mixture of humor and pathos revolving around hobos trying to snatch a duck from a pond in Central Park. The suggestion in the title is, I imagine, that hope can flutter and fly away. My point would be that hope flees only if you choose not to hang onto it. "I don't think hope ever dies," psychiatrist David Morrison once remarked to me. "It is buried in many people, but it can surface again."

Hope is not to be confused with optimism, which focuses always on the best. "Optimizing" opportunities and achieving "optimal" outcomes might be "optimistically" regarded as part of the best in the "best of all worlds." That's not the way it is with hope. Hope is a great deal closer to the human heart—hesitant or forceful, weak or strong—and to the ground on which the have-a-heart person walks (or dances!).

Hope is inextricably bound up with expectation and, of course, your expectations often focus on things getting better than they are right now. This is not to suggest that hope comes into play only when things are bad. You don't have to be ill to get better. The situation doesn't have to be in a deplorable state to begin to improve. Expectation is the thrilling dimension of hope, part of the stretch that's integral to your spirituality.

## "HOPEFULLY"

I have no idea when the word *hopefully* rose to the prominent place of misapplication it now enjoys in the American vernacular. That adverb means "in a happily expectant way." If used correctly, it describes a personal condition similar to the mood conveyed in expressions like "proudly announce" or "gladly welcome." The misapplied *hopefully* (for example, "Hopefully, we will hear from them soon") really means "It is to be hoped that...."

This is more than a simple grammatical quibble. Most of the people I hear punctuating their conversations with the word *hopefully* don't give much evidence of being all that hopeful!

The famous words from Dante's *Inferno* appear (figuratively) above the entrance to many workplaces; at least they are written on the minds of many as they go to work: "Abandon hope, all ye who enter here." This is not the stuff of a sound and practical workplace spirituality.

Give yourself an expectations check-up from time to time, to make sure your supply, your savings account, of positive hopes is abundant. Realize that similar positive expectations are (or perhaps were) on the minds of your associates in the workplace. What were your hopes, your expectations, when you started out on this job? Achievement, money, fame, power, security, influence, creativity, satisfaction, the opportunity to serve, the chance to make your mark? All or some combination of these goals? If you're like most people, few, if any, of your goals have been fully realized. The shortfall could be attributed to one or several of the reversals or wounds catalogued in this book. There's nothing unusual about this shortfall; it's all part of the human predicament.

How, then, do you cope? How do you keep your expectations high and positive? How do you keep your career and yourself in balance and on course into the future?

Hope is the only route to take. Remember, hope is a theological virtue; its object is God. Forge that link for yourself in prayer, and everything else will fall into place.

## HOPE AS A WORKPLACE ANCHOR

Never forget that you can make the God in whom you hope become present in your workplace for the benefit of your co-workers simply by being hopeful. Your centered hopefulness (a quality not to be confused with blind, Pollyanna-inspired optimism) makes you an anchor, a rock for others, and a source of serenity and stability. As is always the case in the realm of

Christian spirituality, in giving this kind of help to others, you are also helping yourself.

You might think of this phenomenon as an example of what the French novelist George Bernanos called "the miracle of the empty hands." You who stand in need of hope can give it to others without necessarily feeling very hopeful yourself. So it is with love, faith, trust, and forgiveness: You can give what you think you don't have. In the realm of spirituality, at any rate, you can; this giving should remind you where the power is, and has been, all along.

A wonderful priest I once knew was fond of saying, "Jesus promises you two things: Your life will have meaning, and you're going to live forever. If you can find a better offer, take it." Build your future on the durability of hope.

Hope is the pillar of the world. Because of it, you're a lot stronger than you think. It might surprise you to learn that John Updike once wrote, "God is a bottomless encouragement to our faltering and frightened being." It will not, I think, surprise you to know that the author of the Pauline Criteria said much the same thing centuries earlier in his letter to the Romans (5:3–5): "[W]e even boast of our afflictions, knowing that affliction produces endurance, and endurance, proven character, and proven character, hope, and hope does not disappoint, because the love of God has been poured out into our hearts through the Holy Spirit that has been given to us."

Your hope will never disappoint as long as the object of your hope is God. When your hopes appear to be dashed, consider the possibility that the God in whom you never stop hoping has something better in mind for you.

## HOPE AS GUIDER AND SUSTAINER

Hope is always future-focused. It fuels your second starts. It sustains your journey through life, especially through life's final stages. Knowing, as you do, that "all the world's a stage," you have to acknowledge your potential (even propensity) to "act," and you have to check the face behind your mask. Are you truly a hopeful person?

What abiding hope can do for you was demonstrated beautifully by Cardinal Joseph Bernardin as his life ended in 1996. "His way of death confirms that this man did not have two faces, one private, one public," said Rabbi Herman Schaalman, a longtime friend. "He was inside with his outside, outside with his inside, which is rare."

That rare quality is the fruit of a functioning spirituality. The ultimate answers come from within because your spiritual guidelines long ago found root there. Your inside becomes your outside in moments of challenge; you can face up to reality without losing either heart or hope.

The memorial card distributed to those who paid their respects at the wake services and funeral held in Chicago for Cardinal Bernardin in November, 1996, had his picture on the front and the "Prayer of St. Francis" on the back. The Cardinal carried that prayer in his coat pocket every day and recited it often. "Lord, make me an instrument of your peace," is the opening petition; midway through a list of subsequent requests, you find these words: "Where there is despair, let me sow hope." Every believer, I think, wants to do just that.

Take to heart these words from Simon Peter, the first pope: "Always be ready to give an explanation to anyone who asks you for a reason for your hope" (1 Peter 3:15). He presumed, apparently, that the Christian believer would always be a puzzle to the world. Truth be told, if you are genuinely hopeful, you will puzzle many even today.

# Chapter 35

# LOOKING UP

We say things are "looking up" when light appears at the end of the tunnel or when we have a sense of something positive about to enter our lives. The advice we often give to a discouraged friend is simply, "Keep your chin up." With the chin raised, the outlook is also elevated.

A positive, upbeat attitude is an essential component of any recovery-and-rebound strategy. The "attitude," as space-flight vocabulary reminds the world, is a leaning, a tilt. Your attitudinal tilt has to be forward and upward.

## KEEPING THINGS IN FRONT, IF YOU CHOOSE TO

Recently, I was impressed by the response of a major college basketball coach immediately after his team, ranked third in the nation, was humiliated by a lower ranked challenger just before "March Madness," the rush to become one of the NCAA Tournament's Final Four. Without missing a beat, the coach told reporters, "We are not going to put this one behind us; we'll keep it in front of us." The spectacle of past mistakes and miscues would, he hoped, guide his team back to the top of the national rankings.

You have the option of putting your reversals completely behind you and looking resolutely up, or filtering your forward and upward gaze through the memory of the past. It's your choice. Use the past, but only if it helps. Wipe it out of your memory if it's preventing you from looking up and moving ahead.

One manager I know keeps his eye on four words from the pen of Emily Dickinson: "I dwell in possibility." This is the mantra that lifts his heart. The words were printed on a card a friend used some years ago to write him an encouraging note after an involuntary separation from a job he thought he could never lose. Those four words "did it" for him, he said.

"Even now," he told me, "I have the card, beaten and battered, pinned to the wall above my desk. I try to live up to its meaning as much as I can." The meaning behind the idea of dwelling in possibility is that no matter where you are in life, you are perched on a pillar of hope. Something good is about to happen. Just keep looking up so that, when it comes, you can see the possibility that's ready to be realized in the circumstances where you now dwell. Remember, dwelling in possibility beats dwelling in impossibility every time.

To dwell in possibility, look up and out, after you have taken your bearings from within. There are steps to be taken, a future to be met.

# THE FUTURE

Sometimes, *the future* is used as a subtle substitute for *God*. I say "subtle" because it can slip into your outlook without you noticing what's going on. Your speech betrays you when this happens. Be careful if you often hear yourself "believing in the future," "putting your trust in the future," or "feeling good about the future." There is nothing wrong with any of that unless the future is all you believe in or trust. First, believe in God; then believe in yourself and your destiny. If your looking up is anchored in God and rooted in the values you hold within, you can rest assured that the future will take care of itself. After all, your Lord, the Lord of the spirituality you've been considering in these pages, is also Lord of the past, present, and future. Trust him.

# EXPERIENCE AND RESPONSIBILITY

Looking up doesn't, of course, mean looking away; it's not abdication of responsibility. Review the topics you've considered in this book. Some of them are still yours to deal with personally; you can't pretend they aren't there. Some of the other issues will no longer be problems for you, but other people in your sphere of influence will have to deal with them, and they might look to you for help. You can't hold your head in the air and ignore the challenges that others lay at your feet. This might be decision time.

You gave some thought to hope in the last chapter. Now you are looking up (and out). Let Shakespeare's words condition your mind for a consideration of what you might want to do next:

*There is a tide in the affairs of men,*
*Which, taken at the flood, leads on to fortune;*
*Omitted, all the voyage of their life*
*Is bound in shallows and in misery.*
*On such a full sea are we now afloat;*
*And we must take the current when it serves,*
*Or lose our ventures.*
*(Julius Caesar, act 4, scene 3)*

There is a current you can take. No need to think of things on a grand "affairs of men" scale. Keep the consideration on a manageable scale; match it up to your experience, your needs, and your opportunities in light of all you've been through and learned so far in life

# REVIEWING WHAT YOU'VE LEARNED

From where you are at this very moment, think about criticism, fear, betrayal, false accusations, sabotage, ingratitude, being passed over, being misunderstood, prejudice, sexual harassment, personal mistakes, failure. (You've been through a lot in these pages!) You might opt to think again about single parenting, accidents, aging, illness, insecurity, addiction, indecision, broken promises, divorce, the death of someone dear, layoff, caring for a parent who is frail and elderly. Then think about moving ahead.

All these brushes with reality, all these elements that are part of normal living, challenge the relevance of your faith to ordinary life and work. If faith can't speak to you there, what good is faith for you? Now that you have had the opportunity to reflect and pray by the promptings you

found on these pages, you know that faith can address all these issues—
and any others that might arise in your life.

You know that faith is good, and useful, and necessary for you, and you
have an understanding now of how spirituality provides an infrastructure
of support.

# THE NINE CRITERIA REVISITED

A practical spirituality functions as a communications network, keeping
you in touch with the source of all goodness and power. More specifically,
each of the nine Pauline Criteria leads you to the source of all goodness
and power.

The list, as you no doubt remember, begins with love. At the end
of every experience of authentic love, you will find God, for "God is love"
(1 John 4:8).

Joy is next. Remember that joy (not to be confused with mere light-
heartedness or hilarity) tops the list of the Pauline Criteria that attest to
the vibrancy of your spirituality. Joy, however, can come and go (or better,
surface and recede). "Gloom we will always have with us, a rank and sturdy
weed," writes Barbara Holland, "but joy requires tending." Tend to the
cultivation of your own deep-down joy, your abiding happiness, and you
will have prepared the solid ground on which your poised and balanced
looking up can stand secure.

Genuine joy can't be described, only experienced. The experience is
not a sudden, surface eruption like laughter. Joy is something that has to be
tended, nurtured, respected, even revered, because joy is the presence of
God to the soul.

Peace, the objective of every soul's search, is a by-product of wisdom.
"The Lord by wisdom founded the earth," says the Book of Proverbs (3:19),
and wisdom's "paths are peace." Those who search for peace are searching,
whether they know it or not, for the God of wisdom. Augustine knew this
when he wrote: "You have made us for yourself, O Lord, and our hearts are
restless till they rest in you."

Patience is another path to God. Who else but God can be there at the
bottom of all reality? Your patience is your deepest possible acceptance of

reality, your persevering acceptance of things as they are. Your patience doesn't preclude the possibility of change; it expresses your obedience to the natural laws of growth and to the will of the God of all reality.

Kindness is, in every instance, a disclosure of what God is like. Your every kindness is an opportunity for the God who dwells within to have a presence, through you, in the places where your kindnesses are seen and felt. Similarly, kindnesses shown to you by others are expressions, through them, of God's love and care for you.

Generosity is another sign of God's presence. It functions like a two-way street that leads the generous person to God, who, as Paul testifies, "loves a cheerful giver" (2 Corinthians 9:7), and it can bring God to any beneficiary of a generous act, who is graced to see the ultimate giver behind the gift.

Faithfulness is required of the believer. God does not require that you be brave, or bright, or outstanding in anything but your faithfulness; in this way, you stand out, despite your doubts, before your God. The faith of your faithfulness is something that can be neither merited nor earned. It can only be given. There is only One who can give the gift of faith. With that gift, you possess the God of faithfulness. All you can be is grateful.

Gentleness is the very atmosphere of divinity. If you are gentle, you are Godlike. If gentleness comes your way, you can find God in that breeze. If your gentle soul is filled with faith, hope, and love, and if veracity and forgiveness are there too, your gentle soul is as strong as steel. Gentleness is the strength of spiritual giants.

Self-control is a lever in your hand. Only you, with God's help, can turn it. God respects your freedom. You can freely decide not to throw the lever of self-control, and that will mean permitting material excesses or spiritual pride to overrun your soul. If it's overrun, the soul is no longer fertile ground for the principles of spirituality. Weeds develop; there is no longer room in the soul for answers from within. Whenever you use that lever, though, you clear away the weeds and move closer to the God who created the self that's now in your control.

With these nine tools and their associated ideas in your possession, you notice that things are looking up. You now know how to deal with the human predicament. It's all a matter of mixing faith with work and with the rest of the wonderful life that is yours. You dwell in infinite possibility. You can take the prophet Hosea at his inspired word:

> *Let us know, let us strive to know the Lord;*
> *as certain as the dawn is his coming,*
> *and his judgment shines forth like the light of day!*
> *He will come to us like the rain,*
> *like spring rain that waters the earth.*
> *(Hosea 6:3)*